My Sister Roseanne

The true story of Roseanne Barr Arnold

Geraldine Barr with Ted Schwarz

Virgin

First published in Great Britain in 1995 by
Virgin Books
an imprint of Virgin Publishing Ltd
332 Ladbroke Grove
London W10 5AH

First published in the USA in 1994 by Birch Lane Press,
an imprint of Carol Publishing Group

A catalogue record for this book is available
from the British Library

ISBN 0 86369 911 1

Typeset by SX Composing Ltd, Rayleigh, Essex
Printed and bound in Great Britain by
Cox & Wyman Ltd, Reading, Berks.

My Sister Roseanne

To Maxine Epstein, for her strength,
love, and constancy.

To my parents, Helen and Jerry, in gratitude
for the way they brought me up.

To Stephanie, Ben, Rick, and Melissa,
who have surrounded my life with life.

Contents

Acknowledgements

My thanks go to Julie Jensen, who has taught me important things about writing and myself and Utah; to Rabbi Eric Weiss, whose soulful counsel made a critical difference; to Marion Fay, for teaching me about editing, law, and courage; to Maxine Margaritis, for her friendship, wisdom, and encouragement; and to Richard Maxfield, for being the ultimate optimist

1 Triumph

*I hate being called a housewife, I prefer being called
a domestic goddess.*
— Roseanne Barr, opening her act at The Comedy Store,
July 1985

We were always outsiders, growing up, Rosey and I.
Part of it had to do with religious bias. We were two
Jewish sisters in Salt Lake City, Utah, where anyone who
wasn't a Mormon was seen as either a potential convert or
a hopeless sinner.

Part of it had to do with the fact that our father was a
struggling salesman in a community where, if you had to
be Jewish, you were expected to be rich. In a synagogue
parking lot filled with Mercedeses, Lincolns, and Cadillacs,
our old Chevy stood out like a sore thumb. Our family
thought that such an obvious display of poverty was
viewed by our fellow parishioners as being only slightly
less sinful than being kicked out of the Garden of Eden for
overeating. We were raised to feel shame for our family's
lack of money. We felt it was perhaps the ultimate blas-
phemy in Salt Lake City, assuring that Rosey and I, along
with our younger siblings, would never be fully accepted.

The frustrations of that life, the five years' difference in
our ages, and the fact that Roseanne decided to become a
hitchhiking hippie while I tried the role of radical Zionist
and scholar, almost ended our mutual story before it
began. Fortunately, we sisters became "Sisters," working
together to show the world the truth about the struggling
yet strong, in-your-face existence of the working class
woman. Comedy became our way to introduce to both
nightclubs and prime-time television a role model for the
millions of women who look more like overweight, overtired supermarket checkout clerks than movie stars. The
Roseanne character reflected all the well-intentioned slobs

1

who would rather spend time with their children than ritually worship such gods as vacuum cleaners, dust mops, and blue toilet bowl liquids. Roseanne typified all women who know that the Health Department will not bar them from their own homes if their husbands and children come home at the end of the day and discover food-encrusted breakfast dishes in the sink. And the blue-collar Roseanne made in excess of $100 million and a place in supermarket tabloid history.

Eventually I was excluded from Roseanne Barr's world when she became Roseanne Barr Arnold. Mutual respect for shared talents that meshed so smoothly degenerated into the attitude of "I'm rich and you're poor." "I'm the star and you're not." "I have suffered great pain in life and you have not." We would be the unappreciated Jewish girls of Salt Lake City all over again, yet the city I had grown to hate had become internalized inside my older sister's mind. Triumph became tragedy, lives were shattered, and only the jokes seemed to continue forever.

But that was later. It was the journey that was the heady time. It was the journey during which we wrote jokes together, traveled and dreamed together, and always working unceasingly for the vision we both shared. From the beginning, I helped with the bookings of her act, then studied her work from the audience's perspective to see how it could improve. Roseanne was the public person. I handled much of the business life and marketing behind the scenes. And when we were ready, when Roseanne was not only comfortable as a stand-up comic on stage but had gained some fame, we moved to Los Angeles. We were going to become the first Jewish sisters to dominate Hollywood like so many Jewish brothers who had founded and run the major movie studios over the last century. We were going to be empowered by our closeness.

But first, like all comics of the 1980s, we had to gain an audience with the then all-powerful god of late-night television, Johnny Carson. Roseanne needed to perform her act on his show, to conquer the most powerful and important audience available to a comic who wants to be successful. And if you weren't around for the ride in those days, you can't imagine how important *The Tonight Show* was for comedians. It was the ultimate mark of respect, legitimacy, and class.

Johnny Carson used to joke that every night in America, millions of women lay down on their beds and watched him through their toes. Other women, and at least as many men, let him come into their living rooms, their factories, bars, hospitals, fire and police stations. He never came alone, of course. Doc Severinsen was with him, leading the Tonight Show Orchestra. And Ed McMahon, his announcer, foil, and occasional fool, sat by his side. But the most important people who accompanied him were the comedians.

Johnny Carson loved comedy, loved showcasting the famous and discovering the little-known performers who could make you laugh with a joke, a story, a characterization. Bob Hope, George Burns, Joan Rivers, David Letterman, Jay Leno, Richard Pryor, Redd Foxx, Slappy White, Garry Shandling . . . the list was endless. An established professional had his or her talent validated by an appearance on *The Tonight Show*. Newcomers proved to the world that they had paid their dues, learned their craft, made their mistakes in small clubs, second-rate resorts, and smoke-filled saloons. To be on Johnny Carson was to be part of the big time.

My father, Jerry Barr, was one of the millions of Carson fans, though he never watched the late-night program through his toes. Comedy was too important to watch in bed, and his love of humor was infectious. He would sit by the television set, a lone sentinel in search of a laugh, watching through commercials, opening theme music, and the banter with the audience. Then, at the appropriate moment, he would shout, "Comedian!" and my sister Roseanne as well as any other interested family members would come running. They would delight in Johnny, then listen enraptured as each of his special guests performed their routines. Ideally, Dad and Rosey would laugh uproariously. At other times, when the comedians seemed to bomb, their jokes leading nowhere, Roseanne would pay special attention. She was as interested in what caused comics to fail as in what made them funny.

Rosey was a teenager by then, allowed to stay up until between eleven and eleven-thirty P.M., always late enough to catch the opening monologue and at least the first comedian on the show that reached Salt Lake City an hour earlier than it was seen on the East Coast. When she was younger, she shared with Dad the joys of Ed Sullivan, whose Sunday evening variety program was her first training ground. Many of Sullivan's comics were from the older generation, men who had worked the Borscht Belt summer resorts in the Catskills. Often Jewish, usually elaborate storytellers, they provided one type of education. Carson was hipper and more upscale.

Roseanne was certain that one day she would be a big-name comic. One day she would be booked as the established pro on whom *The Tonight Show* could rely to increase the size of an evening's viewing audience. It was a big dream for a Jewish girl from Salt Lake City, yet I shared it with her. And though I was only her kid sister, five years younger and even less sophisticated, she and I believed that one day we would be a team, working together so her stage presence could conquer Johnny, Hollywood, the nation, and the world. She would be a famous performer, and I would be the rich, behind-the-scenes producer.

It was July of 1985 when Roseanne first visited Los Angeles, where *The Tonight Show* was broadcast. The visit was actually a stopover, a chance to see people she knew in the comedy business and to meet people she wanted to know. She did not plan to stay for long, having a club date in Seattle where she would perform her carefully refined routine.

Roseanne Barr was in her fifth year as a stand-up comedian. She had begun in Denver, where we both were living. She and I had developed an act for her, written the jokes together, analyzed the success of the material, adding some, dropping some, and improving the rest. She had made two-minute appearances in amateur competitions during open mike nights when comedy club business was slow. She had begun working for minimum pay as her work improved and she developed a following. When she was on the road, I served as booking agent, contact person, marketer, chauffeur, navigator, hand holder, and critic and did anything else that needed to be done. Frequently I was in the audience when she performed, analyzing her work, looking for ways to help her improve. At other times, I babysat her children, easing the burden of her travels on her husband, Bill Pentland. But when I didn't travel with Rosey, she called me every day to discuss what had become our ten-year plan for international success.

Rosey was the sister who wanted to be in the spotlight, to dominate the stage, I was the business expert behind the star. I was the one who went to college, who studied marketing, who learned accounting, whose job it was to help package and sell Roseanne Barr the comedian. And always we were pointed toward Los Angeles, then the comics' Mecca.

Los Angeles was the heart of the world of comedy clubs. It was where the big money was made, where the big talents were recognized, and where success as a stand-up comic could lead to job offers on television and in motion pictures.

There were comedy clubs elsewhere, of course. In 1985 they were becoming as popular as bowling alleys and hamburger stands, in big cities and small towns alike. Roseanne had already seen many of them, had conquered their audiences, had proven she was an emerging talent. But when you arrived in Los Angeles with small-town credentials, you were viewed with as much disdain as if you showed up at Paramount and announced you wanted a movie contract because you had gotten good reviews after starring in your high school play. The worst professional acts in the Los Angeles comedy clubs could often brilliantly outshine the best acts performing in almost every other city in the nation.

Rosey's resumé listed clubs in Aspen, Boulder, Kansas City, and soon, Seattle. She made good money, averaging $300 per week, but in Los Angeles there were "second bananas" playing clubs for that much money per day.

Before driving north to her Washington State club date, Roseanne felt the need to go to the holy of holies in the comedy world, the club from which every major act seemed to be launched – Mitzi Shore's Comedy Store, on Sunset Boulevard next to the Hyatt Hotel. Mitzi was to training comics what Johnny Carson was to selling them. Her Comedy Store had three rooms. There was a small one where acts could be developed by amateurs and beginning professionals working the club's off nights, and a main stage that featured the headliners who were appearing or would soon appear in major markets. The third room, upstairs as I remember it, was specifically for women developing their comedy routines.

Mitzi was the driving force behind developing women comics and giving them a voice. The comic world had long been male dominated, at least for stand-up comedy. Most used a macho character whose humor revolved around what they perceived to be the emotional and intellectual failings of women. Women, especially strong women, were rarities, but Mitzi was determined to change that.

There were great female comic talents working before Mitzi opened her club. Brilliant radio voices such as Gracie Allen, the wife of George Burns, and Jane Ace, who with her husband, Goodman Ace, had the show *Easy Aces*, were well known to the American public. On television, Lucille Ball was a pioneer in the creation of the humorous urban housewife in *I Love Lucy*. And Mary Tyler Moore, playing on *The Dick Van Dyck Show*, took a variation of the Lucy character and brought her to the suburbs. But Mitzi encouraged a generation of strong women – aggressive, bright, and very funny females who neither served as comic counterpoints for men or performed self-deprecating humor. They were as independent as the men. And many of their routines ultimately helped change society, as they caused their audiences to laugh at anyone who would refuse to give a woman status equal to her abilities. Thanks to Mitzi, very talented women were shattering stereotypes in the entertainment world the way rising women executives were changing the business world.

My husband asked me to be more aggressive in bed, so I shouted, "NO!"
– Roseanne Barr at The Comedy Store, July 1985

Mitzi, curious about Roseanne's work after meeting her, asked her to perform a couple of minutes of material in the small room on an off night. She did, and Mitzi liked what she heard. She asked Rosey if she could do twenty minutes in the main room. The twenty minutes represented just about all the polished material Roseanne and I had created, but Rosey jumped at the chance. She also called me to tell me that she would be moving to Los Angeles at least through the summer, after she finished performing in Seattle.

The move was right on schedule. Five years earlier, when we developed a plan to take over Hollywood, we knew that the first four to five years would require paying dues through performing in small clubs and as a minor act in larger cities. By the time she went to Seattle, she and I agreed that she had learned everything she needed to know. It was time to hit the big time. It was time to go to Los Angeles. Mitzi's response confirmed this, and I told her as much. As she later admitted to *People* magazine, my urgings caused her to permanently unpack in the city where she would find her greatest success.

Because we worked so closely together on the act, Rosey and I were rarely apart in those days except when she was on the road performing and I had to work my "day job." The day job was anything where I could use my business skills yet still be able to keep nights and weekends free to help develop Rosey's career. I wanted to be rich, to escape the poverty I had known in Salt Lake City. I wanted a voice in the arts, even if it had to come through the synergy of the act Roseanne and I created. We always agreed that when she reached the top we would create our own production company supporting women in the arts. That targeted future was more important to me than any job I might hold in those early years, any other career my talent and skill might allow me to pursue. It was also the vehicle I knew would lead to both real power and real money.

I did not quit my job and move to Los Angeles when Roseanne first returned there following her appearance in Seattle. Rosey settled into the temporarily vacant apartment of a friend she had there, a fellow comedian named Dianne Ford who was then traveling on the circuit. Dianne's apartment in Santa Monica became a free haven from which to further develop her act. Whether or not she returned to the mid-sized clubs on the comedy circuit would depend upon her performances for the next few weeks.

Mitzi Shore was delighted with Roseanne's return and soon helped her get a part in a one-hour review called "Funny." The show was being produced by George Schlatter, the same man who had produced *Laugh-In*, the television program that revolutionized TV comedy in the 1960s, and that was so popular that even then-President Richard Nixon had appeared in a cameo.

"Funny" showcased several female comics, each with a different style. The show would be filmed, then sold as a special for cable and elsewhere, paying the performers royalties if it was successful. The pay was low, but it was an excellent showcase. In fact, Maureen, one of Mitzi's female comics who was not part of the show, mentioned this new Denver-based talent to her friend Jim McCawley. He agreed to come to the dress rehearsal to see if he liked Rosey's talent.

The job in "Funny," as low paying as it was, was exactly the kind of break Rosey could use to boost her asking price on the road or to gain jobs in the better Los Angeles area clubs. It wasn't the same as being offered a million-dollar contract, product endorsements, and a star in the Hollywood Walk of Fame. But being one of the featured performers in the review was a big enough break for her to call me and tell me to move to Los Angeles. After five years of driving around the country, carefully planning, steady growth, and grinding poverty, she was about to enjoy the next stage of success. She had no intention of entering such unknown performing territory without me. I was asked to pack a suitcase and drive out to be with her for the dress rehearsal of "Funny." I would take notes and analyze the performance. If it went as well as we hoped, I would return home only long enough to say goodbye to friends, quit my job, load Roseanne's car with everything I owned, and move out to Los Angeles to help coordinate our future.

Husbands are never happy. My husband asked me for
more space, so I locked him out of the house.
– Roseanne Barr at The Comedy Store, July 1985

I arrived in Los Angeles exhausted. It was around six P.M., perhaps an hour before the filming. I had no expectations as I parked my car and entered The Comedy Store. Each step of Rosey's career development had gone as planned during the five years since my sister had first started trying her hand at stand-up comedy. She had refined her act to six brilliant minutes of material and another ten that was strong enough for her to hold her own with the competition. However, that did not change how slowly a comic has to develop, nor how cutthroat the competition can be.

The audience sees comics as people who want to entertain them, to expose their own lives in ways so funny, the audience can delight in their foibles, failings, and outrageous insights. Comics see each other as the enemy, and talk of their competition in terms of war. When stand-ups work a club, they say such things as, "I killed tonight," or "I blew all the other acts off the stage." Even career planning is discussed in terms of battle tactics. Thus, with Rosey in the midst of five other women professionals, I knew she was going into battle with warriors who were at least as experienced as she was. But I had no doubts that she would blow them away. I saw the entire picture and had long-term vision. I trusted that the material was very funny, the point of view quite fresh.

I sat in the club as Rosey did her act during the dress rehearsal. I made notes, but my instincts were that there was nothing wrong. She was as good as she had ever been, and while she might not "blow the other acts off the stage" during the filmed special, her performance was a solid one. I was again reminded just how far she had come.

I realized that the pressure was far less than we had endured prior to coming to Los Angeles. The four solid years of work had given her the voice we had been trying to hone from the start. It was a fresh voice, and by coming from Denver, the product was a success waiting to be discovered. We were finally in control, only needing to have others in the industry recognize what we already knew.

Rosey came down into the audience when her segment was over, moving toward my table. The dress rehearsal crowd was made up of insiders – the film crew, lighting techs, a friend or two of Mitzi's and the staff of The Comedy Store. They were often more sophisticated than the usual audience because they heard all the acts, good and bad. Thus I was pleased when Roseanne was stopped by some man who seemed to be saying, "I really liked your act." I was far enough away that I could not fully see Rosey's facial expressions, but her body language was relaxed, friendly. Then he handed her his business card.

The change was immediate. Rosey looked at the card, sagged slightly, and quickly put her hand on the table to support herself. Then she spoke for a moment longer and came toward me, never stopping. Her eyes met mine, yet in the dark I could see little more than shadows, telling me nothing.

Still, I knew something major had happened. We were sisters. We had worked as equals for five years. I could sense that something dramatic had taken place, and I wondered when she would sit down with me to tell me.

Moments later, after Rosey left the theater, the doorman came over and said, "Your sister wants to see you in the parking lot."

It was still quite light out, though there were few strollers where we were standing. Most people were either in restaurants eating or driving to a show. A few were in line, waiting to enter The Comedy Store to see the act in the little room.

The parking lot was as private a place as Roseanne could find. That was why she chose that location to hand me the business card.

Jim McCawley's name was on the card. Although I did not realize this at the time, he was the man Maureen had asked to stop by. McCawley was also a friend of Mitzi Shore's, the reason he had been allowed to attend the otherwise closed-to-the-public dress rehearsal. And then I saw the reason he was a friend, the reason Roseanne's knees had buckled. Jim McCawley was the talented coordinator for Johnny Carson's *Tonight Show*.

I looked up and Roseanne was crying. I started to say something, but tears were streaming down my face as well. We embraced, pressed together in love and fear and triumph. *The Tonight Show*! Johnny Carson! One of us screamed, and then the other. After that, my memories are blurs.

We twirled each other round and round the lot, then feared we could be seen from nearby Santa Monica Boulevard. The boulevard was known for its glamour, but also for its eccentrics and crazies. There was an S-M club nearby, and just down the street, high-priced prostitutes were at work. Police cruised regularly. We quickly moved to the high-rise parking deck serving the hotel, then began crying, laughing, and generally going crazy.

I remember twirling around the support poles. We leaped about as though prima ballerinas. We screamed. We giggled. Tears mingled with snot, mascara, makeup base, and eyeshadow, creating a thoroughly disgusting appearance we knew we'd have to clean before we saw anyone else. I was thankful I had gone to the bathroom shortly before Rosey performed or I could have easily peed in my pants.

Among shrieks, giggles, and tears, Roseanne told me that Jim McCawley had told her to call him. He wanted her to come in so he could approve what material she could do on the show prior to booking her for Carson. He wanted her! She just did not know for which date. Since McCawley had seen her act during the dress rehearsal, she had already had her "audition." Roseanne Barr was about to enter millions of homes, to be watched through millions of toes in millions of bedrooms, to make millions laugh uproariously.

Sometimes Rosey's legs would buckle and she would sag in my arms. Other times I would start to collapse and Rosey would catch me. Then, a moment later, we would be running up and down the ramps connecting the different levels of the parking garage, grabbing each other, trying to toss each other into the air in victorious celebration. We hoped there was no surveillance camera filming our antics, but we could not have stopped ourselves even if there had been.

"This means I can get my own credit card!" I shouted. And we both dissolved in laughter and tears once again.

Finally under as much control as we could muster, Roseanne had to clean her face and return to the rehearsal. I went to the telephone bank in the Hyatt, calling her husband, Bill Pentland, our parents, our brother and sister. "This is it!" I shouted. "This is fucking it!"

I don't know how coherent I was. I do know that at first my mother tried to calm me down, to get the details of the car accident she was certain had occurred.

First I had to convince Mom we were fine. Then, after she understood what had happened with Roseanne, she reminded us that there still had to be an audition for Jim McCawley. Confronted with our hysteria, she reacted, as only a mother can, with a wait-and-see attitude. She said, "Well, let's see what happens next."

Then Mom suddenly understood why I was so excited. Her life had been so far removed from the world of nightclubs and stand-up comedy that Rosey and I had taken the time to teach her the business. We had discussed our plans from the start, and she had seen her daughter's growing success as a performer. Now it dawned on her – the fact that Jim McCawley had given Roseanne his business card

after he had heard her perform. And then she too went
crazy with joy.

> You know, sometimes people come up to me after the
> show and say, "Gosh, Roseanne, you're not very
> feminine." And I say to them, "Suck my dick!"
> – Roseanne Barr, closing her act at The Comedy Store,
> July 1985

I know we slept that night. I know because I remember
awakening in Dianne's apartment. But the time was short,
and we were on an adrenaline rush as we drove to NBC
studios in Burbank in Dianne's little red Triumph con-
vertible.

Roseanne was at the wheel, even though we didn't know
exactly how to get there and I had the better sense of direction. Rosey kept missing the studio entrance, but I couldn't
guide her. I was too busy standing in the moving vehicle,
shouting at all passing cars, "We're going to Burbank!
We're going to Burbank!"

For years we had heard Johnny Carson jokes about the
NBC studios in Burbank. We had heard him mock the
facilities, heard him make constant disparaging remarks
about the NBC commissary, where studio employees were
forced to eat. Now we were on our way to the place
Johnny Carson worked, the Mecca he had discussed five
nights a week ever since the show relocated from New
York. And when I wasn't screaming about Burbank, Rosie
and I were singing along with a Prince tape we blasted over
and over on a small boom box. The song, the most appropriate we could find, was "We're Gonna Party Like It's
1999."

Finally we entered the grounds, stopped by the guard
shack, and were told that a pass had been sent, that we
were expected. *We* were expected at the NBC studios at
Burbank. The Barr sisters were expected at NBC, by Jim
McCawley, the man who held the keys to Johnny Carson's
throneroom. We almost started dancing again.

All giddiness ended as we entered the hallowed corridors

of NBC Burbank, where Johnny walked, Johnny talked, Johnny excused himself to go to the men's room and handle whatever bodily functions Johnny Carson still had to perform without a lackey.

Then we saw it, the NBC commissary, target of a thousand jokes. It was real, and we detoured briefly to step inside what was little more than a glorified cafeteria.

I'm not sure if I really heard music. I suspect that I may have imagined the choirs of angels singing. And I know that when I walked to displays of fruit for sale, touching a banana here, an apple there, an orange, a sliced grapefruit half, that I didn't really have a mystical experience. Yet there we were, two kids from Mormon country who had heard Jim McCawley say, "Call me in the morning."

Finally we broke from our reverie and left to find Jim McCawley's office, and Roseanne entered alone. I returned to the commissary, returned to the magical ambience of a dream come true. And when Roseanne found me, she could barely contain herself as she told me her appearance would be on Friday's show – two days away.

At that moment we believed that all our struggles were over. The Barr sisters had conquered the odds, conquered the competition, conquered *The Tonight Show*! Nothing could ever separate us from each other or the success we had sought for so long. No two sisters could ever be so joyously happy as we were.

Two days later my sister sat in the Green Room of the NBC studios in Burbank, California, the waiting area for *The Tonight Show*. And back in Salt Lake City, when Dad sat by the television set and shouted "Comedian!" the performer who would come out on Johnny Carson's stage to make the rest of our family laugh would be his daughter Roseanne Barr.

2 Childhood

There is never any logic to a dream. Roseanne and I knew little more about Hollywood than what we learned by watching television and going to the movies. We were aware that the major studios frequently had been founded by Jewish men, often brothers, who had moved west sometime after the turn of the twentieth century. We were Jewish as well, and though we were sisters, we somehow came to believe that we could one day take over Hollywood, becoming as much a force to be reckoned with as the Warner brothers, Louis B. Mayer, and the others. The trouble was that not only were we Jewish sisters with a dream, we had the nerve to begin that dream in Salt Lake City, Utah.

In some ways the Jewish community in Mormon-dominated Salt Lake City was reminiscent of a Jewish ghetto in Eastern Europe early in the century. There were approximately five hundred families like ours, some quite rich, others struggling to make ends meet, and most of them in some form of the mercantile trade. It was as though they were repeating an aspect of their history after coming to the United States.

For centuries European Jews had regularly been uprooted from their homes and forced to move to areas where they were denied the opportunity to work in most businesses. Laws often prevented them from owning or renting the land needed for farming. Usually they had to act as bankers or merchants, selling cloth, kitchen utensils, and similar items.

In the United States the Jews settled in cities where they had relatives, where they saw business opportunities, and where they received a certain degree of acceptance. They often faced anti-Semitism. In Salt Lake City, they were viewed as so different that they had to be either converted to the Mormon faith or considered evil incarnate.

At least that is how I saw the world in which we were living. Only many years later, when I made my first visit to Jerusalem in Israel, did I begin to understand the Mormons. In Salt Lake City, the Barrs were among the minority residents of a religious community. In Jerusalem I was part of the Jewish majority. The feelings towards non-Jews in Jerusalem were similar to what I experienced as a Jew in Mormon country. My anger started to subside then. My understanding and growing compassion ended my years of frustration. And later, when our family was in crisis, I discovered the depth of love in the community to which I was once so hostile. My parents and I would be lovingly embraced by our Mormon neighbors while other "friends" we trusted condemned us. But growing up, the blinders I wore from my inner anger and pain caused me to think that our family was often engaged in intellectual and verbal warfare against the Mormon majority.

My mother's mother, a woman we called Bobbe ("Bubby") Mary, was the most aggressive member of the Barr family when it came to dealing with the Mormons. She never singled them out as being worse than other Gentiles. She simply divided the world into Jews and non-Jews, the former to be trusted and the latter to be feared for lack of understanding. She was an Orthodox Jew who was so strictly kosher, she had her meat sent from the nearest butcher she could trust to kill and dress the meat according to Mosaic law. That butcher was in Denver, more than five hundred miles away, and the meat had to be shipped in dry ice. Once I was old enough to drive, I'd have to go to the airport and pick up boxes filled with dry ice and big hunks of brisket. I took it to my grandmother's apartment, where she stored it in several large freezers.

She owned an apartment building which, following World War II, was often filled with Jewish refugees from the ravages of Hitler's army. Those tenants receiving Social Security frequently turned over their checks to Bobbe Mary. She would cash the checks. She would deduct thirty-five dollars a month, usually 25 percent of their check, to pay their rent, then pay their utilities for them. The utilities were in Bobbe Mary's name, which prevented the new tenants from having to make a deposit. Bobbe Mary charged the tenants for their proper utility use, but since the utilities were in her name, each year she was able to include the utility payments in her list of apartment-related business expenses. She saved the tenants one expense while personally benefitting at tax time. She saw nothing wrong with this, since her renters could not have taken such a deduction, which was meant exclusively for landlords.

I never fully appreciated Bobbe Mary when I was growing up. I felt there was a hardness to her that could easily be mistaken for arrogance. When I was older, I came to realize she was not hard but somewhat withdrawn from the deep sadness of a life of intense pain. She was a defender of all things Jewish in a way that seemed like a dismissal of all other religions. Some people would find her hard to understand, but she was always adorable to me.

What few outside the family understood was the world Bobbe Mary had endured in order to stay alive, as well as the price she paid for the life she had to live. Bobbe Mary came from a small Jewish village in Lithuania where pain, suffering, and violent death were all too familiar companions. She was born during the reign of Czar Nicholas II of Russia, a man whose greed and oppression often resulted in the slow starvation of his most loyal and beloved subjects. Those he disliked, and among these were all the Jews in the various villages, were frequently murdered more swiftly. Jewish boys as young as twelve were frequently forced to join the Czar's army, where they were sent to the front line to serve as cannon fodder.

My grandmother, one of eleven children, was the daughter of a couple who owned a successful flax seed farm during a period when the armies of the Czar were traveling through the area. Each sweep of the Cossacks through populated areas carried out a scorched-earth policy to prevent any enemies from benefiting from the riches of the land. The people did not matter. The civilian community could be sacrificed if their deaths were of strategic value.

When my great-grandfather learned that the army was approaching, he took his wife and children, including their six-week-old baby, and hid them in the barn of a Christian neighbor. By the time it was safe to go out, their fields had been destroyed, the land torched. If the Czar's enemies passed through, they could not gain any spoils of war. And if the Czar remained in power, the scorched-earth policy meant that the hated Jewish community would swiftly starve.

My great-grandparents went from being wealthy by local standards to having to fight for every scrap of food, every remnant of warm clothing needed for survival. The usually harsh winter was approaching, and they had been left with little more than the possessions they and their children were wearing when they hid. There were no stores from which to buy more, and no money to use if there had been stores.

Bobbe Mary went from the carefree life of a child of some privilege to having to face the horrors of basic survival. All around the village were the corpses of soldiers killed in battle. They had to be buried before they rotted and spread disease. However, her father also recognized that the clothing that could make the difference between survival and literally freezing to death was that being worn by the dead. He knew that they had to set aside all the Jewish teachings and traditions concerning the handling of a corpse if they were to remain alive into the spring.

First the boots were to be taken from the dead and given to the living. Frostbitten feet were a common source of infection for the underprotected. This led to either amputation or deadly gangrene. The stolen boots were warm enough to protect them.

Then the corpses were stripped of whatever clothing was in good enough condition to be utilized. Day after day Bobbe Mary looked into the vacant eyes of rotting men, removing whatever garments were not destroyed by blood, entrails, insects, and maggots. Someone, somewhere, loved each of them, wondered about their safety, feared that they might not return, never knowing that it was too late to worry, too late to hope. She had to keep reminding herself that, if still alive, probably each of them would be willing to kill her as the enemy. Now they were dead, and in her topsy-turvy universe, their deaths gave her promise of continued life. It was a time of horror and madness, and her heart was hardened to enable her to get from day to day.

The only consistent link with sanity, with a world that had some order, some meaning, some purpose, was Bobbe Mary's Jewish faith. The Mosaic laws were described in the Old Testament, and for centuries they had remained relatively unchanged in how they were followed. And no matter how terrible a nightmare her people endured, God seemed to always look upon them as His chosen people, ultimately freeing them from their horrors. Her life was a little like that of the character Tevye in the play *Fiddler on the Roof*. At one point, while working hard, facing a hostile government, and worrying about the future of his family, Tevye begins talking with God. He complains about his hardships, though he is never disrespectful. Finally he says what many of the Jews of Bobbe Mary's village must have thought. He half seriously says to God words to the effect that "If we're your chosen people, why couldn't you have chosen someone else."

With World War I approaching, my great-grandfather decided to try to save his family by first sending my grandmother, then sixteen, and her sister Anita, eighteen months older, to Kansas, where he had a sister, Shirley. The rest of the family was to follow.

We jokingly called Bobbe Mary's sister Aunt Vinegar (like my grandmother, she pronounced the word in the European manner – "Winegar"). Aunt Vinegar got her name because she used vinegar as an all-purpose balm. In her mind, any skin problem, from a cut to a rash, could be treated by the application of vinegar. (Bobbe Mary's preferred flax seed poultices, herbal salves for infections, and her famous "yolks." A yolk was a cold remedy consisting on an egg yolk mixed with boiling water and five or more

19

heaping tablespoons of sugar served like a tea in her *milchaka* dishes — translucent white china shaped like a seashell.)

Another sister, Great-Aunt Tova, also escaped. She eventually settled in Palestine. Eight other siblings waited too long to leave, though the consequences of that failing would not be known for several years.

Bobbe Mary went from Ellis Island in New York, where she was processed as an immigrant to Wichita, Kansas, where she found employment as a seamstress. She always sent a portion of her earnings back to Lithuania to be used towards passage to America for the rest of the family. She lived with Aunt Shirley, continuing her musical studies in addition to her work. In Lithuania she had learned to play the mandolin. Both she and Aunt Anita also had beautiful soprano voices, and they frequently sang for weddings, though I don't know if they did so for money. She also studied Hawaiian guitar and other stringed guitars while in America.

Bobbe Mary had a strong interest in singing professionally. She studied under a singing teacher who was of such help that when the teacher moved to Salt Lake City, Bobbe Mary decided to follow. My grandmother had a room in the Constitution Building, a residential facility solely for young artists. She knew of the Yiddish theater which existed in several parts of the United States, and it was her dream to join the one in Los Angeles.

My grandfather Ben, the man who would ultimately marry Bobbe Mary, had been born in Austria-Hungary, and came through Ellis Island when he was two years old. His father worked in a family-owned milk company in McKeesport, Pennsylvania. However, they later migrated to Salt Lake City, where he was part of a kosher butcher shop and bakery, a logical meeting point for all the Jewish residents in the community.

Grandpa Ben was a hobo for a while, riding the rails, traveling the country, working at odd jobs. Once he learned to read, he refused to go to school. Instead, he read constantly, educating himself to a level beyond what he probably would have reached if he had attended classes. He was also what we call a "matsia hunter," a man who could not resist bargains. He loved to trade and barter, the chase often more important than the prize.

Mom tells a story of the time he gave her a beautiful white pen which she adored. No one knows if it was valuable, but after a few days he asked to have the pen back. He told Mom he was going to get her something equally special, and though she loved that pen, she trusted her father. When he returned, he brought her a piano which is in my parents' home to this day.

When Grandpa was in business, he so liked trading, he tried to get the customers in his store the best possible buy. He occasionally made no profit, his pride coming from helping the customer, not making money. Naturally this annoyed my grandmother at times, yet she knew he was a good man, a person who would literally give someone the shirt off his back.

Grandpa Ben met Bobbe Mary, six years his junior, at the Bluebird Dance Hall, a popular place for young singles in 1930. They danced, the first evening going so well, my grandfather boldly told Bobbe Mary that she could put her shoes under his bed at any time. Six months later, on December 7, 1930, they were married, each a good catch for the other.

She became a butcher, and together they ran a kosher butcher shop selling meat and poultry to many Jewish families in Utah, Wyoming, and Idaho. There were few of them, but there was little competition for my grandparents' services.

Marriage changed Bobbe Mary's world. The singing lessons ended, and she stopped playing the guitars. Her focus on being a wife, a workmate, and a mother. Her music became limited to lullabies and the singing of Sabbath songs over the candles. Since they were no longer being used, Grandpa Ben traded her musical instruments for something else, promising Bobbe Mary that if she ever wanted to take the time to play again, he would buy her bigger and better ones. She knew he meant it, and the loss never bothered her.

Gradually the butcher shop became a full grocery store, my mother and her two brothers working there. My mother handled the candy counter, my two uncles delivered groceries in the neighborhood, and the family prospered.

My grandmother corresponded with her family in Lithuania for years, though the last reply she received was around 1942. At that time the envelope was marked in such a way that it was obvious the family was not known. Perhaps they had lost their homes and were refugees in another community. Perhaps the area post office could not deliver the mail. The returned envelope was not yet a major concern, because everyone in the United States was either naive or in deep denial about the fate of Jews in occupied Europe. Bobbe Mary knew there was war-time destruction and that civilians were victims, but neither she nor most Americans had any idea that the systematic murder of village after village was taking place. Information came mostly from Pathé newsreels show in movie theaters, and through picture stories in *Life*. But these were done by people traveling with the military, not moving through the civilian areas.

It was only when the Allied occupation forces, the International Red Cross, and other relief groups could go in that the fate of the people was known.

In 1945 word reached Bobbe Mary that every member of her family who had remained in their village had been taken by the Germans, marched to a field at the edge of town, then ordered to dig their own graves. They had to stand in the holes while they were buried alive by bulldozers and other large earth-moving equipment. The lucky ones who tried to resist were killed by gunshots. Burying alive was the preferred method for destroying the people, though, because it saved the Nazis the bullets.

Had Bobbe Mary been raised in America, she might have been able to partially deny the horror she was told. She might have been able to work through the nightmare.

However, she had fled similar violence. She had seen what the Czar's troops had done to Jewish communities. The Nazi atrocities were worse, yet having known one form of hell, it was easy to believe just how bad things had been for those she loved, albeit from afar.

Bobbe Mary remembered the corpses from which boots and clothing had been removed when she was young. At that time, the faces were those of strangers. She realized that other children and their parents were again stealing from the dead so that they might live. Yet she knew that this time, if she returned to where she once had lived, the corpses lining the streets would be those of a sibling, a parent, or a cousin. One nightmare had at least been impersonal. This pain and grief stayed with her the rest of her life.

The news came at a time when there were survivors of concentration camps arriving in Salt Lake City. They had stories that added to the impact of the discovery of her family's deaths. My mother said that Bobbe Mary cried until it seemed as though there could be no more tears wrung from her soul, and then she would weep some more. The grieving never ended. It took its toll on her life in much the manner of a cancer that has been surgically removed, leaving the body safely functioning yet never with its original strength.

Bobbe Mary went to bed a fairly young woman the night she heard the news. She awakened older, haunted, slightly haggard, so visibly changed that it shocked my mother. Within two weeks her rich jet black hair had lost its pigment, turning white from the trauma. And the grief that was never far from her heart resulted in frequent weeping whose sound haunted my mother. She said that Bobbe Mary was never the same again. In truth, neither was my mother. But that was not so obvious.

In 1953 Grandpa Ben became seriously ill. Fortunately, ever practical, he and Bobbe Mary had earlier looked to the future and decided to change businesses. In 1947 they had bought a nineteen-unit apartment building. With the exception of two 2-bedroom end suites, and one slightly oversized two-room unit, each with its own bath, the apartments all were just two rooms without private baths. There were eight additional baths, one bath for every two units. They then sold the butcher shop/grocery store to pay for Grandpa Ben's medical treatment.

The building was a beautiful one, the grounds filled with hundreds of flowers, a grape arbor, three entrance gates covered with roses, and flawless green grass. The two-room units and shared baths were normal for construction at the time. However, after my grandfather died and Bobbe Mary lost her health more than thirty years later, the apartment building became a tenement that was frequently in violation of the local building codes. Any other owner might have been dismissed as a slumlord. Certainly Bobbe Mary, in her later years, did not bother to make as many repairs to the suites as I would have wanted if I rented from her. She maintained the apartment building in a manner that was a comfortable lifestyle for herself. If it looked unkempt to outsiders, that was *their* problem.

If Bobbe Mary had a philosophy of life, it was expressed by the way she lived, not her words. She had that odd combination of anger, fear, acceptance, and determination that comes from knowing that you are a part of a people who may only be one generation from total extinction.

During all this time, her sister Tova was raising her own family in Palestine. The country became Israel in 1948, and eventually one of Great-Aunt Tova's children, a daughter, went to work for Israel's airline, El Al. Great-Aunt Tova and Bobbe Mary had maintained only limited contact throughout the years, but Great-Aunt Tova's daughter eventually arranged for the sisters to meet in the United States.

I was a teenager when the reunion of my grandmother and her sister took place at the airport. It was easy to romanticize the event. Each of these women had left their native land, seeking a chance at a life without hatred. They were strong, courageous rebels. They had adapted to radically different lifestyles. They had endured the agony of

24

knowing that everyone they left behind had been murdered. They had come to love men of different cultures, different countries.

Finally the plane touched down on the runway in Salt Lake City, taxiing to a stop. Great-Aunt Tova was fluent in Hebrew, having forgotten her native Lithuanian. Bobbe Mary was fluent in English. They eventually would share stories of the past in Yiddish, a language in which each was modestly skilled. However, verbal communication was going to be a problem for them. Still, I expected a moment of passion, a tearful embrace, a dramatic catharsis between two women bonded genetically, historically, and by the joys and sorrows of the extremes of life.

As I held my breath, watching the two women come together, it was obvious that, despite the separation of fifty years, each knew instinctively who the other was. They approached as if the meeting had been rehearsed a hundred times. Then, wordlessly, they turned and stood side by side, shoulder to shoulder, touching each other's stomach to see who was fatter, which sister had the greatest sag to her breasts.

One of Bobbe Mary's more eccentric traits was the desire to win at any cost, even against her not-yet-teenage granddaughter. For example, much of my childhood was spent at Bobbe Mary's apartment playing gin rummy with her. I was just a kid, not very skilled at cards, and certainly no competition for my grandmother. Yet she lacked patience with this child who sometimes took longer to play the hand than she wished. When that occurred, she would announce that someone was at the door.

"I didn't hear anyone at the door," I told her.

"Yes. I heard it. It's a tenant come to pay the rent. Go answer it," she would insist. Dutifully I left my cards, went to the door, opened it, checked the hall, closed the door, then returned to find that the next card Bobbe Mary threw was miraculously her gin card. She had cheated me, her granddaughter, in order to end the hand.

The Salt Lake City banks would give away gifts like

toasters, vacuum cleaners, and sets of china with deposits of $1,500 or more. Since Bobbe Mary deposited the rent money, she technically qualified for the premium, and as a result amassed an absurd collection of plates and appliances. Because I was the only granddaughter remotely interested in business, she insisted that I make the deposits and collect her justly deserved rewards.

Roseanne avoided these pressures. She was the oldest and also quite close to Bobbe Mary. They both shared a fascination with the stage. Roseanne was always performing, always "practicing" by standing before a mirror, singing into a screwdriver or other object she could pretend was a microphone. She delighted in the stories of the Yiddish theater and Bobbe Mary's earliest dreams. However, after marrying Grandpa Ben, Bobbe Mary had changed the goals in life, gradually coming to see herself as a businessperson, not a would-be professional entertainer. Thus it fell to me to share her adventures in the world of high (or low) finance.

Bobbe Mary felt that Jews should always stay with their own kind. She saw Gentiles as being incapable of compassion, sensitivity, and understanding of her background, culture, and ways. For example, there was one afternoon when I was over at Bobbe Mary's apartment as she listened to a local talk show. The Gentiles calling in to the show were talking about what made meat kosher, and my grandmother, the local authority concerning all things Jewish, was outraged. She picked up the telephone, dialed the number, and got on the air.

"You're all wrong," Bobbe Mary insisted. "That's not what kosher meat is. In order for meat to be kosher, I'll tell you what has to happen. The critter must chew its cud or have a cloven hoof, and then we get a sharp knife and we slice the throat.

"After we slice the throat so it doesn't hurt – not like the goyim, who take the cows and pound them on the heads until it hurts the poor critters – then we take the yugular wein [jugular vein] out of the throat and we blow it up. And if all the wital [vital] organs that attach to the yugular wein blow up, then we know this is a healthy critter. Jewish people can eat it.

"If it doesn't blow up, and it's not a healthy critter, then we sell it to the Safeway [supermarket] so the goyim can buy it."

The talk show host, sounding both annoyed and bemused, asked, "Then bad meat's okay for Christians?"

And Bobbe Mary said, "Yes, that's what the Torah tells us."

Rather than being offended, the radio talk show host continued discussing life as Bobbe Mary saw it. Despite her abrasive manner and her slightly off-kilter look at the world according to her version of the Torah, the host knew she was trying to educate the public. She had called in before and always enlivened the show. This time the amused host asked her about personal problems, about whether or not there was something she needed.

Soon Bobbe Mary was discussing her greatest nemesis – Medicare. She had only Part B, and somehow all this seemed tied up with Blue Cross. I never quite understood the problem, but the talk show host arranged to get her address. Then, probably as an excuse to meet this eccentric woman, he came to her home to help her with her problem. He found that mistakes had been made and that she did need someone to act on her behalf. He took the paperwork she had received, her receipts, and whatever other documents were necessary, then went to the Social Security Administration office on her behalf.

As it turned out, the nature of the business Bobbe Mary had run over the years, and the law governing such matters at the time, meant that she had not paid into the system for herself, though she did pay for her workers. She was personally eligible only for the one part of Medicare she received.

The disk jockey did all this on his own time. It was not a public service gimmick by the station. And when he was finished, Bobbe Mary was extremely grateful for the fact

27

that her Medicare problem was resolved to her satisfaction. He also kept in contact with her, the two remaining friends over the years.

I tried to be tolerant of my grandmother's extremes, though there were times when she troubled me. She knew she was physically safe in Salt Lake City. Jews who were raised in the community sometimes feared the more extreme among the Mormons. Certainly my mother did at times. But my grandmother had known truly murderous oppression, and knew that the occasional stories of remarks by right-wing bigots among the area Gentiles were not reasons to be alarmed.

Unfortunately, there were times Bobbe Mary acted in Salt Lake City in a manner that had not been appropriate for a half century. This was when I realized how different we were. These times were also the emotional low points of our relationship.

Nothing fazed my grandmother. There was the time she was outside watering her garden when a woman attacked her. Watering the flowers was a peaceful time for Bobbe Mary. She loved flowers, especially roses, and though she later neglected the interior of all the suites in her apartment building, including her own, her gardens won prizes. The woman, quite drunk, was visiting a tenant. Bobbe Mary was determined that the woman would not give her building a bad reputation, and turned up the pressure on the garden hose nozzle. She drenched the woman's face and clothes with the full force of the water. "Calm down," my grandmother screamed. "You're drunk. I'm a lady. Come and talk with me when *you* can be a lady."

She had been emotionally brutalized. But she had standards, and "being a lady" was extremely important to her. She dressed for synagogue, for example, putting on her diamonds and her pearls. The different immigrant groups felt strong class distinctions. And for those who came from an area of money and culture, as Bobbe Mary did, it was important to feel superior to those who came from peasant families.

Oddly, that distinction seemed to find its way into the

synagogue in Salt Lake City as well. Religion was a divisive issue in the community at large. Money was the source of status within the Jewish community, and there was intense snobbery between the wealthy and the struggling. Many of the Jews were doing extremely well in business and in professional careers. They made certain they arrived in expensive cars, giving the impression to those of us in battered Chevrolets that we had somehow failed in life. Even the community that should have joined together did not, and Bobbe Mary reflected that antagonism quite strongly.

This class snobbery certainly kept my grandmother from ever getting along with my father. She was landed Lithuanian and he was peasant Russian stock. I never fully knew why she disliked him. He had a temper that occasionally erupted within our family, but so did our mother. I have memories of each of them, pushed to the limit, becoming overly physical in anger when one or another of us children did something wrong.

When I was in college, I used to take my books over to Bobbe Mary's apartment to show her what I was learning. I wanted to share with her, to bring the world at large into her living room, because I knew she could never see past the Jewish community that was her world in Salt Lake City. I don't know if I wanted to change her, to make her more cosmopolitan, worldly, and accepting, or if I just wanted to challenge her rigidity. Whatever the case, this one day I decided to show her the chart in my anthropology textbook that explained the evolution of human beings.

I told Bobbe Mary about the earliest stages of what would become the men and women who walk this planet. I showed her the apelike creatures from which we evolved. I showed her the pictures of the different stages leading to a human development as we now understand it. I showed her when the use of tools was learned, when humans first stood erect (*Homo erectus*), and when they became what we are today (*Homo sapiens*).

Usually my grandmother had little interest in my courses, but this time she seemed riveted as she looked at the drawings of the different stages of humanity evolving from primates. Finally she looked up at me and said, "Very, very nice. You go to college to learn this. You didn't need to give them the tuition of four hundred dollars to learn that you came from an ape. Everyone knows that your father is a gorilla!"

The Next Generation

Bobbe Mary may have been a liberated, aggressive woman, but her daughter, Helen Davis, my mother, was a very different personality. She spent her adult life in a manner that I often saw as somewhat passive. My mother seemed to be more comfortable appeasing others than standing up to their bigotry. She had the talent and early recognition needed to make a career as a professional musician, yet she was only interested in being a mother and a homemaker. Oddly, she was drawn to an outgoing man who was talented in his own way and seemingly had the ambition for show business my mother lacked. Yet he was not a risk taker, perhaps one of the reasons Bobbe Mary disliked him. Of course, when he settled for what, for him, was a slightly frustrating life of insecurity in business, he was branded a peasant by my mother's mother. And with her class snobbery, Bobbe Mary would have additional reason to look down upon him.

Jerry Barr, my father, was my sister Roseanne's greatest inspiration. He loved comedy and always wanted to be a comedian. He also was a skilled storyteller, as well as being a perfect audience, laughing uproariously at anything he found funny. His tastes varied greatly. He was as likely to enjoy the slapstick of Jerry Lewis as he was to delight in the involved stories of Myron Cohen. And always, whenever a comedian would come on the television screen, he would bellow "Comedian!" to alert Rosey and any other family member who was interested.

Dad never went into comedy, never took advantage of some of his opportunities. Instead, he became a salesman, a good job for someone so outgoing and filled with a love of showmanship. Yet to go into sales, he turned down two football scholarships, one to the University of Utah and the other to the University of Wyoming, ending his formal education and probably limiting his future.

My father's father, Samuel Barr, was born in Kiev, during the same era as Bobbe Mary. He also had to flee the Czar's army, and he, too, made his way to New York's Ellis Island. He had six sisters in New York and a brother in St. Paul, Minnesota. Since the brother ran an import-export business and was in a position to give my paternal grandfather a job, he moved to that city.

My paternal great-grandfather Joseph, who had been a shoemaker in Russia, stowed away on a ship traveling to Cape Town, South Africa. Like many other young men, he did not want to serve in the military. To his delight, he found a surprisingly large European Jewish emigrant community in Cape Town, and he became so comfortable with the life there that he stayed for about fifteen years. Eventually he, too, went to New York and then to Waterloo, Iowa. However, in a manner much like the Mormons, he made the trip from Waterloo to St. Paul on foot. Even the cheapest rail transportation was beyond his means, all his savings having been used for the ship's passage to the United States.

Eventually Great-Grandpa Joe made his way to Salt Lake City, where he became the simplest type of salesman. His place of business was any street corner where he thought he could be successful. His wares were combs, pencils, and similar small items he offered for change. If the customers asked a price, he would say fifteen cents. If they gave him a quarter, he would say, "Thank you," and quickly move on. If they gave him a dime, he would stay where he was and say, "You owe me a nickel."

The work was not done out of desperation. Great-Grandpa Joe loved his business, loved the lack of overhead, and would sell to anyone. My mother laughed about how, when she first met the man who became her grandfather-in-law, he delighted in showing her "combs mit duh fancy handles." He lived to sell, the rare exception being his soon-to-be-granddaughter-in-law, to whom his pre-wedding gift was a pink comb mit duh fancy handle.

Many men made their living from the streets, especially back east. The ghetto areas of Manhattan had men with pushcarts selling dishes and other items, supporting their families in this manner. But while Grandpa Sam seemed content with their life, he was encouraged to do something more by the family he had first met in Minnesota. Those relatives were in the import business, and they wanted to branch out into the West. They saw the Salt Lake City population growing, knew that there would always be money for the right products if they were inexpensive enough, and they recognized my grandfather's enthusiasm for sales.

Soon my paternal grandfather was in the business of selling items imported by his brother and shipped from Minnesota. He went from pencils and combs on the streets to going door to door with such items as rugs, blankets, curtains, fonts for holy water, and pictures of Jesus, the last two for the Catholic market. The pictures were big, gaudy, and often three-dimensional so that Jesus' eyes would seem to follow you no matter where you went in the room.

The merchandise was always stored in the basement of the house. There was almost no overhead, and the profits were what my mother called "feast or feathers." Sometimes the money was so great that they could feast. At other times there was so little, they only had leftover poultry feathers to eat. While their poverty was never that extreme, the family experienced frequent lean times and never got financially ahead.

My father and grandfather never achieved the success of their fantasies, but they were a part of a merchandising effort that changed contemporary American retailing. There were department stores in those days, but they were upscale merchandisers selling for cash. Credit was not given, and the earliest charge options had not yet been devised. In addition, the stores were often not conveniently located except for what today would be considered suburban customers.

The street peddlers understood the potential for making money from those individuals who could not save enough money to buy at the department stores. They recognized that many working people had small amounts of extra money from their paychecks. Like all Americans, they had the desire for an occasional luxury. However, normal merchandising required cash in full when buying anything, and the poor needed credit that was not available to them. In addition, many of the working poor were Hispanic or some other minority group who regularly faced credit discrimination.

My father and grandfather brought the merchandise to the homes of their customers, many of whom were low income or minorities who had known discrimination. They were told that they would be trusted with the merchandise, that they only had to make a down payment to have something special in their homes. A dollar and fifty cents down and four dollars a month, the average charge, does not seem like much money, but there were hundreds of families who could buy only in this way. And selling in this manner was still new in Salt Lake City, giving Dad the chance to dominate the market.

The customers were delighted to have such peddlers come to their homes and they tried to never get behind in their payments. They were being given a chance to purchase a quality of life that had previously been denied them.

The peddlers like Dad and Grandpa Sam made enough money to interest the department stores in the markets those stores previously overlooked. Ultimately the department stores moved branches into lower-income neighborhoods. They developed layaway plans. They instituted store charge accounts, then began also accepting bank credit cards. The peddlers were put out of business.

My mother hated my father's lifestyle because it was so insecure. She wanted him to work with his hands, to have a regular job in a factory or some other location, to have a steady paycheck from which they could budget. Unfortunately he delighted in unconventional sales and managed to fail at the more traditional work he tried.

Part of my father's optimism probably came from his youth. He was just twenty-one when my eighteen-year-old mother gave birth to Roseanne. He was working constantly. She was enduring the nightmare of being completely naive about pregnancy and childbirth.

Bobbe Mary was progressive in many ways, but she was from a background where even the word "pregnancy" was embarrassing. She referred to her married daughter as "being in a family way." She also gave Mom well-intentioned but misguided advice, such as that it was critical for her to "eat for two." As a result, Mom ballooned from the 117 pounds she weighed when she married my father to 197 pounds when she went into labor approximately eleven months later. The excessive weight gain led to severe complications, a surgically enhanced delivery, and the more than one hundred stitches needed to close the opening made by the posterior birth. The pain was so intense, Mom remembered screaming and cursing at everyone.

My father and his and Mom's parents were all allowed in the labor room, though not even Dad could join Mom during the delivery. As the five of them gathered around the bed during the labor, Mom told me she alternated between screaming in pain and cursing Dad, shouting, "Look what you did to me!" She was totally unprepared for the experience.

Rosey was born on November 3, 1952, a time when information about childbirth was not readily available to expectant mothers. The doctors did not bother preparing women for the experience. Since they did not know what to ask, women like my mother usually went through the experience with no understanding whatever. And since the doctor was the man who had delivered Mom, he was considered a family friend. However, Mom's frustrated curses left him in tears, as confused by Mom's momentary venomous hate as she was by what was happening to her.

The biggest shock Mom had, beyond the pain, was the breaking of the water. She did not understand about the natural protection of the fetus in the womb. The sudden break and the volume of fluid released convinced her that, when she was not looking, her doctor had sprayed her with a hose. She was outraged by the indignity of what was either an ill-timed joke or a vicious act. She had no idea that the water loss was possible, much less that it was a natural part of childbirth.

My father was thrilled with the birth of his first child. But my maternal grandfather's reaction was typical of the Barr and Davis family sense of humor. Grandpa Ben went to see Rosey, discovering her to be one of those newborns who actually look beautiful within minutes of birth. However, he could not just tell Mom of his joy. He had to come back and announce, "You know, I've got to be honest with you, Helen. I'm not just saying this because you're my daughter. I'm not saying this because she's my first born grandchild. But that kid looks . . .' ' He paused for a moment, Mom smiling in anticipation of the praise to come. "That kid looks like a monkey."

Mom vowed she would never have another child. She and Dad adored Rosey, whose pictures reveal she truly was a beautiful baby. However, when Rosey seemed to naturally gravitate to Dad, he decided that having more kids was a great idea. Being a salesman, he was also certain he could find a way to "close the deal" and convince Mom to let him get her pregnant.

Roseanne's affection for my father became more obvious later in life. When her comedy success caused her to establish a number of companies to handle various business enterprises, she named one of them the Barr Specialties Company, the same name as Dad and Grandpa Sam's company. It was a way of honoring Dad and letting him know she appreciated their relationship growing up.

My parents worked hard after their marriage, my mother helping with the books in what they considered the family business. She also found time for music, something extremely important in our family.

My mother's childhood had been an emotionally difficult one. Born in 1934, she was eleven years old when

World War II ended and the soldiers who liberated the concentration camps brought back proof of the Holocaust.

She had heard the stories of the world her own mother had fled. She then witnessed Bobbe Mary's shock after the story of the murder of the Lithuanian village people was finally reported. Night after night she endured her mother's uncontrollable weeping. Mom wanted to console Bobbe Mary or somehow flee the pain. Yet the first was impossible, and the second seemed equally unrealistic.

In trying to understand the Holocaust and the horrors being told to her on a daily basis, her imagination created a world of fear. For example, there were the photographs appearing in the newspapers and news magazines following the liberation of the concentration camps. Many of the pictures were of piles of bodies, and many of the victims were small children who had obviously been starved. Mom's little brother, one of my uncles, was four years younger and very Semitic looking. His face was similar to the faces of many of the young boys in pictures of the young victims of the concentration camps. Mom was haunted by the stories and began dreaming of the war, of the pictures coming alive, of hearing the screams, smelling the decaying flesh, being part of the world that had erased a part of her history.

It was a seemingly odd reaction for a child who had been raised safely in the United States. However, there were two other influences affecting her. The first was religious discrimination. She understood that, as the "Jewish girl," she would always be an outsider in the world. She was part of a minority, considered inferior, and sometimes viciously reviled. My own experiences made me understand that a non-Mormon Christian was considered by Mormons to be spiritually naive yet, because they accepted Christ, at least partway to the true religion the Mormons felt they practiced. Very liberal Jews might see Jesus as a great teacher, a rabbi, but they did not feel the Messiah had as yet come. Thus being a Jew was one step removed from being a non-Mormon Protestant or Catholic. A Mormon who converted a Jew would be that much closer to achieving personal glory.

Mother became so conscious of what amounted to the religious caste system of Salt Lake City that I felt she came to fear offending anyone. She chose to lead her life in a nonconfrontational manner, seeking the good to which she could relate in everyone and ignoring the pain they caused. She also learned to not risk putting herself into avoidable situations where others were certain to reject her.

For example, Mom had a severe overbite in her mouth when she was twelve years old. She was taken to a dentist who recommended braces, something my grandparents found the money to afford. She then went to the specialist, being told to return for regular visits. However, the second or third time she arrived at the outer office, she noticed the sign on the doctor's door – Practice Limited to Orthodontia. She had never heard the word "orthodontia," did not know what it meant. In her mind, she assumed that the Orthodontia were members of a Gentile religious group. She was certain that the doctor would not tolerate having her as a patient when he learned she was Jewish!

Mom could not understand why Bobbe Mary would ask her to go to the specialist when her mother knew the discrimination the family had faced over the years. Mom was so hurt by her perception of what she was being asked to do that, at first, she did not tell Bobbe Mary her fears. Instead she pretended to go to the orthodontist's office every week, never going inside. Finally the family realized something was wrong because the orthodontist called Bobbe Mary to tell her that Mom wasn't keeping her appointments. Mom had missed six months of treatment and paid the price of having extensive gum-line cavities to fill when the braces finally came off.

Mom's fear of being hurt for being different was enhanced by one German immigrant family who lived a half block from the Davis home. Mom's school was three and a half blocks from home. There was only one direct route, and that took her past the German family, all of whom were pro-Nazis and who still supported Hitler despite living in the United States.

The German family knew the Davises, knew they were Jewish, and delighted in tormenting my mother. At least once every week or two, and sometimes more often, they would be waiting outside when she went to school. There were two adults and three teens, and all of them hated equally. One or more would stand in front of their house and shout, "You goddamned Jew! We're going to get you, too." It was a singsong chant of the type meant to inspire the masses surrounding Hitler. It was east to imagine being in German territory during World War II and hearing the chants as Jews were systematically forced to leave their homes.

Despite being free and seemingly safe in America, Mother was terrified. The taunts from the family, the realization that her adored younger brother could have been a concentration camp victim, and the horror of the stories of Holocaust deaths were a devastating combination. She also had to watch her mother's anguish, to see the change in the woman after hearing that her family had been buried alive.

Bobbe Mary's aggressiveness, her eccentricities, and her confrontational attitude seemed to stem from the aftermath of her grief. Mom felt desperate to do something to ease my grandmother's internal hell, and helpless in the realization that there would be no solace she could provide. In suppressed frustration and pain, Mom began having nightmares, awakening eight and ten times a night from the time she was a teenager until long after she was married. It took several years, counseling, and my father's loving patience to free her from her nights lived on the edge of madness.

My mother's nightmares affected how she chose to handle herself during her waking hours. She was haunted by what a like-minded community could do to a minority, by the potential danger from the Nazis. She feared the unknown. She understood the potential for harm from the zealous "true believers," and she thought that the greatest safety came from becoming a valued part of what she feared. I had the impression that she thought that if she was active with the Mormons, the handful of extremists among them, especially the former German Nazis, would leave her family unharmed.

Ironically, there are teachings within the Mormon church that fit nicely into the thinking of someone who has been raised in an Orthodox Jewish home.

Among the ideas that Mom respected were those related to food and drinks. The Mormons believed that the body was a temple. It was to be "worshipped" through proper diet. Caffeine was forbidden; the Mormons drank neither tea nor coffee nor cola drinks. Alcohol was forbidden, as was tobacco in any form. The diet was rich in vegetables, brown rice, unbleached flour, and other natural items we now know are important for good nutrition. Fish and fowl served as animal protein, and red meat was seldom consumed (twice a week maximum), again a situation we now try to emulate. They essentially had a macrobiotic diet before it was hip. They also focused on herbal medicines of a type which have only recently become respected in the rest of the country. Vitamin supplements and organically grown produce were standard, low-cost items, not something people saw as special.

Actually even today the only food threat to Mormon health comes from the highest consumption of ice cream per capita in the nation. The high-fat, high-cholesterol treat provides the primary challenge to a true believer's arteries, and many of the families whose children attended my school delighted in such indulgence. Obesity and the attendant risk of heart disease were not major issues among the Saints. They accepted them as the by-products of having ice cream parlors as readily available as neighborhood bars in blue-collar neighborhoods in other parts of the nation.

My mother was also like the Mormon women in her selection of items to bake. We used to have fun decorating gingerbread with five colors of frosting, cinnamon rolls, and other treats. She also made five-color Jell-O, a highly prized skill involving five flavors of Jell-O, special cubing of the cooled dessert, then careful combining of the colors.

Mom had a crafts room where she produced endless

items for the home. She learned to make stained-glass windows, some of which were added to the home, others of which were made small and turned into the sides of jewelry boxes. She practiced calligraphy, needlepoint pillows, and endlessly involved herself in one project or another to benefit her family and friends.

With such domestic traits, my father was certain he had found the ideal woman to provide him with more children as delightful as Rosey. Mom would have none of it, though. She did not want to live with "feast or feathers." His work was too uncertain, their income too unstable. She would not bring another child into such an unpredictable arrangement.

Dad was determined to have more children, though. He informed my mother that he would do anything she wanted. He would even work with his hands and be a laborer worthy of his hire, his hours and paycheck steady.

Mom loved Dad and recognized that he truly seemed committed to being a different, more cooperative husband in exchange for another child. This was more than just a willingness to change diapers. This was a man who would alter his lifestyle for the family he loved. And when Dad became employed at a factory called Eimco, Mom ended all precautions. I think it was the best decision she ever made. After all, the next child she had was me.

This time everything seemed to work much better. Mom learned that she did not have to eat for two. She still feared the pain of childbirth, yet she also anticipated a second child.

Bobbe Mary was excited as well. She was determined that my mother would have a girl, not a boy, the second time around. Bobbe Mary had missed her sisters and regretted that my mother had two brothers instead of the special bond she believed only sisters could enjoy.

Dad just wanted a child, but he also wanted to follow his dreams and schemes, traits that would later be used by Roseanne and me when creating the Connor family for Rosey's television show. With Mom safely pregnant a second time, he quietly went into business with his father once again. They saw an advertisement in the newspaper that said that local salespeople were needed to go door to door with the Atlas sewing machine and Atlas vacuum cleaner. The opportunity seemed perfect for them, and since Dad was working the four-to-eleven shift at Eimco, he had all morning for sales. Because of his promise to my mother, though, he chose not to tell her all that he was doing.

Normally, Dad was always home for a lunch he ate just before leaving for the factory. One afternoon he failed to come home as expected. He had quit his job and was concentrating all of his time on the vacuum cleaners because the company's approach to selling was proving profitable.

Mom found Dad in the area headquarters for the Atlas company. She hustled him into a back room and began verbally attacking him with almost as much vehemence as she had shown the doctor who delivered Rosey. When she finally calmed down, he explained how much money he was finally able to make in sales. He showed her that he genuinely was doing better by going full-time with the vacuum sales than he could do with the factory job.

Dad was the company's top salesman, and Mom and Rosey were enjoying one of those periods of feast. In fact, he was going to be honored at a regional luncheon to be held on July 19, 1957. This originally seemed as though it would work out nicely with her pregnancy, because the delivery of the infant (who turned out to be me) was expected ten days earlier. However, I decided to be late, not arriving until the last minute for both of them.

Dad was dressed for the luncheon when Mom went into labor. With my innate sense of great show business timing, I was born just in time for Dad to make certain Mum was all right, see that I was health, and race to the luncheon with minutes to spare. Not even Rosey, after becoming a star, ever made a more dramatic entrance.

Mom was delighted with the fact that I was a girl. She wanted Rosey to have a sister, the sister she had missed during her childhood. And to her delight, despite the age difference, we bonded intensely. Rosey, being five years older, had friends and her own life, of course. But I looked up to her as a woman of the world, all-knowing and capable of doing nothing wrong. That probably drove my parents crazy when Rosey was at her liveliest, and certainly it must have made me a terrible pest at times for Roseanne. Yet as we grew into womanhood, the adventures we shared also resulted in a closeness each of us treasured.

The days of feast did not last as long as we all liked. Dad was promoted to a regional territory that included all of Utah and part of Idaho. This meant frequent separations, which he hated. However, every summer the four members of the Barr family went on the road together. Mom handled Rosey and me. Dad handled the sales. And everyone was happy.

The only problem was Dad's superior, an immensely successful man whom Dad wished to emulate. Dad went with the man when he demonstrated vacuums and learned new techniques for closing deals. What Dad did not know was that his mentor had taken his high-pressure sales tactics a step too far, apparently getting so deeply involved in fraud, misrepresentation, and over-pricing that he violated one or more state laws. He was sent to jail, and Dad thought it best to enter yet another business.

Mother's earliest connection with the Mormons came through her music. She had won state competitions as a twelve-year-old pianist. She and Bobbe Mary encouraged our family's involvement with music at home. I played the violin, and my younger sister played the flute. Rosey took piano lessons and liked to sing. We would play and sing together regularly at home, just like many Mormons who also enjoyed such family activities.

That encouragement led to what might be considered my brief time in show business. I played in the high school orchestra as well as with various smaller groups, also a part of the high school's music program. But I also became a caroling violinist at Christmastime each year, strolling the mall and playing in department stores. I was truly ecumenical, a Jewish girl playing Christmas carols in Mormon country, though the truth was that I simply loved to play. And when I was playing, everyone focused on the music, not my religion, my ancestry, or my appearance. It was a time of great inner peace and happiness, and while I never thought of a full career in the field, I also knew I would never stop.

Mother's skills with keyboard instruments were, in my mind, more respected than Mom believes. The Mormons convinced her to begin playing piano and organ for the LeGrand Ward Primary, the Mormon equivalent of a neighborhood church. She also once played in the Mormon Tabernacle baptism room in a Temple Square building in downtown Salt Lake City right next to the Tabernacle itself. They called her Sister Barr, because they wanted to make her an honorary Mormon.

I suppose there might seem to be something a little odd about my mother's handling of our religious upbringing in Salt Lake City. Yet when you consider that we were an isolated Jewish community within the rather confined Mormon society, her actions made sense. I think she felt that intense exposure to two different religious cultures would be enriching for her children. I believe that she also felt that if we could be seen as a part of the Mormon activities, we would not face verbal or physical abuse.

While Mum did not have us follow all of the complex rituals of the Orthodox Jewish faith, she lit candles on Friday night and eventually arranged for us to go to a local school of Jewish studies after classes in regular school were over. We honored the Sabbath with a Shabos (Sabbath) family dinner at Bobbe Mary's every Friday, and we always went to Sunday school in the synagogue where Mom was a teacher. But most of the religious studies to which I was exposed were very liberal, very much aimed at getting us to ask questions, to explore matters of faith rather than being given the rigid answers common with the Mormon teachings.

From the earliest age, Roseanne and I approached religion in very different ways. Mom's method for living within the Mormon community ultimately led to Rosey's temporarily embracing the church. By contrast, I showed much greater interest in Judaism and its rituals. But no religious divide would prevent Roseanne from becoming the most important person in my early life.

I Discover My Big Sister

My first memory of my older sister Roseanne, was when she poked pins in my head. She wasn't trying to hurt me. She was trying to make me beautiful in the same way she thought our mother liked to do. As the story was explained to me when I was older, Rosey sat down with me when I was barely a toddler and placed ribbons on my hair. Then, instead of using a bobby pin or whatever my mother may actually have used to secure them in place, Rosey jabbed a hat pin straight down into my scalp. It was a technique that worked with dolls, teddy bears, and other stuffed toys. Certainly, she assumed, it would work with a baby sister.

Despite that rather harsh experience at the hands of my sister, I adored Rosey. She was my first playmate, my first best friend. My mother told me that when Rosey started school, I was so devastated that I sat on the couch, looking out the window, waiting for her to return. There were days when I sat like that for hours.

In my child's mind, I suppose that Rosey was the most mature young woman I could ever imagine encountering. She did not need diapers. She could tie her shoelaces. She had a fairly full set of teeth in her mouth. And she spent a lot of time playing with me.

Later I would learn that one of the reasons Rosey spent time with me, beyond my curiosity value and, I suspect, the fact that our mother would have killed her had she not looked out for me, was that we were limited in our playmates. I did not understand the stigma of being different in a closed society until the day when I made a friend with Amanda, a little girl my own age. We played all day together, and I don't think either of us had ever been happier. We laughed and talked endlessly. We ate the treats and drank the milk my mother provided for us. And then we made plans to get together again the very next day.

There was no second day of play. My friend's parents learned that she was playing with "that Jewish girl." She learned that I had killed Jesus Christ, and angrily she confronted me with this information. She said, "I can't play with you, or be your friend anymore, because you are not a member of the L. D. S. church."

It was my first encounter with irrational prejudice, and I was shattered by it. I don't remember telling my parents, but I did discuss it with Rosey, who, I learned had known similar experiences. She taught me how to deflect the attacks with logic and humor. I learned to say, "I didn't kill Christ. I wasn't even born then." Or "I didn't kill Christ. Pontius Pilate had him killed." Or I might use one of Rosey's favorite lines: "Yes, I did kill Jesus . . . *and you're next.*"

Over the years, I learned that the comebacks did not really ease the pain. They just gave me a sense of being at least a little in control.

There was another problem I faced as I grew. I reached my full height early. I'm five feet eight inches tall, somewhat tall for a woman. However, unlike most girls who reach their first major growth spurts in junior high or their first year of high school, I was five feet tall in second grade. I was also the heaviest girl in class. I was not really fat, but kids did not understand the difference caused by height. I weighed ninety-four pounds, appropriate for my size yet many pounds heavier than my classmates. I was also called the Jolly Green Giant, a constant, painful reminder of what was happening to me.

Again it was Rosey who understood. She grew in a more usual manner, but she was chunky, perhaps fifteen or twenty pounds overweight. An adult would see her as a healthy, normal child. Yet to kids, Rosey was fat, so Rosey was taunted. She endured the pain before me, and thus I could turn to her for understanding and guidance.

Actually, despite a diet that consisted of chicken fat for cooking, Sugar Pops and Cap'n Crunch for breakfast, and

45

whatever treats Mom or Bobbe Mary might make, we were in good physical shape. I rode my bicycle all the time, and Roseanne was always dancing. We just did not think of such healthy activities in the manner of physical fitness. In fact, Rosey had a dread of gym class that led to the one time I physically hurt her.

I don't remember how old we were when the incident occurred, though I know I was still in elementary school. The Kennedy administration had actively promoted physical fitness, including having children test themselves in such activities as sit-ups, pull-ups, and running races of various distances. This program continued after his death, and our school decided to test all the children. Most of the events were no problem for Rosey, though for some reason she was terrified of the 100-yard run.

My age group was still exempt from such testing, so I never learned all the details. As near as I could understand from Rosey's near hysterical demand for help was that a record of individual times was taken. Each child would run 100 yards, alone, in front of every classmate and a teacher with a stopwatch waiting at the end of the distance. If you could not finish, if you collapsed, red of face and gasping for air, every kid was there to taunt you. They would learn who was slow, who was fast, and who was too out of shape to succeed.

Rosey was terrified. She did not want to take the test. She knew the kids would ridicule her when she ran. She knew that she would fail miserably in the effort. And Rosey had to win. She had to be the best. She had to be the cutest, the funniest, the most successful. And if the class was going to run, an activity she knew she could not win, she wanted no involvement at all.

Rosey ranted about what she was facing. She raved. She said things such as, "I don't see how physical education will help me with my chosen career of brain surgery." And then she developed "the plan." Rosey asked me to break her leg.

I was shocked. Being five years younger than Rosey, I could not say I was a giant intellect. But even I suspected that a broken leg was a lot worse than running 100 yards, even if your stomach bounced, your boobs flapped up and down, and you started to sweat like a hog.

"Don't hurt me," Rosey said. She didn't want any pain. She just wanted me to jump on her leg and break it.

There was no reasoning with Rosey, and as I said, I adored her. If my sister wanted her leg broken, then I would break it.

Rosey sat down with one leg outstretched on the ground. I got way back, giving myself a running start. Then I raced toward my sister, jumped into the air, and landed on her leg, just like she asked.

It didn't break.

Wherever I landed required more force than my weight and momentum provided. The leg bruised. Rosey screamed in pain. But she was otherwise remarkably free of injury. She was also outraged that I hurt her when she specifically told me not to do anything of the kind. It wasn't logical, of course. But she had never had a broken leg and I had never tried to break anyone's bones before.

I don't know what happened next, though I assume Rosey ran the 100 yards in her gym class. She was not about to ask her kid sister for such help again.

Rosey could not stay mad at me for very long. She dominated my world and could get me to do anything she desired. Sometimes this meant playing Army. She, being the older sister, was Sergeant Barr. I, the younger, was Private Barr.

"Private Barr, make my bed," she would order when we were faced with domestic chores we both hated.

"Yes, Sergeant Bar," I would say, saluting. And then I would make her bed as well as my own.

Sergeant Barr always had the upper hand, though such games were not as humorous as the way Rosey convinced me to do the dinner dishes alone when we were both assigned the chore.

First Rosey convinced me that witches frequently came into homes at precisely the time that dishes had to be washed. They apparently attacked little girls only when the dishes were still dirty. Thus we were quite vulnerable after dinner each night when it was time to do our chores.

Rosey, the braver of the two of us, decided to "save me" from the witch attack. Selflessly she went outside to watch for the coming of the witches. If one arrived, she would fight it to the death or until I put the last dish, newly clean and sparkling, into the drainer on the sink.

Terrified of the witches, exhilarated by the hint of danger, and thrilled with the courage of my sister, I washed the pots and pans as fast as I could. And each night when I was finished, I was thankful for brave Roseanne who had once again saved our lives and, perhaps, the lives of every member of our family.

Not all the games involved Rosey taking advantage of my gullibility. For example, we all loved to play beauty shop. As usual, Roseanne was in charge. She was the oldest, and she was able to convince the other kids that she knew what she was doing.

At first everything went reasonably well. Roseanne gave one girl a dramatic new look by taking her very long, well-maintained hair and working it into six braids. Then she cut off every other braid. We never heard what the girl's mother thought, and we survived that artistic endeavor without repercussions.

The problem came when Roseanne gave Cindy Atherton a facial. Not having any other devices to use, Rosey appropriated a heat lamp that my parents had in a closet. Then, telling Cindy that the lamp was part of a facial needed to rejuvenate her skin cells, Rosey had her sit in front of the heat lamp for a prolonged period of time, absorbing the restful warmth. Unfortunately for Cindy, the exposure was long enough to blister her face. She had to be taken to hospital for treatment, and I think she still has to wear dark glasses in the sun. Rosey felt terrible for her pain but was not punished.

One time when Rosey was truly mean to me occurred when Dad went fishing. I hated fish. There was something terrifying for me about the eyes of a whole dead fish. And to my regret, the catch, cleaned but not beheaded, would be placed in the freezer until it was time to prepare it for dinner.

Every once in a while, when Rosey would become thoroughly annoyed with having a little kid follow her everywhere, she would take a fish from the freezer and chase me with it. We would race all over the house as I tried to get away from the staring, dead eyes. Then, if I was lucky, I would succeed in reaching the bathroom, where I would lock myself inside.

The bathroom had a heat register at the bottom of the wall, the other side of which was my parents' bedroom. It was the middle of winter, and I was covered with sweat, scared and cold. I stood by the heat register to try to get warm as I calmed myself down, knowing I was safe at last.

Rosey, determined to "win," ever so quietly sneaked into my parents' bedroom. She took the fish to the hot air register that linked both rooms, then put it through the register to where she could see my feet.

Suddenly I felt something cold around my ankles. I looked down, and there was the head of the fish sticking through, the unseeing, dead eyes rubbing against my skin.

I tried to scream but no sound came out. My face turned red as I hyperventilated in terror, opening the door, my mouth wide open, silent in horror. Even Rosey knew she had gone too far when she saw me, and she left the fish, took me aside, and desperately tried to calm me.

It was that day that I came to understand that there was a cruel streak in Roseanne. I realized that she could go too far, that she could torment beyond a point where others would show more restraint. She seemed to enjoy what she had done to me, stopping only when she feared that my extreme reaction might get her punished.

This is not to say I was perfect either. Twice during our childhood I felt as though I was being teased too much, pushed too far, treated with too little respect. I would start screaming to the point where the neighbors sometimes complained. I also was likely to physically attack Rosey, and because I grew so tall so young, my strength was such that I often hurt her during those moments.

But the majority of our time was cherished. And each summer, when Rosey and some friends decided to put on a show, I was honored to be allowed to be an integral part of the effort.

Mormon country was the ideal place to be when a kid had enough "ham" to want to put on shows. Mormon families took great pride in such activities as playing musical instruments together, singing, and entertaining one another with what were called road shows. And in typical small-town fashion, every July 4 the Liberty Park bandstand came alive with the music of John Philip Sousa and other patriotic composers. Everyone sang, and the immigrants who were new to the area took a special pride in singing of their new American home. Thus when Rosey and I and our friends decided to put on a production, it was easy for us to gain cooperation from the neighbors.

First came the cast and crew for the show. At least fifteen to twenty kids were used for each production, not because the shows were that elaborate but because I was a good businesswoman. I knew that the more kids we recruited, the more parents who would come.

These shows provided a glimpse of our future together. Rosey wanted to be on the stage and worked to be a star. I was the one who understood how to bring the elements together that would give her a place to perform and provide an audience to support her.

If I remember correctly, we sold admission tickets for a quarter each, but that was not where we made our money. We made a killing on cookies and punch, and usually we made enough to afford ice cream for the entire cast, pay any expenses, then be able to split the net proceeds among the performers.

The program was a mixture of the Ziegfeld Follies, a television variety program, and an episode of *The Little Rascals*. We always tried to use a stage, usually the crumbling outdoor stage of a former Baptist church that had a large parking lot on which the parents could be seated.

However, the show might also be in someone's yard or anywhere else we could perform.

The kids nobody liked were assigned tasks that were important only because we were limited in our equipment. At least two would operate the sheets or blankets we hung over the clothesline to serve as curtains. Another would come out with a large easel card announcing each new act. And if they really were a couple of doofuses, there was always the act that delighted the other kids yet which no one rational would perform. For example, I remember one year when two boys I'll call Orin and Dwight, both doofuses, came out, ran across the stage, and butted heads.

That was the act. Two boys butting heads. It was very short, but they were quite willing to repeat their presentation any time I asked them to do so. Children on the block trusted me and would do whatever I said was of benefit to them. In hindsight, I was a little like a Hollywood agent. I can see myself wearing a miniature pinstripe suit with pedal pushers and saddle shoes, smoking a big chocolate cigar, and tell them their act was genius. "You might butt your heads a little harder, though. Get a great cracking sound echoing through the audience. It will bring the house down. Trust me."

Dale, another boy of perhaps seven years of age, had a webbed foot. Skin linked the toes so his feet looked a little like flippers. It was a genetic defect he delighted in showing off to all the neighbor kids, so he had his own place in the show.

First there was a massive drumroll handled by the sound effects expert – me. I used two metal bowls held together, a large metal spoon placed in between. Then I would bang the spoon back and forth against the hollow insides of the two bowls, the sound thundering across the parking lot. Or so I envisioned as Dale proudly walked to the center of our stage, sat on a chair, and revealed his bare feet to the audience. This was the one act where everyone in attendance was encouraged to participate, so they all crowded around to look at his feet and see the webbing. Once they had satisfied themselves that he did indeed have webbed feet, they would applaud politely and Dale would leave the stage.

In addition to the drumroll, I was in charge of most of the backstage equipment. I ran the portable phonograph that provided the music for lip-synching songs and dances. I handled the flashlights that served as roving spots, sometimes shining one on the performer, sometimes shaking it all around for a "spectacular" lighting effect. I never was positioned where I could see the performer, so I had to guess when serving as follow spot. However, it really didn't matter because the shows were done outside in daylight. No one could see the flashlight beam anyway, though I tried. I used a black curtain that sometimes caught a hint of the beam. In my zeal I even created my own version of a gel – a piece of tissue paper held over the lens to alter the color and intensity. In reality, it made the light softer.

I just wanted to make certain that every aspect of the production was worthy of our inspiration – Ed Sullivan, and when we reached our teen years, *The Sonny & Cher Show*, Flip Wilson's shows, and, of course, the acts on *The Smothers Brothers Comedy Hour*. I knew that one day I would be a real producer. The stage equipment would be the same as used in professional shows. Thus I had to be true to my calling, going as far with each production as our resources allowed, yet always trying to top the previous performances.

We even had commercials, none of us realizing or caring that live theater was different from what we saw on television. Usually the commercial had to do with some food item requiring a mixing bowl and a demonstration. We mimicked what we saw on TV, and cooking demonstrations were popular back then.

Rosey was always the star of the show – opening, closing, and performing in the middle as well. She would sing and dance while lip-synching to Beatles' songs or other popular music of the day. But her best numbers were the butterfly dance and the twirling cape.

The butterfly dance involved obtaining some relative's massively oversized robe. Then Rosey would hold out her arms and gently move them up and down, waving the material in a way that was meant to imitate the wings of a butterfly. It was silly, of course, yet Rosey was always a talented dancer and musician, and she did outperform the other kids.

The twirling cape was also impressive. A large piece of material was mounted on a dowel or other barlike object that could be grasped and manipulated like a baton. Then Rosey would combine twirling movements with a dance of her own creation. Her choreography and the flowing material again worked.

The shows were an important part of our summers and the one time that all the kids in the neighborhood, no matter what their religion or ethnic background, truly came together. They also were the first indicators of my future with Roseanne. The shows reinforced her love for entertaining, for being in the spotlight, for controlling her destiny. In my case, I was the person who delighted in being backstage, coordinating events, making the spotlight possible for my big sister while never challenging her right to be the sole occupier of its glow. Somehow I knew that without people such as myself, there would be no show, no place for a performer's talent to be seen.

I Discover Religion

There were many ways to look at the Mormons who so influenced everyone's life in Salt Lake City. Bobbe Mary ignored them, carrying on her life as much as possible like that of a Lithuanian village dweller. She made no effort to learn about their religion but was always willing to correct their ignorance about hers.

My mother was different. She felt that the best approach was to get along, to become involved with both Judaism and the Mormon faith. Ultimately they both worshipped the same God. They both had concerns for the health of their people, and similar morals and ethics. By neither denying her faith nor joining the church, she could walk a safe middle ground. She felt that we children would benefit from such contacts as attending the Wednesday after-school religious education programs open to Mormons and those interested in the church. And ultimately she expected us to emerge as loving, tolerant adults, enriched by a cross-cultural experience.

By the time I was entering junior high, I saw the Mormons as a target for humor and satire. For example, there was the night when some close friends of my parents stopped by. They were devout Mormons, and though they genuinely cared about my parents, they inevitably felt compelled to say something on each visit that related to the idea of joining the Mormon faithful. They wanted my parents' friendship, of course, but they were excited about the possibility of assuring my family's celestial presence as well. They were convinced that the Mormon church held the word of God and, to my mind, were overly enthusiastic about sharing.

My mother, the musician, was almost saved in their eyes. My father seemed more distant. And Rosey and I were disgusted with what was taking place. Rosey had not yet become seriously active in the Church of Jesus Christ of Latter-day Saints. I was already fed up with a religion whose answers for everything seemed based more on intolerance than on love.

It was not unusual for Mormons to entertain each other when visiting. We lived in a relatively low income neighborhood where everyone was struggling to support large families. Home musical events, variety shows, and similar forms of self-generated entertainment were extremely popular. Thus when Rosey and I announced that we would perform, everyone was genuinely pleased. These were people who not only encouraged the budding talents of the young, they truly found great pleasure in them. Until that evening.

I'm not certain what made us do what we did, but we found a couple of my father's hats, a pair of canes, and some other props. Then Roseanne, in her early teens, and I practiced a soft-shoe routine, with gestures, for the beloved song "The Old Rugged Cross." We did some quick run-throughs in my parents' bedroom, then came down to perform.

The performance was blasphemous in everyone's eyes but our own. We weren't trying to mock the death of Christ. We weren't challenging the religious beliefs of my parents' friends. Yet the end result was admittedly offensive. We performed a line dance, tapping our way around the canes for some of the music, contorting our faces in agony when the words related to crucifixion.

At first everyone stared in amazement. Our actions were so outrageous that no one knew quite how to respond. Then they moved swiftly, my father exploding in anger, sending us to our bedroom. There were no apologies necessary because the friends knew my parents were not supportive of our actions, yet they did go home early that night, too upset to stay.

In hindsight I realize that this was typical of my grade school rebelliousness. I had too long encountered the hypocrisy and bigotry of the Mormons. I did not like being constantly reminded that my religion somehow gave me inferior status with the same Lord in whom they believed. I wanted to mock them, to shock them, to spit in their eye. Yet I was too young to understand all that, just as I did not realize that my father was almost as angry.

I first became aware of the tension between Mormons and non-Mormons when I experienced the shock of Amanda's not being allowed to play with me. Because I was Jewish, I was called Christ killer, something I could not even understand. I had hurt no one. Mom and Dad had hurt no one. My grandparents had done no harm. Yet because of a religion I had yet to comprehend, I was condemned by the girl I thought to be my new best friend.

Gradually I learned that the hostile feelings were between some bigoted Mormons and *all* non-Mormons in Salt Lake City. Growing up, I placed all Mormons in the same category because of the volume of criticism by the few. They were anti-Semitic if you failed to convert, but they were also hostile to other faiths. Eventually my friends

55

were Catholics, Greek Orthodox, Jewish, Episcopalian, and of every other locally practiced faith – but not Mormon. At first I understood the subtle and blatant bigotry only as a Jewish child focusing on the hate I encountered, never letting myself see any love. And from this understanding, I gained empathy for all the oppressed minorities I learned about, though I failed to realize that my attitude towards the Mormons was one of stereotyping.

My original perceptions of the Mormons stemmed as much from the immaturity of my age as they did from reality. Children and teenagers generally see life as black and white. They have little perception of the gray areas in which most people live, and I was certainly no exception. Often the most vocal people in society are the frauds and the bigots. They substitute hatred and blind absolutisms for the real practice of whatever faith they profess. Others live out their religion in the conduct of their lives, speaking with their actions more than their words. I made the mistake of looking at the actions and words of a minority, then assuming that they reflected the attitudes and beliefs of everyone. It would be years later, when I returned to Salt Lake City as an adult in pain from a family crisis, that I would discover the truth of the majority. We had more in common in our seemingly different faiths and values than I had ever let myself see and understand.

It was in elementary school, after I became an avid reader, that I became so sensitive to the extremists among the Mormons. I hated my life, hated being different in so many ways. I was teased about my size. I was hassled because of my religion. And I intended to be an intellectual loner.

I tried to reduce the pain by mocking the Mormon children. Who could relate to kids with really dumb names like Orin and Dwight, Darryl and DeWitt? I asked myself. Okay, so maybe they weren't so dumb. But they were different from those with which I was familiar, and since I was being teased for being different, I saw no reason not to mock them.

Since many of the Mormon kids wouldn't reach out to

me and I was afraid to reach out to them, I tended to spend a lot of time reading in the library. I had some friends, of course. We'd make our first encounters by quietly asking, "Are you L.D.S. [Latter-Day Saints]?" If the person said no, we automatically shared a common bond, like members of a secret society meeting halfway across the country, delighted that each knows the forbidden handshake of the other. But most of my free time was spent with books and magazines, especially *National Geographic*. I desperately needed to explore other worlds, other cultures. Where else could I learn about blacks, either in the United States or in Africa. Where else would I encounter Chinese, Japanese, Koreans, and Vietnamese? Where else could I learn that Salt Lake City was not the center of the universe, that the customs and mores were not the standard around which the world revolved. They were simply part of one culture, a very small one at that, and no more right or godly or special than any other.

Salt Lake City, like most isolated areas, had its special bias against those who were both different and unfamiliar. Now that I am an adult who has traveled throughout the United States and abroad, I have seen this phenomenon repeated elsewhere. Any time a group of people share a radical, ethnic, or religious background that dominates the community, there is a distrust of outsiders. When those same people spend their entire lives within that small territory, seldom if ever going more than a few miles from where they live, the prejudice, born of ignorance, is reinforced.

Stereotype becomes truth when you are as isolated as the Mormons of Salt Lake City had become. They rarely saw a black person, so they developed their attitudes based on stereotypes in the mass media and whatever racist propaganda came their way. The term "nigger" was used even among many "respectable" people. Everyone "knew" that the "niggers" would steal from you. "Nigger" men had large sex organs. "Niggers" were stupid. "Nigger" men were violent. "Niggers" could be saved through the faith, but their ability to participate was sharply controlled; they

57

were treated like trained pets that have been housebroken but are still denied entrance to restaurants and supermarkets because they might forget what they have learned.

The result of such prejudice, like prejudice of all types, was that the children were taught conflicting ideas. Since kids are quite literal in their thinking, and since I was always questioning what I was learning, I began asking the "wrong" things in class. For example, we were taught that the Founding Fathers developed a Constitution that declared all men to be created equal. Yet we also learned that both George Washington and Thomas Jefferson had slaves.

I asked about this seeming contradiction. The relation between a master and his slave was obviously not an equal one. Yet my reasoning was not acceptable. I was told, "Yes, Thomas Jefferson and George Washington had slaves, but everyone knows they were very, very good to their slaves."

The contradictions disturbed others as well. By 1978 the Mormon hierarchy was changing radically. Blacks could be a part of the church priesthood, though not yet the leadership. Still, by being a part of the priesthood, they could also become a part of the highest kingdom of heaven, something previously denied them.

Every Wednesday I attended what was called Primary. This was an after-school religious class for elementary school kids. Primary was run by Mormons for both Mormon kids and any of the rest of us who wanted to attend. Mom participated in the music portion of Primary, and Roseanne had long been involved. My joining the group was naturally expected to follow.

I learned more of the Mormon faith in Primary than I was comfortable knowing. I was taught that all of us begin life as spirits in heaven and choose what we will be on earth. Some spirits choose to join with Jesus, and they come back with a white body. Other spirits choose to join with Satan, and they are not allowed to come to earth and get bodies. And some spirits are stupid. They do not know if they want to become joined with Jesus or with Satan.

They aren't bad people. They're just too dumb to think clearly and make up their minds. They are given the derogatory name "fence sitters," and it was believed they evolved from Cain.

I began challenging the teachers. I understood the teachings to mean that unless you embraced the Mormon church, you would not go to heaven. You would not be reunited with your loved ones after death. A belief in Jesus did not appear to be adequate. Instead, you needed to believe in Jesus in the same manner as the Mormons did.

I knew from my *National Geographics* that members of other faiths far outnumbered the Mormons. "Does this mean that the Chinese can't go to heaven?" I asked. "Does this mean that the Arabs can't go? What about the Japanese? There were billions of people who were not Mormon in the world, and if God created and loved us all as the Mormons taught in Primary, how could God abandon the vast majority of his people.

I was reading the Bible and learning about the Old Testament, and I was fascinated with the Song of Songs, which tells of Solomon. He was David's son, and therefore in the lineage of Jesus. In the writings, Solomon says, "I am black and beautiful," a clear indicator that Jesus was black or the descendant of blacks, something that matches a study of the lands of the Old Testament. In order to try to get the best of the Mormons, I brought up the issue of Jesus as a probable black man in Primary. Naturally, the teachers could neither tolerate such a comment nor deal with someone who was trying to challenge them with the Bible. I quickly learned that, at least within this group, though the claim was that the Bible was the foundation for the Mormon faith, when the Bible contradicted Mormon teachings, other writings, including the Book of Mormon, were utilized.

Roseanne did not feel as I did. At best our family seemed to have a mixed reaction to our heritage, though I always knew I was Jewish. To me Mom's Mormon involvement was part of her mishegash, her craziness, and Dad reinforced this idea. He said, "Your mother, she's a little . . .'

Then he would point his finger at his temple, circling it in the sign of being crazy. This was Mom's "trip," and I knew it was right to align myself with Bobbe Mary in pursuing my Jewish heritage, tolerating the embarrassment of my mother's Mormon connections.

Bobbe Mary seldom came into our home because we failed to keep a kosher house. She was also mildly agoraphobic, and later her health was not at all good. She would go out to get her hair done and go to synagogue, but that was it. The groceries were delivered and even the utility company sent someone to pick up the money for her light bill.

We lived close to Bobbe Mary and used to walk over there all the time, including for a weekly family gathering. But she never knew that Mom and Dad put up a Christmas tree each year and that we kids decorated it. However, she did know that we went to Primary.

I was less of a concern for Bobbe Mary. I eventually attended a California-based Zionist summer camp for Jewish children. It provided me a stronger grounding in my heritage as well as exposing me to children who lived in what I considered more normal communities. I discovered the intellectual side of Judaism and realized that Salt Lake City was not typical of where other kids were raised. It was as a result of the camp that I decided to have my bat mitzvah, a rite of passage for Jewish girls. I had to learn Hebrew and extensively study the history, the teachings, and the writings of Judaism, something in which Roseanne had little interest.

By contrast, Roseanne found fame, acceptance, and love in the Mormon faith. She became the chorister for the Primary, leading the kids in song while Mom played the piano. She also was very active in Mutual, the program for older kids her age.

It was on Sunday, at Fast and Testimony Meeting, that Roseanne began to give her testimony. She was introduced to the others as "the Jewish girl" who wanted to tell what she had learned about the Mormons. Then she spoke of her discovery that the Church of Jesus Christ of Latter-Day

Saints was the only true church. She embraced their doctrines and informed our mother that she wanted to be baptized. She was too young to convert without parental approval, and she assumed that Mom would be accepting of her decision.

In hindsight, while I was comfortable being a loner, Rosey needed friends. The conversion assured many close relationships that she seemed to think she could not get any other way. Admittedly, after I started going to camp, most of my friends were in other cities, becoming pen pals. Yet we were close and they reinforced my decision to stay with my faith.

Up until the request for baptism, I think Mom had discounted the impact that the Mormon church involvement was having on Rosey. Mom felt that we could be solidly grounded in our heritage at the same time that we were exposed to the culture and more public activities of the Mormons. Besides, Rosey was with kids who did not drink, smoke, or involve themselves with drugs, a wonderfully conservative peer group that was keeping her from going wild.

The baptism request changed that fantasy. Mom decreed that if Rosey wanted a complete break from Judaism, she would have to do it when she was an adult and able to speak for herself.

My father was never part of these emotional struggles. He went along with my mother when it came to having the Christmas tree, and he did not object to us kids going to some of the Mormon gatherings. But he did not share my mother's beliefs about religion.

The most blatant example I recall from my childhood was when I became concerned about the meaning of death. I don't know if other kids were obsessed about such ideas, because I never asked. The Mormon kids were rigidly taught and did not seem capable of thinking for themselves. I often thought that the way to truly be happy in Salt Lake City was to either be mentally retarded or a Mormon. The former did not have the intellect to think about the questions of life. The latter might have the innate intelligence, but they were taught from birth that the faith provided all the answers they would ever seek. I, by contrast, had only questions and would endlessly weigh the many possible answers.

What happens when you die? I asked my mother. She told me it was a joyous time. She said that your body is left behind, but your spirit floats up to heaven like a large bubble. Then in the heavenly mists you meet God and are reunited with your loved ones who have gone before. It is a joyous time, a time of celebration. You are happy. And you are never alone again.

I thought about that awhile. It was a gentle image, calming, but I was also very young. The bubbles I knew about were the champagne bubbles that used to float about the set of the Lawrence Welk television show I had watched with Bobbe Mary. Welk and his dance music were popular with older adults, and his program used a bubble-making machine for what passed as special effects in those precomputer days.

One night I went to bed, thinking about death, and there were the Lawrence Welk bubbles floating my spirit up to heaven. I heard his accordion music, but instead of seeing the dancers he showcased, I saw old Jewish men, obviously my ancestors from centuries back, each with long curly hair and the clothing worn by the Orthodox. With them were old Jewish women attired in peasant clothes, all of them with big breasts.

The dream was too much for me. Three weeks after having asked my mother about heaven, I went to my father and asked him what happens after you die. He responded with his typical bluntness:

"Have you ever seen a dead dog in the road that has been rolled over fifty or sixty times by cars until it is all scrunched up? That's what you look like. Then you're placed in the ground, the maggots eat your skin and eyes, your bones rot, and the dust goes back to being part of the elements of the earth. You're just dead!"

"But Dad, Mom says there's heaven."

Dad dismissed such a concept. "Your mom needs to believe that. When you're dead, your bones dry up and that's it."

That's when I stopped dreaming about Lawrence Welk. I stopped thinking about heaven and began to question all kinds of religious beliefs as concepts to be studied and not necessarily absolute truths.

Dad and Me

Our family's history is a rich and at times luxuriantly textured quilt of recollection embroidered by the differing viewpoints of succeeding generations. We children saw my father as a man caught in the midst of cultural contradictions in a community where he could never quite find acceptance. As we remembered his story, he was primarily raised by his mother, Frances, and her father, Joseph. His biological father, Samuel, was home only intermittently. Bobbe Fanny's sister Sophie died when she was only eleven days old.

I never did learn what killed Sophie. Family history says it was rheumatic fever. But the Jewish families I knew in Salt Lake City only claimed two causes of death – rheumatic fever or pneumonia. Someone could have terminal cancer, diabetes, leprosy, and a bad heart, then break his neck when falling from his house while trying to patch some shingles, and his relatives would say he died from rheumatic fever.

Whatever the case, my great-grandfather Joseph never recovered from the shock of the loss. He began drinking, essentially climbing into the liquor bottle and never really coming out. He was an alcoholic his entire life, and that included the time when my father lived with him.

My father's father, Sam, was a storyteller and compulsive gambler. My father must have suffered greatly from his emotional absence, though this was something he would never say in so many words. Living with these two men and their problems took a toll on my father as a young boy. Dad seemed to feel responsible for the problems in the family, despite the fact that he was really the victim of his family's excesses, not in any way a cause.

Once Dad was facing the prospect of becoming a parent, he made the decision to be different from his ancestors, to not drink, to not treat his children as he had been treated. Much of the time Dad was successful. Certainly he was one of the most positive influences in Rosey's and my lives.

For example, it was around the third grade when it became obvious that I was going to be a child who had nothing but questions. My mother would try to paint life pretty, but my father took me by the hand and said, "Come on, darling, I'm going to open a world for you."

We went down to the Salt Lake City Library and he introduced me to this librarian. I'll always remember him going up to her and saying, "Excuse me. I'm wondering if you could help us. This is my daughter, Geraldine, and I wonder if you could help her find books that would be interesting for a young lady."

The woman said, "Certainly, I'd be glad to." And then he said to me, "I'm going to leave you now with this librarian, and she's going to help you. I'll be waiting for you here."

So this librarian talked to me and said, "What are you interested in?"

What I came out with was this book called *The Endless Steppe* about a Jewish girl who lived on the steppes of Siberia. And she didn't have any paper, since paper was an expensive commodity, and she struggled to get paper so she could write. And then she got her period . . . It was an incredibly important book to me. I was in the Siberia of Salt Lake City, and here was this girl who had written of the isolation and longing that I felt. It was like reading my life, and that was the first time that I fell in love with books.

Every week my father would take me back to the library. Whatever we would discuss in terms of literature, whatever questions I would have, he didn't always have the answers, but he made sure that I had access to information. I think that without him, I would have been lost.

In addition to the books, the library had a collection of classical records, players, and earphones. Each visit, if there was time, Dad would select different records — Vivaldi, Mozart, and others – then have me sit and listen to the music. He broadened my taste and sensitivity in ways I would never have known to do myself.

Dad also taught me about the periodical collection. He went to the catalog and looked up all the newspapers and magazines published on my birth date. Then he had me discover what took place the day I was born. From there I learned to truly explore the library's resources to understand what was happening during any period of history.

He also showed me *National Geographic*. We would read it together, Dad helping me learn of the world outside Mormon teachings.

Dad's memories of his past focus on other matters. The stories of his childhood were about Europe and the pogrom against the Jews. As Dad recently related his history:

"I came out of a house of humor and pain. My father came to America when he was nine years old. [He lived] on the streets of New York, in the typical Lower East Side.

"My father was a salesman most of his life. And he was a storyteller. He was a man who could tell a lot of jokes. He had a tremendous background and repartee, so to speak, of jokes. But he was mainly a storyteller with dialect. He could do any kind of ethnic background — black, Irish, English, Scotch, German, also Russian . . . heavy Russian. He had the brogue and all the ways. And he used to be a fabulous storyteller. We'd sit for hours and just listen to him tell the stories."

The stories, according to Dad, were often about his youth in Russia, and about his parents, my great-grandparents. Dad mentioned that Great-Grandad owned an inn in Kiev. "My father had seven brothers and sisters," Dad explained. "The Russians came to the door. They said to my grandfather, 'you no longer own the inn.' They gave him a piece of paper – it was called a pogrom in Russia – and they told him, 'You don't own it.'

"And he said, 'Listen, this is my income for my family. This is all I've got to raise my family.'

"Two soldiers, Cossacks, took him and grabbed him and threw him head first down the well. In those days they didn't have running water. They had outside wells. They broke his neck and this killed him. And that's when they started to slaughter the Jews in Kiev and in Russia, and the pogrom took place.

"My father's mother took the eight children – I'm not sure – and walked from Kiev into Poland in the cold of the winter. We think of Stalingrad when the Russians were fighting Hitler, but here's a woman with eight children who crossed the border to get them out of the Ukraine to save the children."

Dad told about all the funny stories his father told in addition. He had hundreds of jokes that he learned from his parents and grandparents. Certainly there was an aspect of Dad that had wanted to be a stand-up comedian. When he graduated from high school, each senior was asked to write a paper about what they wanted to do with their lives. Dad noted that he wanted to be a stand-up comedian. However, instead he became a salesman with his father, my grandfather doing most of the actual selling to the two thousand customers that formed their base in Salt Lake City, and Dad handling the collection of the one dollar per week that they charged.

Dad did not exactly fit into the *Father Knows Best* world of the 1950s. The creation of the suburbs was a post-World War II phenomenon that took millions of Americans from living with extended families on farms and in cities to the new suburbia, where everything was different. Although many women had worked during the war, the "proper" role for a white suburban woman was to raise the children. The father would commute to work each day, seeing the children at breakfast and dinner, if that. Then, on weekends, the father was expected to cut the grass, shovel the snow, and maintain the house. The suburbs were a matriarchy, though often a frustrating one for the women involved.

Dad was part of this generation, but his situation was

worse. As a poor Jew in a Mormon community, the social pressures on Dad were tremendous. He had neither a prestigious job nor a meaningful estate. His pride, his legacy, the jewels of his life were his children.

The good about Dad was wonderful. We each have fond memories of his surprises. For example, I remember when, without warning, we kids would be awakened before sunrise by his gentle hand stroking our foreheads. "We're going to Strawberry," he would tell us, and we would hurriedly get dressed.

Strawberry was a small community where there was a lake in which we could fish. We would take our equipment and drive there before sunrise, stopping at a coffee shop for cones, renting a little boat, then fishing for what could be hours. Nobody cared if we caught anything. What we loved was the joy of the early morning, the beauty of the ascent of daylight, the sights, the sounds, and the smells of being on the water.

When we were frustrated with Dad, sometimes those frustrations came from well-intentioned acts that did not go far enough. I still remember when my eleventh birthday was approaching and Dad asked me what I wanted. I told him I wanted a watch and to go horseback riding with him.

The morning of my birthday, Dad awakened me and handed me my watch. Then we drove to a stables where they brought out a large horse for him and a Shetland pony for me. I was pissed off. My father had the nerve to give me this dinky little animal when he got the big horse that I wanted.

Dad tried to explain that he didn't want me hurt. He felt that the gentler, smaller pony was ideal. I was certain I was too big for such an animal, that my body weight would squish him into the ground. And if it didn't, how exciting could so little an animal be? We rode without incident, but I also rode without the pleasure I was anticipating from a "real" horse.

Maybe Dad had a point. Maybe the stables we used only had large horses that required a reasonably skilled rider to handle. Maybe I was too inexperienced for anything but a pony. But that did not reduce my anger, and to this day I can't tell this story without remembering that frustration. I wanted a big damn horse!

And then there were the extremes of behavior. Dad, trying to do the right thing, put down by others at every step of the way, often too poor to meet all the family's needs without Bobbe Mary's help, would explode. For example, my brother Ben remembers Bobbe Mary having to help with his dental care and, occasionally, paying for his clothes. Dad tried to help her in return, but Ben remembers incidents where he was put in the position of practically having to beg her. It was humiliating at best. Yet it was also impossible for him to take out his frustrations on the people who caused his pain. Instead, the rare displays of violence would happen at home. To feel that he was held in disdain when he was doing everything he knew to do for his family was extremely upsetting for him. And a couple of times in our young lives, we each bore the brunt of Dad's pain and frustration.

Two facts were never questioned by any of us kids despite Bobbe Mary's hostility to Dad. One was that Dad loved us intensely. We four, Roseanne, myself, Ben, and Stephanie, were the family jewels, the part of his life that validated his existence. Everything else might go to hell, but we children were Dad's riches. We were valued beyond measure.

The other fact was his intense love for our mother. While he may have found other women attractive, Dad both loved and lusted after Mom as intensely thirty years into their marriage as he had when he first courted her. She was the sole object of his sexual desire, and he had no interest in experimenting elsewhere. He could be cold at times. He could overreact to perceived disobedience by his children. But Mom understood Dad's heart, and because of that was always willing to endure the hard times as well as the good.

Dad's sense of humor was outrageous. He loved a good story and was a comedian's best audience. Yet he also loved what amounted to slapstick in his own life. For example, there was the hot summer's day when Dad and we kids were having a water fight outside. It was growing late and finally Mom and Dad called a halt to it. We kids had to go in, get dry, and settle down. We obeyed Mom, but Dad lingered behind. Then, a few minutes later, the front doorbell rang. I don't remember which one of us kids answered it, but there was Dad, holding the garden hose. He raced inside, spraying everyone with water.

The wildness had an irresponsible streak to it. For example, there was the time when Mom and Dad still had a growing family. Roseanne was in elementary school, but I was little and Ben was just eighteen months old. Mom could not work outside the home because of her responsibilities, and Dad was not earning all that much money. It was dead of winter, the family car was a 1950 Chevrolet with no spare tire and an engine that had probably been driven many miles longer than the manufacturer thought it would last. Yet Dad came home early from working with his father and announced that we were all going on vacation.

Mom was cooking a roast, but Dad informed her that she should put it in the refrigerator. Then he took several large empty boxes and wedged them on the floor in the back of the car, so that with the back seat they would make a wide bed. Then he and Mom gathered whatever supplies we needed and we set off to California. There were stops in Las Vegas, Reno, Hoover Dam, Disneyland, and Knott's Berry Farm.

At one of the stops along the way, Dad bought a big washtub from J. C. Penney in which to bathe Ben, who was terrified of the shower that was all that existed for bathing him in one of the cheap motels. He also bought a cheap mattress for use on the boxes. These were all strapped to the roof of the car. In addition, the back doors of the four-door sedan were tied with rope to the handles of the front doors so that we kids could not open them and fall out. By the time he got done, Mom said that we looked like a family of refugees from the Oklahoma dust bowl in the 1930s.

Dad and Mom thought it was the greatest vacation the

family ever had. The weather was perfect, storms that devastated both Salt Lake City and other parts of the country having passed or not yet struck as they drove from city to city. They did call their respective parents when Dad stopped for the time to rest, but basically Dad acted irresponsibly, wiping out their money and abandoning his responsibilities on the job.

There was an impetuousness to Dad's actions that occasionally got him into trouble. Yet it was a childlike impetuousness; he did things because they seemed appropriate at the moment without any thought to the consequences. He never meant to hurt or inconvenience anyone else, though there were times when that did occur, and frequently Dad did not understand this fact.

For me, Dad's excesses were always tempered with his quiet show of stability during time of real need. In addition, there were the stories that taught us to appreciate the oddities of life and led to the type of comedy writing Rosey and I developed for her act. I never knew how much was truth and how much was exaggeration. I do know that we never forgot Dad's genius when first writing jokes of our own.

There was no question that our family would never be honored for its exemplary relationships and the maturity of our father. But despite the aspects of Dad's personality that everyone found negative, he was our stability, our nurturer and guide in the confusing world of Jewish/Mormon society, and the inspiration for our love of laughter.

The Accident

It was September 17, 1968, when Roseanne and her girlfriend were walking the four blocks to East High School to go to classes. I didn't remember the date, but our mom did. Twenty-five years later, when I asked her recollection of the experience, she knew the date, the hour, and the minute. Her love for her oldest daughter and the near loss she experienced forever etched the moment in her memory.

Rosey was walking east, into the sun. She was crossing the street diagonally, not a good idea under the best of circumstances. Unfortunately, this time there was a young woman driving a car in the same direction, her eyes temporarily blinded by the harsh light. She struck Roseanne with such force that the hood ornament of the car hit Rosey in the head, opening a serious gash. She was also dragged twenty feet before the horrified driver could stop, and when the car did come to a halt, the wheels were on Roseanne's legs.

The accident was the start of a nightmare for my parents. I was in school when they were notified, and they did not concern themselves with telling me at that time. It was too important to rush to the hospital, where they needed to give authorization for whatever procedures might be necessary. Roseanne was unconscious, her injuries so severe that the wrong treatment would leave her a vegetable – if she lived.

Mom and Dad raced from the house, their drive to the hospital taking them past the scene of the accident. The ambulance and police cars were long gone, but a crew remained, hosing down the street. As they drove by, they realized that the water was the deep reddish brown of human blood, their daughter's blood. And from the quantity remaining, it was obvious that Roseanne had lost a great deal during the accident.

The family pediatrician met my parents at the hospital, warning them to *not* sign any of the consent forms for treatment. The emergency room staff wanted to stitch up her head, seemingly the proper treatment for a severe head wound. However, the pediatrician asked them to wait until she could be seen by a nationally respected neurosurgeon who had privileges at a different facility. Roseanne would have to be transported again, but the pediatrician felt that she needed the best qualified doctor.

It turned out the pediatrician was correct. The neurosurgeon cleaned that wound but did not stitch it. Had he done so, the accumulated blood would have severely damaged Roseanne. Instead, by waiting several hours for the internal bleeding to stop, there would only be the routine danger of infection. There would be no other complications.

Later other doctors confirmed the neurosurgeon's decision. Roseanne made a complete recovery. She would have suffered some degree of brain damage had the doctors at the first hospital been allowed to stitch her wound. They were not incompetent, just less experienced.

Rosey's condition was hell for Mom and Dad. They were with her from the start. They saw her unconscious. They were present when she awakened in the intensive care unit. But I was only concerned with whether or not she would be okay, and by the time I heard of the accident, there was reason to be optimistic. By the time I saw her, she was already on the way to recovery.

The accident was the beginning of a radical change for Roseanne. She had been the perfect "good girl" in her choice of friends and activities, even though she had been somewhat wild in school. In fact, I always cringed when one of the teachers asked me if I was Roseanne Barr's younger sister, because the question usually reflected the memory of some problem with Rosey five years earlier. Yet overall she was conservative in her lifestyle, fitting nicely with the Mormons she tried so hard to befriend.

Being struck by the car changed everything. Roseanne was sixteen years old, a time of rebellion and extremes of emotions under the best of circumstances. But Rosey had gone through more than many kids. She told me later that two things shocked her about the accident. The first was the fact that she nearly died. She had the classic near-death experience others have reported. She saw a tunnel of white light and was drawn into it. Although she lived, although it was not yet her time, she had a glimpse of an afterlife and thus was forced to accept her own mortality.

The second shock was the fact that she did not remember getting hit by the car. She never even heard the vehicle.

Because the driver was blinded by the sun, there was never a warning horn or a screeching of brakes. She came out of the coma trying to figure out how she had gone from crossing the street to being hooked up to monitoring equipment in a hospital's intensive care unit. She was angry at the loss of control.

I think that at the moment she awakened, she realized that she could never again be certain of anything in her future. She was determined to grab life and explore it her own way.

Mom felt that Rosey was changed as a direct result of the physical trauma of the crash. She believed that every negative experience Rosey had was the result of her mind somehow being altered by the crash. However, the doctors proved otherwise. The physical recovery was complete. There were no residual mental aberrations.

Instead, Rosey had to deal with adolescent angst, raging hormones, sudden isolation from friends, and the awareness of her own mortality all in the same few weeks. She no longer wanted to be a good girl. She no longer wanted to abstain from sensual experiences to win the favor of her Mormon friends. She wanted to drink coffee, smoke pot, lose her virginity, and wear the wild hippie clothing then in style. She wanted to be out from under the odd mix of Orthodox Judaism and ecumenical acceptance that defined life with Bobbe Mary and my mother. She wanted to flee the strictures of Salt Lake City and discover all aspects of life that she could imagine trying.

That car accident was the defining moment in the creation of the character that would become Roseanne Barr Arnold, the comedian who conquered the nation.

3 And Baby Makes Complications

Growing into young womanhood in Salt Lake City, Rosey and I were fascinated by those we called Protestant girls. Like the stereotypical blonde of the 1970s, these imaginary creatures always had more fun than Jewish girls and Mormons. Not that we knew very many. Mostly we knew Mormons, Jews and Catholics. The occasional Protestant girl we encountered was so much like ourselves that we were convinced they were exceptions.

From almost the moment I reached puberty, I wanted to be a Protestant girl. Rosey was the same way, and it was one of the fantasies we shared once I achieved the start of my sexual coming-of-age.

It was not that any of us were inhibited. Jewish girls fucked, though they did it on a limited basis and usually felt guilty afterward.

We thought that Mormon girls fucked the most of anyone we knew. They weren't supposed to do anything like that. There were all sorts of taboos involving sexual relations between unmarried teenagers. Yet the truth was that Brigham Young University had the highest rate of illegitimate pregnancies of any school in the state, and the majority of those accidental mothers were Mormons.

I think the reason the Mormon kids fucked so much was because of the church teachings about the afterlife. Good Mormons would be resurrected with full genitalia, becoming gods of their own planets. It was a goal sincerely to be pursued, the reward being an erection in the resurrection. And while only sex in marriage was officially condoned, all that talk about the glories of fucking your brains out to populate some distant world was a great turn-on for naturally horny teenagers.

But somehow none of this was the same as what "Protestant" girls got to do. In our naive fantasies, these girls lived life to the fullest without guilt or such repercussions as pregnancy and sexually transmitted disease. They could smoke dope, get high on any manner of recreational drugs, seduce any boy who struck their fancy, stay out late, and generally enjoy a sensual existence that even *Playboy* magazine's most sophisticated reader would envy.

It was not that we wanted to abandon our family or our culture. We just wanted a measure of sophisticated pleasure in our lives, and that could only be achieved by "Protestant" girls.

After Rosey's accident she decided to come as close to our ideal as she could. She dropped most of the Mormon girls who had been her friends, stopped leading the singing at Primary, and was not concerned with being accepted by any of the people whose approval she once wanted.

The change was remarkable. Everyone noticed, of course. The doctors said it had nothing to do with brain damage, as much as Mom thought it did. All anyone could see was that Rosey was going wild and out of control. None of us could see that she had had a severe near-death experience, had just reached adolescence, and was trying to find herself.

For someone older than Rosey, the near-death experience probably would have led to what is often called a midlife crisis, during which the person gets a divorce, takes a lover, or changes a job. When you're sixteen years old and experiencing the crisis, there are few ways in which you can rebel. One of Roseanne's choices was to tempt fate. She went out to the scene of the accident and began dancing in the street at the spot where she was hit. She was caught doing this by the school administrators, and it was then that counseling was arranged for her.

Rosey's actions were never suicidal in nature. She was not severely depressed. She was not hoping that a car would hit her once again. We talked about this off and on over the years, and she was apparently only trying to deal with the reason she could almost die without knowing she was about to be hit. She was also seeing if she was charmed, cursed, or something in between. And while her approach was stupid, she was also sixteen years of age with no close adult she was willing to talk to about any of this.

If anything, rather than trying to die, Rosey wanted to live on the edge. Part of her lust for testing the limits of teenage experience may have come from the isolation she endured following the accident. Although eventually she returned to school, at first she had to stay home and have her schoolwork brought to her.

Like so many kids of the period, Rosey joined the "hippie" movement – or what passed for it in Salt Lake City, a community that was always a few years behind the times. She was never extreme. Wearing a maxi-coat, she would take her guitar to the park and sing folk songs and read poetry. While there were plenty of drugs around, she was quite conservative at heart, probably using nothing stronger than marijuana.

Her main form of rebellion came from doing that which she knew was wrong but which she did not think would hurt anyone. Like the night she stole the family car.

The incident occurred the night Mom and Dad were out with my Uncle Perry and his wife. Perry was sick at the time with an illness that would take his life in less than six months, even though he was only thirty-one, with a fourteen-month-old baby. (My mother has never really gotten over his loss.)

That particular night in 1969 was a happy one, though. Rosey was old enough to be the sitter for the youngest two kids, ably assisted by Private Barr. And just like the days when we played our Army game, Rosey used me to do the dirty work while she pursued her own agenda. Unfortunately, her idea of fun was to take the family car for a ride.

Sixteen-year-old Roseanne only had a learner's permit. This meant that she could drive so long as there was a licensed driver sitting next to her in the passenger seat. Rosey also had only the most rudimentary knowledge of how to handle the car. She knew how to accelerate, steer, and stop, though not necessarily in a smooth or safe manner. However, that did not prevent her from coolly suggesting that since Mom and Dad had driven with Uncle Perry, she would take us for a ride in the family car.

"You don't have a driver's license," I said to her.

"Oh yes I do," she replied proudly.

"Then show it to me," I told her, thinking my calling her bluff would end it all.

Roseanne produced her learner's permit, which I recognized immediately as not really being a license. Still, I agreed to go with her, placing Stephanie and Ben in the back seat.

We didn't go far before I panicked. I was scared from the moment she turned the key in the ignition. By the time we had driven half a block, I was fantasizing about our fate.

A policeman was going to spot us. He was going to check Rosey's license, discover it was only a learner's permit, and then arrest us all. We kids would be placed in the back of the police car, handcuffed, our rights having been read as they were on television cop shows.

Then we'd be taken to jail and given striped suits, have balls and chains attached to our ankles, and be forced to endure hard labor, bad food, and the violence of our fellow cons. Our lives would be over, our futures destroyed. Terrified, I ordered Rosey to turn around and take us back, which she did. During that brief time, Rosey slammed on the brakes and Stephanie was tossed backward, though she was not hurt.

I took the kids into the house, telling Rosey to park the car and come inside. She told me that she would not do that, that she was going to go for a ride with us or without us.

Time passed. Maybe it was fifteen minutes, maybe a half hour or more. I paid no attention. I just remember that suddenly the telephone was ringing, and when I answered it, a very shaken Roseanne told me she had been in an accident, hitting another moving car. The driver of the other car was pregnant, but fortunately she was unhurt.

Although the accident did not cause serious damage, my active imagination caused me to recall all I had ever heard or read about hit-and-run drivers. If you leave the scene of an accident, even to call the police or an ambulance, it is hit-and-run and they can lock you away even longer than for driving with only a learner's permit. "You have to go back," I told her in a panic. "You have to go to the car.

Probably Rosey was just a few yards from where the two cars had hit each other and no one minded her using the telephone. For all I knew the police may have been called, may even have started to arrive. Facts did not matter. Instantly my mind flashed on the television show *Dragnet*. In my mind I heard Jack Webb speaking over the sound of Rosey's conversation. "Roseanne Barr was found guilty of hit-and-run by a jury of her peers. She was sentenced to fifty years in a jail cell with two Mormon missionaries, two Jehovah's Witnesses, a Tupperware Lady, an Avon Lady, and the top Utah salesperson from Mary Kay Cosmetics. She never should have left the scene of the accident to call her sister Geraldine!"

Rosey agreed to immediately go back to the scene of the accident. I felt better as I hung up the telephone. Jack Webb's voice trailing into the oblivion of my overactive imagination.

It was perhaps an hour later when a man called, asking for Mom or Dad. I explained that they were out for the evening, at which time he informed me that his name was Sergeant Peabody. He said that there had been a car accident and that Roseanne was in Juvenile Hall. It was important to contact our parents.

Juvenile Hall did not sound as bad as jail. They probably had Mormons there, but I was fairly certain Jack Webb would never use her arrest as the basis for an episode of *Dragnet*. I did not know how to reach my parents that evening, though probably wouldn't have the nerve to telephone them if I had known. Instead, I waited, every half hour enduring yet another telephone call from Sergeant Peabody.

Finally, some time after midnight, my parents came home. "How is everything?" they asked cheerfully.

I wasn't going to lie to them. I also wasn't about to tell them what was taking place. "Ben is upstairs in his bed," I said. "Stephanie is upstairs in her bed. And I'm here on the couch."

I smiled, hoping they wouldn't think about Rosey. Sergeant Peabody had probably called a half dozen times by then. Perhaps he would not call back that night.

"Where's Roseanne?" Mom persisted.

"Ben's upstairs in his bed. Stephanie's upstairs in her bed. And I'm down here on the couch." Had I known how to smile like some adoring child star and convince her that she had only three children, I would have done so. There was no way I was going to break the news that my sister had gone to jail for crashing the family car.

The telephone rang before my charade could go any further. This time Dad answered and listened to Sergeant Peabody telling him that Roseanne was in juvenile detention and the car had been impounded following the accident. Dad's face grew livid with anger. "You have my daughter in Juvenile Hall? Keep her. I don't want her."

Rosey did not spend the night in jail. A bunch of kids selling drugs were arrested and filled up the Juvenile Hall holding facilities. Rosey's bed space was needed for more serious offenders. A uniformed officer was dispatched to take Rosey home around six in the morning of what was Easter Sunday.

I did not stay around to find out what happened. I was just glad that I did not have to face my father's wrath. As it was, from the bed upstairs I could hear my father and Rosey talking. Rosey was extremely upset, having seemingly learned her lesson, promising to be good, something Mom remembers her accomplishing for at least a couple of weeks.

In the aftermath of her accident and her subsequent rebellion, Rosey did agree to go to counseling, much to my parents' relief.

I gave little thought to Rosey's dealing with her own mortality, and I was not concerned with her going for counseling. Those were worries for my parents, who were supportive of Rosey's going to a professional to work

79

through her problems. So far as I was concerned, the biggest change in Roseanne was the same change I eventually went through. She was becoming a woman in a culture that was quite restrictive.

While all kids change in adolescence, in Mormon country the girls are encouraged to focus on marriage, children, and family. Their future will be in building the church, and that means suppressing their identities and following the desires of their faith's leaders and the men they will eventually marry.

The Mormons have a sense of family continuity that is first intensely drilled into them at about age eleven or twelve. That is when the children experience the ritual of baptism for the dead. Using genealogy studies, church elders identify often long-dead relatives who were not baptized in the faith. The children take their place as living stand-ins, being baptized in the names of those who came before. Each participant undergoes numerous baptisms for the dead, making them extremely conscious of how much their lives are connected with the past as well as the future.

With the onset of puberty, the Mormon girls are taught to be more conservative in all aspects of their lives. They are prepared to be wives, not to think about a career or a life that might delay their having a family. Their lives may ultimately be more complete than that, yet their focus is marriage and childbearing before all else.

This is not to say that the planning for monogamous marriage makes perfect kids. By high school it seemed like secret sex was the most popular extracurricular activity we heard about. The difference was that there was supposed to be tremendous guilt attached to such matters. Any experimentation that would be considered normal in any other big city or small town was taboo in Salt Lake City. Thus Mormon kids led circumspect public lives yet were privately as wild as kids anywhere. The elders would not admit it, though, and what the elders said was true, no matter how it flew in the face of reality.

Roseanne chose to be wild in public like we imagined the

Protestants outside Salt Lake City to be, not hiding in the shadows like her former friends. Eventually I became a rebel as well, though the differences in our personalities were such that mine was a quieter rebellion. My world centered around books and serious movies. When an art movie theater called The Blue Mouse opened, I practically lived there, entranced by the foreign films. As for the future, I decided I might become a geologist, and loved to study rocks. I knew I would go on to college, and not just as a way to pursue a Mormon boy I wanted to be my husband.

My parents were proud of my choice, of course, but the more vocal Mormon kids in my class seemed to see my desire for an education and career as further proof that I was from Satan.

I withdrew in order to stay sane. Roseanne was more outgoing and had no interest in formal education. She hated school and could not conceive of ever going to college. Years later, when I was a student at the University of Utah, she told me. "Only fucking assholes go to college. That's no place to learn anything." She believed in experiencing a variety of lifestyles, hitchhiking, and exploring new sensations, new relationships. She had no time for academia, a fact that added to her problems.

Roseanne's first break from both school and family came in an odd way. She began seeing a counselor, trying to deal with the mixed emotions troubling her following being hit by the car.

Mom remembers the counseling helping Roseanne, and she expected her daughter to continue as an outpatient, going for regular sessions until she decided she was fine. Our family was extremely poor, yet Mom and Dad were willing to make any sacrifice necessary to help her. The problem came when Roseanne decided she wanted to check herself into the state hospital in Provo. I was about ten or eleven at the time, old enough for everyone to talk in front of me, not holding back any of their concerns, yet young enough so it didn't really matter to me. Rosey's actions always fascinated me because I adored her. She was a drama queen, and if I thought about what was happening much at all, it probably was in seeing the hospital as the next scene in a continuing saga.

It is not that I was callous about Rosey's problems. What I understood most was her having been hit by the car. My big sister was safe following the accident, and nothing else mattered all that much to me. I was hitting puberty, dealing with my own problems, like every kids approaching their teenage years. But I did know that my parents were upset with Rosey for wanting to go to the state hospital in Provo, and with her therapist for agreeing with her that checking in would be good for her. It was what she wanted, he explained. And the adolescent care program was an excellent one.

The therapist was comfortable with the world of hospitals and psychologists. To my parents, any in-patient treatment that appeared non-essential seemed to be a condemnation of how they had raised us kids. They felt the social stigma attached to such voluntary commitment.

Our father was especially upset. We were poor but he had insurance that would cover mental health care. He was willing to get her any therapist she wanted, either through the Jewish Family Service Agency or someone in private practice. He remembers begging her to not commit herself to the state hospital before trying the other options. She would hear none of it, planning to put herself into treatment.

Rosey's memory of that conflict was slightly different from my father's.

When I helped her write her first book, *My Life as a Woman*, she claimed that Mom was the one who thought about having her hospitalized. While I'm certain Rosey remembers it that way, so far as I have been able to learn, the statement was not accurate. Mom was embarrassed by having a daughter in the nuthouse. She would never have encouraged such a thing unless she thought it was the only way to help her.

Rosey also wrote about how bad her life had become prior to hospitalization. She spoke of staying awake for several days at times. She talked of passing out. She talked about becoming obsessive. She talked about things I honestly don't remember being so extreme.

I know from what was constantly discussed at home that Rosey checked herself into the hospital around the middle of November 1969. She was seventeen and headstrong, and under the regulations of Provo as I understood them, that was old enough for voluntary commitment. Rosey later implied that Dad signed her in because of papers he filled out. However, the papers were for the insurance. She was in full charge of her stay, being free to check out of the hospital any time she requested. No drugs would be administered without her approval. No therapy would take place without her consent. The only drug she was given of which I am aware was Mellaril, a product meant for short-term use to combat problems with anxiety, sleep disturbances, depression, and tension. And there was certainly no risk of some horrible operation of electric-shock therapy being used against her. She was in control of her stay, and she was never considered insane.

Mom and Dad were embarrassed at having their daughter in the state mental facility and certainly did not encourage her stay. But I think Rosey thought it was more dramatic to imply in her memoirs that she was somehow there against her will. Years later, when interviewed for the February 1994 cover story of *Vanity Fair*, she took the drama a step further. According to Kevin Sessums, the writer of the article, " . . . her parents . . . put her away for almost a year in a state hospital. To this day she refuses to go into details about her life there."

In fact, Rosey has told variations of the same story often enough that she probably believes it. Yet if Rosey had taken the time to reread *My Life as a Woman*, she would remember that we spent approximately ten pages recounting many of the details of that hospital stay.

Dad drove 150 miles every weekend to bring Rosey home and return her to the hospital. Mom and Dad were never comfortable with her being an in-patient. They were constantly hoping she would want to come home permanently and see a therapist here.

The first time I saw Rosey in the hospital in Provo, I was greatly upset. She was in a locked ward, though probably everyone was. Still, I felt a little as though I was seeing my sister in prison, even though intellectually it was obvious that some of the patients were so confused and disoriented, they would have wandered off the floor if the door had been open.

Ultimately the state facility proved to be Roseanne's first experience with theatrical improvisation. Some of the staff members and some of the teenagers got to travel to various schools, talking about the importance of mental health and the danger of drugs. Most of the kids in the hospital were placed there because of serious problems with drug addiction. They made great "bad examples" for the other children, and the staff felt that their open discussion of their problems was therapeutic for them. The kids fighting their former addiction gained a sense of pride in being applauded for giving up their earlier destructive lifestyle. Rosey had never been a serious drug user. She just wanted to be a part of the road show.

Roseanne talked with the drug addicts, learning the slang terms for both the drugs and the paraphernalia. She also learned what the kids had experienced at home and during withdrawal. Then she ad-libbed her "experiences," gaining as much of the spotlight as the kids who had endured a genuine problem.

I never knew if the staff of the state hospital was aware that Roseanne was lying about drug use. If they did know she had never been an addict yet brought her along because she was a dramatic speaker, it is a sad commentary on the quality of their programs. More likely Roseanne gave the staff a plausible enough story so that they believed her, just as the school kids believed her. What is chilling to me now is how many "facts" about Roseanne's personal life and the actions of herself and her family were created in the same manner as the drug addiction story. She later admitted in her first book that she had lied, yet whatever she said about drugs and the reasons she became an "addict" became part of the hospital's permanent records.

She created a life she had never led, then spoke with such conviction that seemingly no one knew or cared that nothing she was presenting was the truth. That time, presumably no one was physically or emotionally hurt by what she did. Later her words and actions came close to destroying our family.

The nuthouse road show played to great audiences. Rosey touched many hearts with tales of sin and degradation, as well as the importance of doing whatever is necessary to achieve sound mental health. She also chose to obtain weekend passes to come home, giving her a chance to see friends and relatives.

I had mixed feelings about Roseanne during this period. I was an extremely withdrawn adolescent and was becoming increasingly dedicated to the study of Judaism. I loved reading the Torah, the first five books of the Old Testament. I also loved the various commentaries that are a part of Jewish history and tradition. I was thinking seriously of using my talent as a singer to become a cantor, someone who is an integral part of the services as well as acting as a teacher. There was a certain amount of enjoyment of the peace I gained without my older sister, the "Drama Queen."

It was years after Rosey's hospitalization, when I was in my early thirties, that we finally talked in depth about this period in her life. We had become not just friends but probably closer to each other than to anyone else in our lives, including her first husband. We talked endlessly, coming to grips with our pasts, understanding our present, and working through the path we wanted to take for our futures. We discussed her mental problems prior to the hospitalization, and I became convinced that her troubles were mostly the result of growing up in Salt Lake City.

Everything in Salt Lake City was difficult, and her adolescence was compounded by the emotions resulting from her near-death experience. Provo was an escape from the schizophrenic world of being Jewish in Mormon country and from the whole family.

Roseanne may have thrived during her time in the hospital, but it was during her weekends at home that she decided to explore life more fully and perhaps more recklessly. Her next escapade involved a boy from the neighborhood.

Hell-bent on breaking all the rules, they got high, began kissing, and before too long Roseanne lost her virginity, just as she told me she planned.

Considering the pain of what happened next, it is important to put Roseanne's experience in perspective. We were sexually naive in Salt Lake City. The schools offered nothing in the way of sex education, and even the Mormon church was rather lax given the high out-of-wedlock pregnancy numbers. Our mother was certainly no help, for she was raised with so little information, she had no idea that there were separate openings for sexual relations and urination.

My parents had an active sex life. In fact, we kids used to joke about their supposedly secret signal to each other. Dad got Mom one of those sexy black lace negligees. When it was hung on the door and we kids were encouraged to go to bed early, we knew they were going to have sex.

Their signal backfired one day, though. It was Sunday morning, and Dad wanted to get the morning paper. His robe was in the wash and he thought it was too cold to step out on the porch without an extra covering. Since it was handy, he grabbed Mom's negligee, put it on, peeked out of the window, then stepped out when no one was around.

Roseanne had been hiding, watching Dad's actions. The moment he was on the porch, she slammed the door shut, locking it. Then, as she roared with laughter, Dad, dressed in Mom's negligee, frantically tried to find an open door or window.

It was late enough so that within minutes of Dad's being locked out, our Mormon neighbors began going to services. No one said anything, though they had to notice Dad. Each passerby politely wished a good morning to Brother Barr, and Dad, just as politely, wished a good morning to each of the neighbors. Then he'd turn back to his frantic efforts to get inside, finally being able to enter through an unlocked dining room window.

The love was strong. The sex was frequent. But when it came to understanding female biology, I had to explain the facts of life to Mom when I was about nineteen, an awkward role reversal for me.

The teenage Roseanne was aware that sex could be a pleasurable experience, but she had no idea how a woman got pregnant. In her mind, first a woman lost her virginity. Then, at some future time, probably after numerous experiences of intercourse, she could become pregnant.

Rosey soon discovered the truth. I don't even know if she really enjoyed her first sexual experience. It was more like a rite of passage. She came home from the boy's house sick and scared. She was sure that my parents would smell the pot she had smoked and certain her loss of virginity would be noticed. What mattered, though, was that she had broken taboos of the teenage community in which she had been so active. The boy had been a means to an end, and by the time she returned to the state hospital in Provo, she was again feeling good about herself. She didn't know she was pregnant.

I was shocked when I learned of the pregnancy, because Rosey had always been my source of knowledge about sex. She was the one who told me how to fuck people and where babies come from. She was also the one who revealed the truth about my parents, that they had sex more than the four times necessary to have four children.

"They do it all the time," Rosey told me.

I wanted to believe she was lying. I wanted to believe she was just trying to shock me. Yet when Rosey roared with laughter at my naïveté, I had the sinking feeling that she was telling me the truth. Mom and Dad had sex more than four times? They were maybe still having it even though they were old, almost forty? It was truly shocking. It was also when I first understood the regular appearance of the negligee.

Maybe my parents had sex, but that didn't mean I would trust Mom in any sort of discussion about my body. I had Rosey buy me Kotex when I started getting my period. It was too embarrassing to bring up the need to my mother.

Roseanne was my friend. She was my sister. I loved her and trusted her completely.

Still, the difference in our ages was just enough to cause us to take two different paths. For example, there were no organized sports for girls when Rosey was in high school. Five years later, there was a department dedicated to girls' athletics.

In 1970, when Rosey was seeking magazines to help her to understand what being a woman might mean, she was limited to publications like *Cosmopolitan*. Although the editorial matter was freer in discussing such areas as sex before marriage and the possibility that a woman might live with more than one man before marriage, it still focused on marriage as the goal for womanhood. It might have been seen as a risqué, corrupted version of how to achieve the Mormon girl's dream.

Five years later, when I went to the newsstands to find magazines that would teach me about womanhood, I could obtain *Ms.*, the first widely circulated feminist publication. I learned about having a life of my own. *Ms.* didn't put down the idea of women marrying. It just considered marriage as one option in life.

Thus Roseanne was able to be my guide into womanhood and my friend, yet we were not influenced in the same ways. I think she sensed that, and perhaps that was why she came to me first when she realized that she was pregnant.

I was in the basement, doing the wash, when Rosey told me she was going to have a baby. "You need to tell Mom and Dad," I said, suddenly frightened. I had just become a teenager. I had been preparing for my bat mitzvah. I had been having trouble at school, doing well in the classes where the teachers were not Mormon, being criticized by those who were. I couldn't understand my own life. The idea that Rosey might want me to help her as well was beyond comprehension. This was one time she had to talk with our parents.

What followed next affected the various family members quite differently. I was not overly concerned. I really didn't understand what the pregnancy issue might mean. I suppose abortions were available in Salt Lake City; abortion had been practised by all manner of people over the years in every major city. But abortion was never discussed, because Rosey would never take that way out. She had not meant to get pregnant. She had not thought it was possible to get pregnant the same time you lost your virginity. But once she realized she had been wrong, the only question was what she would do with the baby after it was born. It was not something she needed to discuss with me, so I never was part of that process. I came to feel that I was living in the midst of a soap opera, part participant and part audience, and just wondered what she would ultimately decide.

My mother's feelings were quite different, though apparently no one ever discussed them with her. She had come to love children over the years. After Rosey had been born, my father had to seduce her into having a second child by promising to change his ways. He didn't, of course, yet she found such happiness with the two of us that she had two more.

Over the years, Mom's capacity to love children seemed to grow. She is the type of woman who can still go into a family restaurant and be immediately deep in conversation with a delightful toddler. There is something gentle about her, something that causes children to treat her as a favorite aunt from the moment they meet her.

Mom could never have tolerated the idea of Roseanne's having an abortion, but that was never a consideration for my sister. Instead, the question was whether Rosey would raise the baby herself or give the child up for adoption.

The decision was difficult for Rosey. She was too young to raise a child, too immature, too busy trying to understand herself to care for a newborn. She was essentially a child having a child, and this she seemed to instinctively understand. She came to the conclusion that she would give up the child for adoption.

Rosey never asked Mom her feelings. Neither did I. Neither did the people who counseled Rosey through the pregnancy. I don't even know how much help Dad might have been. All I know is that Mom was determined to let Rosey handle the difficult time in whatever way her daughter felt was best. However, what Mom did not say to anyone, so far as I know, is that she wanted to adopt her daughter's baby.

Mom was still quite young and healthy, and though there were three of us at home, we were all old enough to be reasonably self-sufficient. The idea of raising a fifth child, of formally adopting her grandchild, was exciting for her. She had no illusions about the frustrations of raising an infant. She understood the stress. She understood the financial burden. She even understood the potential for local scandal, since everyone would know Mom was never pregnant during that year. None of that mattered. She had love to give and wanted one more opportunity to spread it around.

Rosey never considered Mom's adopting her baby after it was born. She did not ask, of course, and Mom did not volunteer her desire. However, I think that had Mom discussed it with Rosey, the end result would have been the same. Rosey would probably not have allowed our mother to adopt her child, if for no other reason than she would not want to see another member of the Barr family have to endure Salt Lake City.

Whatever might have been, the fact that Mom was not considered hurts her to this day. She still says with anguish, "No one ever asked me what I felt. No one ever asked me if I wanted to adopt my grandchild."

This is not to say that Mom has been totally cut off from the girl who was eventually named Brandi. Many years later after she became famous, Rosey was reunited with her daughter, and our family became aware of the identity of her parents. To Mom's horror, Rosey has stated that Mom never agreed to meet her "bastard baby." The truth is that Mom has always been eager to meet her first grand-daughter, and she has been in contact with Brandi's mother and has tried to keep track of the young woman's progress in life. She hopes that Brandi will one day want to meet

90

her, but for now she is comfortable letting Brandi initiate any involvement she may desire.

At first Rosey wanted to endure her pregnancy alone. She was seventeen, and she moved into a cheap, fleabag apartment with the help of a girlfriend who lived in our street. Rosey took some food and old furnishings we had in the basement, but she only lasted about three days there. She became so ill from morning sickness that she returned home briefly, then was referred to the Jewish Family Service Agency in Denver, where my Uncle Perry lived. The referral came from a counselor with the Salt Lake City branch of that agency.

Denver was an exciting place for Roseanne, a big city where Mormons, if there were any, were definitely in the minority. It was cosmopolitan, with a growing, diverse population. Denver could provide the break Rosey so desperately sought while still keeping her under the watchful eye of a family member.

The Jewish Family Service Agency was extremely helpful. They knew of a Jewish family with a large house and several children. The couple agreed to help Roseanne by giving her a room and board during her pregnancy in exchange for Rosey acting as a live-in babysitter, nanny, playmate, and general helper. Roseanne agreed, then quickly balked.

Rosey later claimed that she felt herself to be in the midst of pressures akin to indentured servitude. By contrast, the couple apparently claimed that Rosey was lazy and self-centered and that she seemed to feel they should wait on her since she was enduring the pregnancy.

I can believe both stories. I don't know which one is true, nor does it matter. Rosey had to leave.

Finally Roseanne went to the Booth Memorial Home, which was sponsored by the Salvation Army. For years, the Booth Memorial Homes provided pregnant single women with a warm, friendly caring environment where there was no stigma attached to being pregnant and single. Rosey's experience, as she told it, was not typical. One of the people in charge was hostile to the girls and made Rosey's stay extremely unpleasant. Roseanne's baby was adopted by a pair of Jewish professionals who had desired a baby for many years. They could not have children of their own and welcomed Roseanne's newborn, a little girl whom they named Brandi.

Roseanne returned briefly to Salt Lake City. She was grossly overweight and looked terrible. Mom helped her get involved with Weight Watchers, where she both began regaining a decent figure and had her self-esteem restored. She took a job in the food business, starting as a salad girl at a place called the Chuck-A-Rama. I never did know why it had that name. We used to joke that the carryout bags were the same ones the airlines supplied in case of air sickness. But I suppose the appeal was primarily one of its specialties – the famous Sunday, all-you-can-eat for $2.99.

The Chuck-A-Rama had great appeal to Mormons with big families. Every Sunday buffet offered a tantalizing display of ten – count them – ten different kinds of Jell-O. That meant a greater variety of Jell-O than some restaurants have wines. You could get your Jell-O plain, with marshmallows, with fruit ... The list was seemingly endless – a cornucopia of Jell-O. And the selection came *after* such gourmet items as chicken-fried steak and steam table vegetables.

Roseanne was restless, walking around a lot. She had a friend named Linda who lived in Denver. Rosey told my parents and siblings that she was going to visit Linda for a little while, then prepared for the Denver trip. They believed she would be gone only a few days. Rosey made clear to me that she was kicking off the dust of Salt Lake City and planning to make her life in Denver or anywhere else outside of Utah.

I cried when Rosey left, knowing she would never return. I would miss her, and I was torn apart by the pain she was inflicting on all of us. Rosey lied to our parents. She didn't have the nerve to face Mom, Dad, and Bobbe Mary and tell them the truth. I was the one who would have to pay any consequences once she was gone. And I felt that I was adding to whatever pain they might be feeling because I knew the truth yet was not saying anything.

The other reason for my tears was the fact that I had to stay in Utah. There was tremendous frustration over the fact that Rosey was getting to move on while I had to stay in the midst of the Mormon madness.

Roseanne did not understand how I envied her and hated being stuck in Salt Lake City. She would later write in her first book that I had "feelings of hatred and abandonment" toward her. She also said that it would take me eight years to speak about those feelings. That was not the case at all, but Rosey was in her own world, making a painful break. She found it necessary to focus on her own self-interest in order to reinforce leaving her roots, and I was just as self-centered in my grief over having to stay behind.

Once in Denver, my sister experienced the sexual freedom of the period, which was completely at odds with what we had been taught. My mother's relationship with Dad had led us to feel that monogamy was the only way to live, and we knew she thought that premarital sex was a big mistake. Her philosophy could be summed up by the old expression, often repeated by Dad, "Why buy the cow if you can get the milk for free?"

Once on her own, Roseanne immediately discovered that Mom had lied. Sex could be fun and a profound part of life. It wasn't some medieval notion of buying cows or owning property! It was, in the liberated language of the day, part of the journey of self-discovery. If you had sex and it didn't work out, you weren't destroyed or tainted, just a little more experienced.

I learned all of this both from Rosey and from sexuality courses I took when I eventually went to the University of Utah at nineteen. I went so far as to become a psychology major just so I could read the books that would give me the understanding I was seeking and listen to the professors who told about life as it really was. I even told my mother and one of her friends what I was learning.

Eventually my mother believed the biological explanations I showed her. But the reaction of her friend was like that of a small child whose cherished and trusted older sibling announces that there is no Santa Claus.

For Mom, though, the experience brought us closer. My mother was fascinated to learn about her body, and I felt as though I was beginning a relationship between adult women, not just parent and child.

While I was finishing high school and preparing to work my way through college, Roseanne was living the hippie life in Georgetown, Colorado. This was a ski area that had not been discovered by the big-money people who had taken over areas such as Aspen. Everyone seemed to be poor in Georgetown. Everyone had long hair and casual clothes they wore even in situations that would have called for semi-formal attire in Salt Lake City. They smoked. They drank beer. They enjoyed sex. They were friends to one another despite being of the opposite sex. And almost immediately after arriving by bus, Rosey met the long-haired night clerk at the nearby Motor Inn, a man named Bill Pentland who would radically change her life.

Linda and Rosey shared Linda's apartment, which was three miles out of town. There was a rock and roll bar directly above it, which guaranteed rather raucous late nights. There were also other room-mates, the area being one of those places where "crashing" with both new and old friends was common. Everyone lived together in one form or another because most available jobs paid salaries too low for them to afford decent apartments.

Denver was a revelation after Utah. Just an eight-hour car trip away from Salt Lake City, even an eighteen-year-old could order a beer with his or her pizza. In addition, there was Bill, the night clerk, who was a hippie, who had a real job, and who, the first night he and Rosey were together, fixed dinner for her. It was a combination plate – leftover Hamburger Helper and salad. It was also the most erotic meal my sister had ever enjoyed, because a man had cooked it for her and served it to her. Until then, every man

94

she had ever met expected women to tend to his wants and needs. The reversal was as arousing as the most sophisticated foreplay.

Food was an important aspect of Jewish life as we had known it. Food was the balm that eased every physical and psychological pain a human could endure. Food was a focus of rituals such as the Sabbath dinner, the Sunday morning breakfasts with Bobbe Mary, and Passover, and was the focus of the kosher dietary laws. Food was also meant to be a uniting experience, a shared delight. And food had been the province of women. They planned meals. They fixed meals. They served meals. (They also used the time to gossip about their men, the women delighted in the time away from husbands and fathers.)

Men were fed. Men received. A man's reaction to whatever edibles were placed before him helped determine the woman's standing, at least in her own mind. For Bill Pentland to understand the importance of food, then reverse all Rosey had known by preparing it, then serving it to her, was one of the most romantic and oddly erotic experiences she had ever known.

Rosey's affair with Bill Pentland became intimate that first week, according to her recollections. They stayed at the motel where he had a room, enjoying a sexual relationship that was as intense as is possible for a horny Jewish girl who has just cast off the strictures of a naive conservative mother, a repressive religious community, and her own fears of real intimacy. There was little else they shared, each frightened of what was happening to them, yet neither willing to quit at first. However, once the intensity of the relationship settled a bit, once they parted for a while, Rosey staying with friends and taking a job in a French restaurant after becoming a largely self-taught French cook, they found they were in love.

In addition to food, sex, and love, Roseanne's life centered around work and hitchhiking with Linda. She considered being on the road her version of a college education.

Eventually Rosey married Bill, and over time they had

three children. Mom and Dad were thrilled, because they liked Bill, and from what they could see, he and Rosey were good for each other. Mom remembers loading up the car with presents and driving to Denver to wish them well. However, Mom also says that no one knows what goes on between a couple behind closed doors and assumes that there were eventually problems with the relationship not evident to her during the early years.

None of this was my concern, though. While Roseanne was being a hippie, discovering America, getting married, and entering what might be considered her earth mother phase, I was trying to be a scholar. Despite my mixed high school record, I entered the University of Utah, exploring everything from psychology to business marketing. I also worked at K mart for five years, a relatively high-paying job (for Salt Lake City) with hours that let me be flexible with my studies.

My job at K mart was a learning experience. When work was slow or I was taking a break, I tried to learn about the other departments. I talked with people in other positions to learn about retail buying, display marketing, and the other aspects of the business. I began to see how each aspect of a business interrelates, how all the employees affect the success of the store. Such knowledge motivated me to take business, marketing, and accounting courses in college.

It was around 1978 that I finally broke loose from all the constraints of my upbringing. Unfortunately, I did it in a manner that almost got me killed.

As a budding feminist, I was passionately in favor of the Equal Rights Amendment (ERA). This was a simple constitutional amendment under consideration by the state legislatures in all fifty states. It would end any form of discrimination based on sex.

Technically the ERA was not necessary. There were enough laws relative to civil rights so that women were equal to men under the Constitution as it had evolved over the previous two centuries. Yet the truth was that women were consistently discriminated against.

The ERA would not end most of the problems, especially those where the people in power had found ways around them, within the corporate structure. But it would be a symbolic victory, and it could lead to genuine equality of opportunity over time.

Some states rushed to ratify the ERA. A total of thirty-eight were needed for ratification in order for the amendment to become a part of the Constitution. There was a set period for the passage to be possible, and women were lobbying in state legislatures throughout the country. Some states passed the amendment quickly. Other states defeated it with equal speed. And some had legislators who dragged their feet, afraid of political repercussions whichever way they went.

Utah was experiencing a serious problem when it came to ERA. One of the pro-ERA leaders was the wife of a Mormon bishop. She loved her church, believed in the Mormon teachings, and had friends who were equally devout. Yet all of them were pro-ERA. They saw no reason why discrimination against women, or a constitutional amendment outlawing it, violated their faith. They were in a minority, however, and eventually the woman was excommunicated by the church.

A group calling itself Mormon Women for ERA was formed, and they began protesting at the state capital. They were verbally militant, and some took physical action, such as chaining themselves to the building where the legislature was meeting.

The most important protest occurred during the semi-annual general conference of the Mormon church in Temple Square. Thousands of Mormon representatives from all over the world were present. KSL-TV, the Mormon-owned television station, was broadcasting the event. And for a week there would be meetings, prayer sessions, and other activities.

Tensions were high when the rally began. Most of the delegates to the convention were hostile to both the ERA and the idea that Mormon women would support it. They resented the fact that they had to pass the demonstrators, and a number of them made hostile remarks to the women.

But the real hostility to the protest came from several sources. First there were the delegates' spouses who did not go into the temple but remained outside, angrily confronting the women. Then there were the locals gathered for the excitement, who hated the idea of Mormon women demonstrating for something they felt was against their teachings. And finally there were the fanatics who came specifically to do something about the pro-ERA Mormon women.

You have to remember several things about Mormon faith and history. First, the church leadership comprised conservative white males at whose head was one or another old white man who was always believed to be God's prophet. This meant that when the leadership spoke against ERA, the people were expected to believe that the pronouncement came from God.

Second, these were extremely strong, often insular people. It was not unusual to hear a Mormon in his or her seventies talk about a parent or grandparent who had literally walked across the country to get to Utah.

Third, the history of the Mormon church was one of violent attack by outsiders. Many had been murdered just because they were different from the members of the communities in which they had lived. Others had been murdered for having different concepts than their fellow Mormons. Whatever the source of the violence they encountered, the survivors were defensive. They knew that continuing the faith could be a life-or-death situation, and their history was one of fighting back.

Being the typical young, naive, fired-up college student, hating most things Mormon and very much pro-ERA, I joined the demonstration. And being an insensitive idiot when it came to reading the mood of the crowd, I was ready to do battle. I was determined that the force of our presence – Mormon women and non-Mormon women, as well as many men, united for a common cause – would overwhelm the opposition. I was certain that a few well-chosen words of explanation and some catchy slogans would cause those who were against us to think for the first time, to change, to support ERA. I was sure our enthusiasm would overcome their fanaticism. I had forgotten that the difference between a radical and a fanatic is that a fanatic will kill for his or her belief. We were radicals confronting both radicals and fanatics.

The day of the demonstration was bright and sunny. We gathered with our signs that made such statements as "We Want Our Tithing Back" and "Brigham Young's 27 Wives Never Got It. We Want It."

The slogans were especially offensive to the Mormons. Brigham Young was revered by all Mormons for his early teachings. He was also the role model for the polygamist Mormons who still practiced their illegal multiple marriages in a number of smaller communities around Utah and Arizona. The polygamist Mormons were also the most radical, the most prone to violence, and present in disproportionate numbers because they were trying to convince gatherings of more mainstream Mormons of their beliefs. Thus a statement about Young's twenty-seven wives not having a proper opportunity was a slap in their faces.

The tithing comment referred to the standard 10 percent of income routinely paid to the church by its members. Many faiths have tithing or something similar as a way of fund-raising and paying for clergy, buildings, educational programs, and the like. But the Mormons seem more totally committed to the idea than the members of other religious groups. And these women were saying that if the church did not come out in support of ERA, they could not in good conscience continue financial contributions. Again the sign touched a lot of nerves, adding to the tension.

I had seen both the radicalism and fanaticism of Mormon extremists such as those who were present to attack our rally. For example, a friend of mine named Paul Wine fell in love with a Mormon girl and converted to the Mormon faith in order to win her hand in marriage. He loved her deeply, yet she left him after he changed religions. Feeling betrayed by her and not really believing in the Mormon teachings, he decided to get excommunicated. I planned to become a writer at that time, and thought that I could sell an article based on the ritual experience of excommunication if I could go with Paul to see the elders.

Paul met with the Bishopric, a gathering of elder males who make all the decisions. I was informed that I could not attend as a casual observer. However, under the rules of the church, someone seeking excommunication is allowed to bring a legal counsel. We lied and said that I was a law student who was attending to act as his legal representative, a fact that enabled me to be present.

"Brother Wine, why do you want to be excommunicated?" the old Mormon men asked him.

Paul didn't want to say that lust, not faith, brought him into the church in the first place, that he had joined just to win his girlfriend. Instead he said that he had come to disbelieve the teachings. Among the examples he gave was his belief in such heretical (to those Mormons) ideas as Darwin's evolution of the species. He said that science had taught him how humans evolved from fish who came out of the water and developed the ability to breathe pure air, not just oxygen filtered through water.

The elders immediately set him straight concerning the "fallacy" of his ideas. I still remember one old man saying, "If man came from little fish men in the sea, there would still be little fish men in the sea."

The elders argued other points as well. Finally, exasperated, I said, "Paul just wants off your rolls." It seemed like no big deal. They should have been glad to get rid of a nonbeliever.

Eventually the men who interviewed Paul did remove him from their rolls. They were computerized by then, and so the removal was no big deal. Yet the challenge to the church was so great that Paul lost much of what he valued. He had been employed by a Mormon in Ogden, Utah, and he quickly was released from his job. Denied the ability to earn a living, he quickly lost his house and car.

Then there was another man I knew, a journalist who decided to research the polygamous Mormons. These men and women were not united under one belief or leader. Instead, there were many factions, some of which dominated entire towns. There was often violence among rival groups of believers, and the journalist thought there might be a fascinating story in telling the truth about the people. He moved into a cabin that served as a base for his going out each day to conduct interviews. Then, after he and his work-in-progress had become known, the polygamous Mormons stopped him. His corpse was discovered, his head bashed in by what was probably a shovel.

I did not connect the emotional and physical violence I had known so well with the ERA fight. I attended, shouting slogans and confronting about a hundred angry militants who were determined to stop us.

Suddenly the women Mormons who were there to fight against the ERA began throwing rocks. Those who were there with children carried shoulder bags which they gave to their kids, telling them to hit us with the purses. To me their violence seemed as senseless as the biblical stoning of adulterers.

I just freaked in outrage. There had been too many appeasements of these people in my life. Some in the crowd were neighbors. My mother had played the piano in their ward. I had endured taunts for my religion, which did not have doing violence to others as one of its teachings. All the insular bigotry I experienced over the years came to mind as these people suddenly chose to add physical violence to what I had endured.

I began shouting slogans and telling off the people, using rather extreme feminist rhetoric. When I announced to this violent group that God has two round breasts and a vagina, I suddenly found myself being silenced by someone whose hand was covering my mouth. My arms were pinned and I was hustled away from the angriest of the counterdemonstrators. Only when I was freed did I see that it was my friend Rick, whose family was Mormon.

Rick understood the dangers far better than I did. He

understood the mood of the crowd and their potential for real violence. He had reason to be certain that I was going to be severely beaten and possibly killed if I said more. The police presence was mostly Mormon and they seemed willing to let us be taught a lesson. He did what he had to do to get me out of there alive.

I was livid, not with Rick but with the entire situation. I wanted to do battle, but Rick would hear none of it. He forced me into his car, then drove me to the woods to calm down and collect leaves. I knew Rick was right. I had gone too far. I also realized, as he did, that there was no turning back. I had reached the end of my patience. I would only get into deeper trouble if I stayed in Utah.

The next morning I packed my clothing and left town. It would be many years before I could reconcile myself with the reality of Salt Lake City. It would be many years before I had the maturity and perspective to distinguish my many loving, caring Mormon neighbors from the few vocal extremists. For the moment, my anger left blinders on my eyes.

My goal was to move to Denver. I had visited Rosey there several times, and, given my limited experience, it seemed as cosmopolitan a place as I could imagine.

Up until then my most "worldly" experience was when I was fifteen and accompanied my friend Melinda and her father on a trip to Las Vegas. Her dad let us gamble and took us to the MGM Grand Hotel to see the show. There he bought us Shirley Temples to drink so we would feel like part of the scene.

The show was unlike anything I had ever seen. There were beautiful women, bare breasted, wearing sequins, G-strings, giant feathered headdresses, and generally showing me an erotic side of life I had never imagined possible. I still remember when I suddenly became aware of Melinda's father taking my hand in his. Then he gently raised it to my chin. "Sweetheart, please," he said, smiling with amusement as he used my hand to push my jaw up, closing my mouth. I had been gaping and never knew it.

That night when I was fifteen had done more to prepare me for adulthood than anything else in my life. I stared at the performers, trying to be cool so as not to embarrass Melinda's dad, and thought to myself, "God, it's going to be great to be a grown-up."

I had also visited Rosey during the time we were separated. The visits were few, most of our contact coming through letters and telephone calls. Her world was far from mine, and she was still living in a small hippie community in Georgetown, Colorado. Yet there was something exciting about starting a new life with the sister I still adored, and she was willing to have me, if only because I could help with the children.

I like to think that I made my move at a critical time. Roseanne was ready for changes in her life in ways quite different from the past. There had been a period, early in her new life in Colorado, when she had become almost agoraphobic. She and Bill were living in a trailer. For some reason the constant isolation had taken its toll and she reached a point where she was uncomfortable going out. Her days were spent inside the small trailer, and she was putting on weight, becoming severely depressed, and generally degenerating.

Rosey was really spooked by the movie *The Exorcist* and was literally afraid the devil was after her soul. I suspect she was overtired. When we later discussed what happened during this time, she told me she believed she was getting a special message. I did not, though I was certain her mind was not just on the movie. She told me that she began to see herself in mortal jeopardy.

Then there were the drugs. She smoked a lot of pot. This can make anyone paranoid, particularly an isolated, frustrated woman living in a very small rural town. Bill believed in space aliens. Their other friends were often not very sophisticated. And it all seemed to unite to fuck up her mind.

To make matters worse, two Mormon missionaries came to the door of their tiny trailer. My not particularly religious sister told me that she suddenly saw the visit as a sign from God. She immediately asked for the blessing of the pair of missionaries, or so she related to me.

After that incident, Rosey became increasingly uneasy. She stayed in the trailer a lot, and even when she went out, she kept to the more isolated sections of the tiny community.

The relationship with Bill did nothing to ease her emotional discomfort. He had to work long, hard hours, so he was unable to be encouraging when she needed someone to push her back into the world during the day.

Fortunately, I visited her during this period. I brought news from Salt Lake City and a reminder of a world at large. I managed to convince her to go out for a pizza and a salad. We spent a lot of time talking. Gradually she overcame whatever was troubling her. The relationship with Bill grew stronger, and soon the couple was able to afford a larger house for their growing family.

I would like to think that I moved to Denver at a time when Rosey was ready to break out into the world again. Sometime before my arrival Bill had a one-night stand. As I understood it, he and the woman in question were drunk and one thing led to another. It was not a serious affair. Yet he felt guilty enough to confess, and that only added to Rosey's emotional distress. Not only was she isolated and paranoid, now she had been betrayed by the man to whom she had been faithful, and she reacted by making herself both desirable and available to others.

While many people think of Roseanne as fat, we were both in great shape when I moved to Denver. I was looking good, if I must say so myself. Roseanne looked equally good, after having lost a lot of weight in reaction to Bill's confession.

The result of all this was that Rosey and I were ready to explore the big city. After leaving home, I wanted to taste sexual and personal freedom. Rosey wanted time away from Bill, the kids, the too small house, and sexual monogamy. We were ready to hit the night spots together and to pick up men. We were also ready to explore new ideas.

Although we did not know it then, we were about to get more seriously involved with radical feminism in a manner that would "open" my consciousness far more than the ERA rally in Salt Lake City. And all of this would help develop Rosey's unique sense of humor. Without deliberately planning such an action, we would soon learn that Roseanne Barr Pentland was uniquely able to see life in all its absurdities. She was a natural comedian waiting to be discovered, both by herself and, later, the world at large.

4 Denver: The Adventure Begins

While Rosey and I embarked on our journey of sexual and personal liberation, back home, things were pretty damned messed up.

Our family seemed to have emotionally fallen apart by the time I reached Denver. People talk about dysfunctional families today, though in hindsight, I see our problem was both the family and the fact that we lived in a dysfunctional community. We were Jewish in a city dominated by what I felt was cult-like Mormonism. We were poor in a Jewish society that I felt lauded the wealthy. Three of us children were girls in a city that said only boys had full value with God. And even our brother did not escape a special stigma, for by the time Ben discovered his sexual orientation shortly after finishing high school, he realized he was totally monogamous and dedicated to just one person for life – another man.

Ben's teenage years were much like those of many gay men of my acquaintance. They are just beginning to get intense sexual urges, and they focus on the opposite sex with the intensity born of denial.

Ben had a girlfriend whom he thought he loved and who certainly loved him. Unfortunately, they were both fifteen years of age and not capable of using the best judgement. She became pregnant, and Ben was determined to be responsible for the child she was carrying. Ben quit school, got a job as a janitor, and lived with his girlfriend for two years, until his sexual desires for males were so obvious to him, he knew he was gay. He has always been monogamous to the mother of his child, though his refusal to marry her and his reason for leaving her were obviously shocking to her. However, he, his lover, his former girl-friend, and her husband have all worked closely together in the raising of the daughter they all had together.

Dad was irate. Roseanne had already had a child she gave up for adoption and was living the hippie, earth mother life in Denver. I was coming into a rebel, feminist stage. And the pressures were too much for my father to handle. He tried to set rigid rules for Ben to obey, even though it was too late to prevent the pregnancy, and one of the rules was that Ben could not talk with his girlfriend after eleven o'clock at night.

It was two A.M. when Dad discovered Ben in his room, the door closed, but the sounds making it unmistakable that Ben was talking on the telephone with his girlfriend. Dad freaked, kicking in the door, grabbing Ben, and, as Ben later commented, "beating the shit out of me."

There were no apologies later, no obvious recrimina-tions. Ben was wrong. Dad was right in punishing him. The fact that he totally overreacted, losing control, estranging himself from his son in ways he never expected, was not something he would think about.

I know now that the extreme anger we felt toward where we lived reflected, in part, the natural rejection of the fami-liar when first breaking into adulthood. That was why I felt hostility to almost all Mormons instead of recognizing how many of the members were loving people. They didn't believe in the extremist pronouncements of their leaders any more than all Catholics accepted the Pope's teachings, or even all Jews embraced the extremist leaders of my faith. But if I let myself feel the love that was always present, per-haps I would not have had the courage to make the transition into an independent adult life.

Ben took out his frustrations in perhaps the most posi-tive way, focusing on work and raising his daughter. Stephanie, the youngest, who was seventeen at the time, had the greatest difficulty with the least support within the family.

In many ways, Stephanie was the shortchanged sibling, because she was just enough younger than the rest of us that we usually dismissed her as the "kid." Rosey was teaching me about tampons while Stephanie was still playing with dolls. As a result, I would later project my own feelings on to her instead of trying to know her when she was in turmoil. I assumed that her attitude towards the Mormons and Salt Lake City was as hostile as my own. I also suspected that she might resent Rosey's freedom, which, because it was in another state, would seem glamorous. I didn't really talk with her about all this because I was too busy with my friends, work, and school, "adult" pursuits I thought she wouldn't understand.

The truth was that Stephanie was the inadvertent victim of everyone's emotions. When she was seventeen, our parents were in turmoil. In a relatively short period of time, Mom and Dad experienced the nightmare of almost losing their oldest daughter in a car accident. Then Rosey checked herself into the mental hospital. Finally Rosey had an out-of-wedlock baby she gave to loving strangers when my mother intensely wanted to adopt her newborn granddaughter. And after that she became involved with a man they knew nothing about and settled in an unfamiliar city.

The stress of that combination of life crises would have been enough to shatter many marriages. But Mom and Dad also had to contend with the fact that their only son "came out of the closet." He admitted to the mother of his child, then to our parents, that he was gay. He was the first, and while he would not be the last in our family, I had not yet admitted to myself that I would spend the rest of my life with a woman. Besides, in most families, and especially in a Jewish home where sons are often more respected than daughters, having a daughter in love with another woman is less traumatic than having a son in love with another man.

Ben was extremely mature for his age. He accepted full responsibility for the daughter he loved. But neither of his parents could emotionally handle the idea that their son was in love with another man. Today Ben is a loving father and actively participates in the raising of his daughter.

Ben's coming out became the focus for my parents' frequent arguments. Mom and Dad seemed to be angry, hurt, and in denial, not only about Ben's life, but also about what "made him" gay. They were certain it was a choice, and my mother was convinced at first that the "choice" was determined by Dad's failings. "You should have played more baseball with him," I remember Mom wailing.

Against this background of pain and confusion, Stephanie became a teenager, never an easy time under the best of circumstances. Bobbe Mary's health was seriously in decline, another stress factor for Mom. And both my parents were adjusting to the changes all families face when their children are about to leave home.

Finally Stephanie decided she didn't want to continue living in the midst of such tension. All of our tempers were on edge. Even the most seemingly minor conflicts resulted in explosive confrontations. When one fight escalated to a point where Stephanie felt she wanted to endure nothing more, she decided to go to Denver to be with Rosie.

Stephanie was extremely bright. Her course load and grades in Salt Lake City were such that, as a junior, she had enough credits to graduate. Still, she liked school, and enrolled in a Denver high school that proved to be less advanced than the one in Salt Lake City. Bored after her first week, she left that school and enrolled in Barnes Business College, completing their course over the next ten months.

Barnes Business College required financial aid. The school had a loan arrangement that needed to be signed by a local parent or guardian. Since Mom and Dad were in Salt Lake City, Rosey and Mom arranged for Rosey to be Stephanie's legal guardian. Stephanie was given the school loan with the understanding that Rosey would be liable only if Stephanie failed to repay it. Stephanie did repay the loan, taking a total of five years to do so, never missing a payment, never having a penalty. Roseanne never had to put even a dime toward Stephanie's schooling.

Stephanie also took a part-time job at a rib joint in order to pay for food at the Pentlands'. She was even given her own refrigerator shelf to hold the food she bought. In addition, she acted as a babysitter for Rosey's kids and helped her with the housecleaning. Rosey took advantage of the help to go barhopping with her girlfriends, Stephanie spending evenings talking with Bill and working with the kids.

As it turned out, Stephanie's stay was not very long. Four months into the relationship, Stephanie and Rosey had a fight. Stephanie was tired of Rosie yelling at her over how much assistance Roseanne claimed to be giving Stephanie. One night, after one of their fights, Stephanie packed her bags and walked to her job at the rib joint, uncertain where she would spend the night. A coworker lived across the street in a small apartment and helped Stephanie get a room there.

Stephanie lived in that room until I found an apartment we could share. I had lived with Stephanie at Roseanne's, getting a job as manager of a mall store. Stephanie's fight with Rosey occurred during a training session while I was at the corporate headquarters in Cincinnati. I returned from my training, found the apartment, and Stephanie move in as my roommate. She finished her education at Barnes, then returned to Salt Lake City in time to graduate with her high school class.

Finally, in 1981, the last nightmare occurred. Bobbe Mary was near death and I went home to see her in the nursing home before she died.

Bobbe Mary had spent the last months of her life in increasingly helpless circumstances. She could no longer maintain the apartment house to the minimum standards of the various city agencies concerned with housing. The building was at risk of being condemned, and when Bobbe Mary moved into a board-and-care home, Mom promised she would rehabilitate the structure. That satisfied Bobbe Mary, though Mom had no such intentions at the time. (Only later, after my grandmother's death, did Mom and Ben decide to get a loan for the money needed to restore the place. The number of suites was reduced so that the existing rooms could be enlarged, making the place more desirable. The electrical, plumbing, and other problems were corrected. New flooring was added. And ultimately the apartment was made into an attractive condominium building called "Mary's Place," in which my brother lives to this day. The roses have been restored, and the landscaping is again quite beautiful.)

What do you bring an Orthodox widow who is dying? Everything Jewish that's good to eat. When your life is being measured in hours or days, who cares about diet? I packed all the kosher specialty items I knew Bobbe Mary either had not had in years or could no longer obtain. I brought gefilte fish, lox, and numerous other "Jew foods." I also brought my violin, eventually playing every song she wanted to hear.

There was something deeply moving about the experience. Sometimes Bobbe Mary was calling to God, speaking of the strength the Creator provides. At other times she was delighted to see Ben and Perry, her husband and son, both long dead. They were in the room, sitting at the edge of the bed, giving her great pleasure. Yet no one else could see them.

The Jewish faith has a belief in Malchamovitz, the Angel of Death. Malchamovitz stays around the family for a week after death, a time when the family sits shiva. This is a seven-day period when the family gathers in the home and friends come to pay their condolences. The mirrors are covered because the Angel of Death will also take anyone who sees his or her reflection. The funeral is held within twenty-four hours of the death, though, because Jewish tradition does not allow full embalming.

As I listen to Bobbe Mary say her prayers, talk with Ben and Perry, and grow increasingly pale, I knew that Malchamovitz was near. Before I left for Denver, I turned to her and said the only words I could speak. "Bobbe Mary," I said. "I have loved you as much as you loved me!"

Two days later she was dead.

Rosey's life was a mess during this period, not only because of Bobbe Mary's death, but also because of the stresses at home. In addition to her three children – six-year-old Jessica, Jennifer, who was approximately a year younger, and two-year-old Jake – there were problems with Bill. Around the time of the birth of their first child, he had gone to work for the Post Office. This eventually resulted in several moves and the family's having to adjust to changes in his work shift. Rosey was supplementing the family's income by working as a window dresser in a clothing store. She thought all was well with the family, despite the financial pressures and overcrowding in their small home we shared before Stephanie and I moved out on our own. Bill's confessed affair had only added to her worries. She was never again able to fully forgive or trust him. Despite her onetime flower child existence, she had actually been an extremely conservative housewife and mother. Adultery was beyond her comprehension. That was why knowledge of the affair effectively shattered the marriage forever. The fact that they stayed together for several more years didn't alter the fact that the bonds of love and trust had been broken.

Roseanne, who was extremely obese, channeled her anger into changing her appearance, and lost about 120 pounds in a way only Roseanne could. She made up a diet called the Dilly Bar Diet. She was determined to eat her favorite sweets, and she was equally determined to reduce her weight. She was a Dairy Queen fanatic, so her daily meals consisted of one Dilly Bar (vanilla ice cream covered with hard chocolate) and salads. The salads were nutritious and the Dilly Bars satisfied her sweet tooth.

By the time Rosey ended the Dilly Bar Diet, she looked great. She was beautiful, sexy, and desirable, and she soon used her appearance to her advantage. Although she continued to live with Bill, she had at least two relatively serious affairs that I knew about.

I don't think that this was revenge. Rosey had missed the excitement of adolescence. She was thin, attractive, and no longer totally committed to Bill. Her affairs, at first, seemed more an adventure than a conscious desire to hurt her husband.

One affair was with a nineteen-year-old boy. I used to

take her to his apartment, and she would go inside for approximately forty-five minutes while I waited in the car. The boy was too young and inexperienced for her, though. She told me that he "fucks like a bunny," and she eventually dropped him.

Then there was the lover she took after I had moved into my own small apartment. By then Stephanie had returned to Salt Lake City and I was sharing the place with my friend Rick. The man's name was Mark, and he was an "artiste" who performed at a coffee house called Muddy's. Bill knew about this affair because Rosey moved in with Mark for a short time, a situation that upset Bill. He never forgave me for helping my sister cheat on him, and I don't know if he was mature enough to realize that his unfaithfulness had helped create the problems they were having.

Of course, the kids suffered more than anyone for the tension between their parents. They were loved, yet Rosey, at least, seemed to live her life with a narrow focus. Once she decided to act out, she was so single-minded, she did not see the greater ramifications all around her. She acted based upon what she had to do for herself, seeming to never think about how others might be affected. I have never had reason to question Roseanne's intense love for her children. No one ever wanted a child any more than Roseanne wanted Jessica. She carried her newborn everywhere, singing to her constantly. She bought books on the Indian concept of baby massage, studied them, then massaged her tiny daughter's body in the way she had learned. The action was meant to relax the baby, and to bring parent and child closer together, something it seemed to do.

The Pentlands were extremely poor, and the baby was a financial strain. Rosey took Jessica to the park to play, for walks, and to anything else that cost no money. She was the classic "earth mother," the hippie fulfilled with baby raising.

Rosey and Bill loved their children despite being in a situation where money was always tight and living space was always too small. When their two daughters were very young, Bill went on nights at the Post Office, the few cents an hour extra that he earned on the third shift being desperately needed. But that meant he had to sleep days. Rosey had to find ways to keep two active, growing kids away from their father when they wanted to play. (By the time Jake was born, Bill had switched to days.) She had to quiet them when they wanted to be noisy. She had to take them to a nearby park to wear them out when she herself was exhausted and needed a nap.

For the first few years, there was something romantic about the struggle. Rosey delighted in the unique personality of each new infant. Bill adored the confusion of the children and the discovery of life with a growing family. But Bill spent very little time with his daughters when he worked nights, and even when he switched to days, Rosey at first had to cook clean, care for the kids, care for Bill, and usually be the one to handle a crisis.

During the time when Stephanie was living with Bill and Rosey, everyone seemed to have their prayers answered. Bill was then working days and could spend his evenings eating and watching television. Rosey and one or more girlfriend could go to bars for entertainment. Rosey had to spend some time with the kids when Stephanie was not around and Bill was either sleeping or at work.

After Stephanie left, Bill took growing responsibility. He made the kids' dinners. He fixed their lunches when they began going to school. He helped clean the house and do laundry, and greatly eased Rosey's burden.

Rosey developed some eccentricities during this period. For example, she decided to become a cat whenever she was at home. Instead of talking, she would meow. She developed inflections so that it sounded as though she was asking questions or talking in "cat talk." "Meow meow meow-meow?" she would ask. And often the kids would curl up with her and respond the same way. "Meow." Or, more emphatically, "MEOW!" Although everyone else would talk normally, and Rosey would use English when she went shopping or otherwise was in public, at home she would only say "Meow."

Everyone but Mom and Dad thought it was hilarious. No one in the Pentland home was frustrated, though Mom wondered if her daughter was a little nuts. It was one of her eccentricities, but it was done with love and made the kids feel part of something uniquely special. When the kids were young, Rosey also played another game. She would pull a child to her breasts, then suck on each cheek, giving the kids hickeys. It was silly, but the kids let her do it.

No matter what Rosey did, it was intense and totally absorbing. But catering to the needs and wants of three kids and a husband to the exclusion of all else was too much for her. In the end, Rosey could take no more. She burned out.

Later Rosey make a joke out of the experience and inevitably won laughter and applause from other women in similar circumstances. She said, "I love my husband. I love my kids. But I want something more – like a life."

There were other problems as well. Rosey had been raised in a family where our father often overreacted. He could be more violent than necessary when punishing us, and we all hated his temper. She and Bill decided to be relaxed and casual about the kids. This was the era of permissiveness, a time when the baby boom generation was trying to figure out how to settle down and raise families of their own. Some formed communes, sharing the chores. Others believed in lax child rearing, letting the kids learn on their own, with only a minimum of discipline.

The end result was that young Jessica threw temper tantrums, and Jennifer would scream through the house. Little Jake was much too young to show his personality, though as he got older, he was the quiet, sensitive, curious, philosophical child. Although I used to scream in rage and frustration as a kid, much like Jennifer was doing, my personality was more like Jake's. In any case, it was obvious to me, and I think to Stephanie, that there needed to be more of a structure to the lives of our nieces and nephew.

Rosey realized that the stress of her poverty, the frustrations with Bill, and her lack of direction for the future were causing her increased depression. It was then that Rosey threw herself into the task of "getting a life" despite the inevitable trauma it would cause the kids. They went from having a mother who made them the center of her universe to having a mother who almost totally ignored them as she began looking for excitement by hanging out in bars and flirting with men she met there.

By 1981, when I was first living full-time in Denver, Rosey had tried seemingly every home decorating project imaginable, both for the artistic pleasures they provided and to keep from being totally frustrated. She often spent hours redecorating her small house. She would go to thrift stores, flea markets, and Salvation Army outlets to see what she could find. She purchased decorated sheets, velvet paintings of dogs playing poker, and similar items that sold for a few cents to just a dollar or two. She would mix and match. She made curtains. She created the most bizarre combinations I had ever seen. It was Rosey's version of interior decoration as visual comedy. Some people thought it was funny; others thought it was as strange and disturbing as her habit of talking like a cat.

Despite her best efforts, Rosey was becoming burned out. In large measure this was because neither she nor Bill had any parenting skills. They loved their children, but they didn't know how to create a structured environment for the family – how to discipline their children, to set limits, to not cross the line between nurturing love and unhealthy overindulgence. And this resulted in problems that none of them knew how to handle.

I wanted to be buddies, and it was a f——n' disaster.
– Roseanne Barr Arnold quoted by Frank Swertlow in the June 1993 *Redbook*

Having an extended family in Denver did not help with the needs of the kids. We three sisters were in Denver, beginning the relationship that ultimately launched Roseanne to the top. But Stephanie had no plans to stay for very long, and no aunt can substitute for a parent. Rosey shared with me some of her dreams for the future, for the life she hoped the kids would lead. But at first our relationship primarily involved learning about each other and the absurdities of the world that we would utilize in the creation of her humor.

After I settled in Denver, I spent almost all of my free time with Rosey. I was always willing to work at any job, and over the years I had worked in a psychiatric nursing care facility, at K mart, in the field of bookkeeping and account-ing, and other areas. But once in Denver, I at first combined the work necessary to keep body and soul to-gether with exploring the city, cruising for men with Rosey, and learning the community's peculiar ways. Once Rosey and I were almost arrested for sharing a salad at a fast-food place. It's the darkest blot on my record, and one reason I may never be able to run for the presidency of the United States.

The incident occurred in Wendy's, where Rosey and I had innocently gone for lunch. Unwilling to endanger her drop-dead gorgeous figure, Rosey ordered the "one-time-only" salad bar, while I risked the wrath of calories and cholesterol and had a hamburger with the works.

As fate would have it, I finished my hamburger well before Rosey was done with the salad, so I reached across and stole the cherry tomato she had placed on top. Sud-denly the manager and an armed security guard were at the table. Stealing the tomato caused us to violate their rules and we would have to pay for two salads. To be honest, there were signs all over strictly forbidding the sharing of salad. Each person whose fork dared touch the container had to have paid full price. When we refused, we were ordered to leave, evicted under armed guard, Rosey carry-ing a bag filled with the remains of her by then rather soggy meal.

After the Salad Bar Police Officer returned to his inside duties, Rosey suddenly turned to me and said, "You bitch! Why did you do it? Now we'll both get demerits. It will go on our permanent record.

"Do you know what that means? Do you know how

117

that will affect the rest of our lives? Do you know . . . how fucking ridiculous that was?" And then we both began laughing uncontrollably, the salad dressing slowly dripping from a hole that had formed in the bottom of the bag.

And people wonder where comedians get their material.

While we did not return to that Wendy's, not even daring to use the drive-through, we did make Muddy's our hangout. Muddy's was a combination coffee house and theater space providing a small stage for poetry readings and similar activities. It was also where the idea of a career as a performer began to jell in Rosey's mind. Muddy's was the type of place where you could hang out for hours, eating, drinking coffee, and discussing world events, philosophy, literature, and similar intellectual concerns. Everyone seemed young, intense, and extremely naive.

If you have ever been to a party where the only thing the guests have in common is a love of alcohol, you have probably experienced a variation of the talk in Muddy's. Bad jokes poorly told are a turnoff to sober relationships. But get everyone a little drunk and suddenly every conversation is witty, every joke hilarious.

With Muddy's, the conversations were superficial, pretentious and fun. The more you knew about the subject, the less you were appreciated. It was always easier to make insightful comments about a book neither you nor your conversational partner had ever read. You could say anything you wanted and the other person would agree in order to win your approval. Muddy's had a lot of shallow people making "deep" comments with empty heads.

This type of crowd proved to be a supportive audience when there were open poetry readings on the small stage. Everyone was applauded enthusiastically, even if they were bad. The reasoning seemed to be, "If I give you a standing ovation despite the fact that I didn't understand what you wrote and it probably would have bored me even if I did understand it, then you'll give me a standing ovation when I read my poetry. I get to feel loved so long as I make you feel loved." Yet with all the pretentiousness, with all the "artistes," including Mark, Rosey's boyfriend of the moment, Rosey's writing was actually quite good. She had worked at developing her poetry and had read extensively. She hated the idea of college and was hostile to most formal education. Yet she was enthusiastic about learning and willing to tackle any book on a subject that interested her. Over time I found her reading about feminism, ancient religions, and other topics.

The poetry Rosey read on Muddy's equivalent of open mike nights was probably good enough to be published. She preferred to perform, though, to experience the audience, to be the center of attention. It was a very nurturing phase for her, and the beginning of what would become her career. The audience for the poetry readings became a surrogate spouse, providing her with loving support.

I loved her poetry, and I was deeply moved by the quality of her work. I felt, and still feel after all these years, that she has great power as a writer.

Gradually Rosey added jokes and comments to her poetry. She also became the emcee for others performing. She was learning to handle an audience, seeking a way to comment about her life, her frustrations, and her lack of community respect. She was also becoming quite popular with the regulars.

Discovering the Women's Movement

Our life was not totally involved with evading the Salad Police and hanging out at Muddy's. We ran around in all the neighborhoods. Among these was a low-income, blue-collar, very integrated area where the Woman to Woman Bookstore was located. It was from this bookstore that Roseanne would begin the changes that led to her success.

The women's movement was still relatively new to Rosey and me. I had been what might be considered a feminist as early as 1978, but this was limited to protesting what I felt were blatant injustices and discrimination against women in Salt Lake City. The writings of Betty

Friedan and others were not readily available in Mormon country. We missed *The Feminine Mystique* and other popular books on the subject. When I moved to Denver, Rosey and I thought we were part of the vanguard when, on a national level, we were really just catching up to those who had been working for almost twenty years.

We were reading publications such as *Ms* magazine that raised our consciousness, and like many in Denver, we were demanding the right to "have it all." In Rosey's case, that meant ending the family focus and being able to aggressively pursue a career, and expecting Bill to be responsible for most of his own wants and needs. She bought the idea of the "Superwoman" in much of the feminist literature, the concept that she could be a whole person, a lover/mother/home caretaker/businessperson/corporate head, and otherwise successfully manage a complex life. The husband was expected to overcome tradition and be a full partner, not a user whose whims are respected because he has the higher-paying job.

On another, deeper level we were learning about the real history of women in society. We both came to know of the women who dominated medicine in Rome during the time of Christ, medicine so sophisticated that many of the same surgical techniques were used through the first half of the twentieth century. We learned of the goddesses who dominated religion. We discovered times and places when women were to politics and religion what men are today.

Woman To Woman Bookstore introduced Rosey and me to a wide range of women we had not previously encountered. There were blacks and Hispanics, blue-collar women and those with advanced education. Some were married to frustrated men who worked assembly-line-type jobs, then drank beer and watched television in the evenings. Others had husbands with more complex jobs and greater interests, yet often they were the type to verbally put down their wives and see them as secondary. They seemed to want their wives to behave as their mothers had. Woman To Woman gave us all a chance to come together to bitch, to support one another, and, to my delight, to learn our history.

One of the first discoveries Rosey and I made was about the ancient world. We read of digs throughout Europe and elsewhere that uncovered a goddess-centered culture. It's impossible to describe how important the idea of the goddess had been to Rosie and me. It was exciting, almost intoxicating to learn that in the ancient world, the major deity had always been a women, and that she was celebrated, revered, and worshipped for her female attributes – her fertility, her nurturing nature, her wisdom.

We wanted to bring aspects of the ancient goddess worship back into the modern age, on to the TV screen, and into the minds of working women, mothers, and young girls. We wanted to see feisty daughters, strong mothers, and wise grandmas depicted in popular culture.

After we discovered goddess culture, it amazed us just how much effort had gone into eradicating that history. It seemed like all of so-called Western Civilization was based on eliminating her. In the Jewish tradition Yahweh replaced the Canaanite goddess Asherah. In the Bible, the powerful woman Lilith was replaced with Eve, the temptress, born from Adam's rib, a guilty woman responsible for the Fall. In Greek legend, Zeus replaced numerous gods and goddesses. Athena, the goddess of wisdom, was said to have been born from Zeus' head. And in Christianity, the dogma of a virgin birth was rigidly enforced to ensure that Mary, the "Mother of God," would not be considered a goddess herself.

It was amazing and depressing at the same time to see how thoroughly and consistently the goddess had been driven underground, made evil and effectively silenced. We also saw how, by creating God and gods in the male image men had effectively silenced women for centuries. What does it do to a little girl when the only deity she ever encounters is male? How will she feel about herself and other women? How are her imagination and ambitions limited by that?

We knew that the goddess had to be reborn.

Perhaps it was best that we were naive back then. Sometimes it is necessary to generate the anger that comes from seeing a circumstance purely in terms of black and white in order to change your life enough to see the shades of gray. Certainly we had a thirst for knowledge about history and a zealot's passion when we discovered that the world was not quite what we thought it was.

The feminist movement was new and exciting to me, but it was the study of history, archaeology, and ancient cultures that changed my life. I saw how this could relate to economic empowerment. I also saw how much of the feminist movement ignored or was hostile to blue-collar women. Yet what I was learning could strengthen working-class women, could return them to the ideal that had once been dominant in the world.

The history of women and the various women's movements has not been lost so much as it has not been regularly told and retold. For example, I learned that the Old Testament stories sometimes came from the stories that had been part of the goddess religions. There are two major Jewish goddesses mentioned in the Bible — Asherah and Ashtoreth. Asherah was goddess of the sea for some, associated with growth and trees for others. Their definitions varied in different cultures, but they represented the feminine side of creation.

Deborah was my guide to many aspects of the movement, the bookstore, history, and my self. She was a large black woman married to an abusive Marine. For several years she endured physical abuse as they made their home on one base or another.

Deborah's background helped me to start to understand aspects of the women's movement I had originally not comprehended. Had she been white, thin, and married to a businessman, she and her ideas would have been more accepted. Her parents were wealthy intellectuals who had raised her in a world of privilege and education. However, because she was black, obese, and the wife of a Marine, she had faced discrimination within the women's movement. The women's movement had its own hierarchy and snobbery.

As I gradually became involved with various study sessions and books concerning the history of women, I had an idealistic image of Sisterhood. I was sharing an apartment with my friend Rick. His interest in me was that of a trusted, respected friend. However, there was a period when all I could see was that he was male, and I was hostile to males for the history they had suppressed. He later explained that I had become somewhat of an unobjective man-hater in my early days of study. I came to think that if women ran the world, there would be no violence, no hatred or prejudice. Obviously I've had to revise my opinion since then.

I was amazed that there was so much history not taught in male-dominated curriculums in high schools and colleges. Ironically some of it was part of the Jewish lore and tradition, such as the story of Lilith, Adam's first wife.

The story of Lilith, which is sometimes called Jewish mythology, is like the story of Noah. It is one of two creation stories, and though she is not named in the Old Testament, it is obvious how the idea of more than one wife to the first man came about:

"So God created humankind in his image, in the image of God he created them; male and female he created them.

"God blessed them, and God said to them, "Be fruitful and multiply, and fill the earth and subdue it" (Gen. 1:27–28).

The first man and first woman were two equals, and they were both in the image of God. This was not a story about a Father in heaven in whose image only men were made. This was a story of humans being equal with each other and, together, being like God.

It is in the next chapter of Genesis (Gen. 2:21–24) that the idea of a woman made from Adam's rib is introduced. Yet few people bother to explore the Babylonian and Sumerian religious ideas that were popular at the times the stories of Genesis were being written. Those stories had to do with sexuality issues, with the concept of whether a man faced heaven (woman on top) or earth (man on top – the so-called missionary position) during intercourse. The idea of woman as equal was gradually rejected in favor of the woman as inferior to the man (taken from his rib, under his protective arm).

The story of Lilith had numerous variations in religion and myth separate from the Old Testament, and her name is slightly different in a variety of stories. In one culture she is the cause of wet dreams in men. When a baby boy laughs in his sleep, it is the result of Lilith's stimulating his penis. In other stories she cavorts with demons, delighting in sex and giving birth to one hundred babies a day.

Some of the stories are positive. Some are negative. Yet the earlier in history the story was told, the more likely it is to portray her as a good being.

Roseanne and I both became avid readers of history, mythology, Jungian psychology, and related studies. We were discovering the extensive body of literature that existed from ancient times through the present day, all of which was limited in circulation because it presented information counter to that found in male-dominated societies. Yet in this discovery we became not only avid feminists anxious to spread the information we were learning, we also came to understand how shifting power-bases – sometimes shared by men and women, sometimes dominated by one sex or the other – affected society.

Over time we would be tempered in our feelings by the men in our lives and conflicts we discovered within the woman's movement. Eventually Bill Pentland became a feminist and an ardent supporter of Rosey's evolving work. Rick also was an accepting believer. We discovered that it was one thing to declare ourselves Sisters, and another to have to face women who judged one another based on skin color, education, and socioeconomic status. But we did not know that until we were in the midst of trying to bring our version and understanding of truth to the masses.

Some of what Roseanne and I were learning at Woman To Woman Bookstore would lead to the jokes we wrote for her comedy act. We realized that no one wanted to listen to a lecture about Lilith. We knew we had to go for laughs. A joke can introduce people to ideas and cause those who might otherwise be uncomfortable to laugh.

For example, one of the earliest comments Rosey used in her evolving act started with the statement that God is not a single parent. She then said that there has to be a Mrs. God. She has just been silenced for six thousand years, and now She's had enough. She's beginning to bitch at her husband, telling the old man to get off the couch and clean up the lakes, clean up the rivers, clean up the air. Then He can stop the famines, stop the wars, stop all the macho bullshit.

Woman To Woman Bookstore was a cooperative of women from all walks of life. Most were living in blue-collar neighborhoods in a low-income area of Denver. But we had our share of white, Protestant suburban residents. There was tension within our cooperative, but it was not yet blatant. We were the only local source for books, magazines, and bibliographical material solely for women. The bookstore had a basement meeting area for discussion of all sorts, from groups of lesbian and bisexual women discussing their orientation and their lives, to groups discussing history, religion, mythology, and related matters, to groups concerned with contemporary feminist literature. It had a clothing bank for any woman in need. It provided bus tokens to women requiring transportation, a resource even used by prostitutes trying to change their lives. It had a referral line which could help women find assistance if they were being battered, had financial problems, needed short- or long-term housing, and so forth.

It is important to remember that this was the beginning of a movement that is only now being widely discussed. The issue of battered wives was still not a national concern, even though it was happening in frighteningly large numbers. Today the American Medical Association looks upon battering as an epidemic and recommends that its members screen patients for abuse. Back then the attitude was that marital problems were best kept in the home, even if the home was a place of ongoing terror.

There were numerous shelters for men, but few places for women and even fewer places helping women with children. There were few places women were allowed to discuss their private lives openly without fear of social stigma by other women. As a result, there were universal truths about relationships that were widely known but so seldom spoken publicly that women did not realize how common were their thoughts and feelings

The lesbian community, both in our bookstore and in other, similar groups, was the primary one speaking boldly about female experiences. I am not talking about sex. I am talking about concerns of empowerment – personal, professional, psychological, and spiritual. Lesbians were saying things in groups and in their writing that the straight women felt they dared only whisper.

The homosexual community was able to step back a bit, to look at human relationships differently. Because the straight culture was denied to them, they often became acute observers of the world around them. They were like the small boy in the story of the Emperor's new clothes, the only person able to perceive the naked vanity of the Emperor.

Gay and lesbian writers were often years ahead of their time, saying things that took five to ten years to reach magazines and talk shows. The unusual part of our bookstore was that Roseanne was about to become the straight woman's vehicle to speak the observations only lesbians had previously dared express in public. Her act, once professionally polished through experience, touched the hearts of housewives and mothers in ways that little else had done before. She would gain unprecedented wealth and media access because so many millions of women could listen to her and say, "I was right. She's saying what I've been thinking. She understands and she's saying that my thoughts and feelings are valid."

The act had been planned in part around our understanding of the women's magazine concerns at the time. There were numerous articles about the problems men and women had with communicating. We, along with Bill Pentland, developed a portion of the act that addressed men as a separate species. Rosey talked about how women have to translate what you say into male language, how you have to understand the difference between what they say and what they mean. The jokes that followed were examples of this.

Ironically, it was the men, not the women, who were sometimes the most vocal about all this. There were times when men came backstage after the act and said to us, "Wow, what if my wife thinks that way? I wonder if life is like that for her?" And then they talked about the possibility of their needing to change. The men "got it," not just the women, and we felt as though we had reached a previously untapped market for both understanding and entertainment.

It was because Roseanne was straight, married, and had kids that she became the sister to speak out. She and I talked hour after hour for days, weeks, and months about communicating the ideas we discovered. We tried to determine the best vehicle, both in terms of the media and as sisters. Ultimately we realized that Roseanne had to do the talking because she was one of "them."

Rosey had a husband and three kids. Bill had gone from being a hotel night clerk to working for the Post Office. They had lived in a small trailer. They eventually moved to a blue-collar neighborhood whose residents considered their modest homes and small plots of land the high point of their lives. She was one of them, enduring the same problems, relating to many of the same pleasures, and paying the same bills. As a single woman, I could not be accepted in the same manner by the vast majority who shared Roseanne's lifestyle.

Roseanne also represented something different to women. The women's movement leaders often had tremendous bigotry against women like Roseanne. Only women who came from above-average incomes, who were college-educated, were respected by many of the feminist leaders. This economic bigotry hurt the poorer women, who were often at least as intelligent, and sometimes far brighter, than their higher-income "Sisters." Yet they were denied a voice in the movement. Roseanne was beginning to provide that voice for the economically disenfranchised.

Woman To Woman was linked with approximately 280 other feminist bookstores. We were part of a grassroots network of women trying to change society and help one another. We believed in total equality, in personal and professional empowerment through the sharing of differing, complementary skills.

We also dealt with such issues as displaced homemakers. These were women who had lives outside the workplace that were suddenly disrupted, forcing them to seek jobs for which they were no longer qualified. This might occur through divorce, widowhood, or a financial crisis. Whatever the case, they needed skills they did not have yet were capable of learning.

Deborah soon became both a close friend and a guide to the inequities within the movement. There was tremendous tension among the members of the first group of women we encountered in the bookstore. Racism was intense, and when Deborah was talking of "women of color," she began calling white women "women of noncolor." The liberal white women who came from the suburbs of Aurora in their new Volvo and Mercedes Benz station wagons were biased against the blacks and Hispanics. There was hostility between the rich and the poor as well, including among women of the same racial and ethnic heritage but different economic backgrounds.

One of Deborah's greatest frustrations came when the white suburban women kept repeating the line, "We must concentrate on our similarities and celebrate our differences." She hated the idea. She said that the differences were what were causing tension among us. It was critical to discuss the differences, to resolve them where possible, in order to ease the tension. Celebrating them meant that we would never discuss the shit that oppressed blacks, Hispanics, working-class women, and others who did not fit their world

On the surface, the mix of rich, poor, and multiple ethnic and racial groups seemed constructive. We had anarchists mingling with socialists mingling with radical revolutionaries mingling with Democrats and liberal Republicans. I was naive enough to think we had an ideal uniting of all races and creeds, everyone working for the same goals. Instead, we had distrust, bigotry, and intolerance. Frequently I found myself in the midst of a bitch-fest, either in the bookstore or at the International House of Pancakes next door, where we would sometimes adjourn to smoke cigarettes, drink coffee, and talk.

This was not what I wanted, yet it was bringing me into a sharing of ideas that had long troubled me. For example, during my bat mitzvah I had not only read from the appropriate section of Proverbs, like other Jewish girls experiencing this rite of passage, but I had also read from the Torah. This reading from the first five books of the Bible, the ones containing all the laws, was normally the dominion of males. But I was one of the serious Jewish females seeking changes that were leading, during that period, to women becoming ordained as rabbis.

I was already hostile to some of the traditions. For example, Jewish tradition requires that there be ten Jewish males over the age of thirteen in order to have a proper group for public prayer. This is known as a minyan, and at the time I was getting my bat mitzvah, the idea was being challenged by women coming of age, including myself. Why not have a minyan with nine males and one female? Or eight and two? Or whatever combination was possible to achieve ten people over the age of thirteen? God created men *and* women in God's image. Surely the Creator would listen to ten of God's people coming together in worship.

Although this was tradition, not a requirement of the laws of Leviticus, the Jewish elders treated it as though it was demanded by God. Given the strong female origin of so much of the early Old Testament books, I was outraged that I could not be considered as a participant for public prayer.

Such ideas could not be expressed with most people. I had one close friend whom I had met at the summer Jewish camps, a young woman named Maxine Epstein, to whom I wrote letters, exchanging such ideas. She knew my turmoil, my emerging feminism, my anger, and my secret passion for change. But we were friends only by letter and telephone. Rick, the other friend in my life, was the one male I felt could understand women's issues, though I also felt that we needed to fight over concepts. He often had to take the brunt of my anger, but he cared enough to listen to me. Thus the discovery of women with whom I could speak openly about issues normally too controversial to express was a wonderful experience.

My discovery of women's history also constantly challenged and changed my personal relationship to Judaism. Among other topics, I learned the origins of Rosh Chodesh, the monthly celebration of the new moon that is a part of Orthodox Jewish tradition. I had not realized that in ancient times the moon was considered female, and the celebration related directly to the menstrual (lunar) cycle of women.

I learned that Sara, the wife of Abram (Abraham), a major prophet for Judaism, Christianity, and Islam, was originally a respected priestess. She was the important person, yet the feminist aspect of her history was gradually ignored.

I was excited by the knowledge, thrilled to be in a community where such information had been gathered. In Salt Lake City nobody would dare challenge the patriarchal ideas of the Mormon church. If such books were available, I didn't know how to locate them. Thus, for me, Denver and the Woman To Woman Bookstore proved both enlightening and emotionally liberating. But none of this meant that I could avoid the type of bickering I might once have classified as being "male."

Our worst encounter with the tremendous bias inherent in the movement came when we were invited to participate in a conference on women in labor. It was being held in Rock Springs, Wyoming, and Roseanne, Deborah, and I were to be among the presenters. We had purchased a filmed program about pornography that was offered by one of the feminist bookstores in San Francisco, and we planned to share it with the others.

The film presented evidence of the racist and exploitative nature of this $80-billion-per-year industry. We felt that the movie was a fast way to reach people who didn't have access to scholarly literature and resources, allowing them to pursue in-depth study later if they so chose. But for most of the viewers throughout the country, the film would be their only exposure to this important issue. Thus if you knew about the film and purchased it, you felt obligated to present it to others as a way of Sisters sharing. As I say, we truly believed that we could change society through a power-shared corporation of women. Each woman would do whatever she did best, and we would come together in synergy.

At Rock Springs, Deborah spoke to the group, using a chalkboard to make several points. She also misspelled one word, and that misspelling became the focus of attention for several women. They stopped paying attention to her presentation. They stopped focusing on the issues being discussed. All they saw was an obese working-class black woman who was "obviously" only semiliterate. It was a vicious stereotyping that brought out the worst in the attendees.

Later, at a women's program held at the University of Colorado, it was Roseanne who had the problem. She was on a panel with a female professor who was an intellectual snob. The professor wanted to talk about quantitative learning differences, age-based factors, and other concerns with raising unbiased children. Rosey was talking about societal perceptions affecting the way girls were treated, the way women were viewed, and the like. She was focusing on the impact of popular culture on women, on advertising, on the characterization of women in books and movies, and other serious concerns. She was not looking at statistics.

By the time the two presentations were over, we realized where we had problems within the movement. The wealthy, the well educated, and the academics did not care for the large number of women who fell into the blue-collar category. Racism and classism dominated the movement. Rosey's interpretation was factual and effective, but she lacked academic credentials, a fact on which the snobs focused.

As Deborah pointed out, feminism had been very good for some women. They had middle-management jobs and three-piece suits. They got to act like men. But those women were usually middle-class and almost always white. Feminism rarely touched black women, rarely touched Hispanic women, rarely touched women who were raised in poverty.

I also was discovering something else, something extremely sobering. The experience occurred when I was visiting Rosey and Bill after I had my own apartment. They had a neighbor, an extremely docile woman whose husband, unknown to us, was extremely violent. Apparently in the past he had been careful to hit her so that any marks on her body would be hidden by her clothing. This one night he had gotten carried away, beating her about the face. She arrived at Rosey and Bill's with a black eye, missing teeth, and blood stains she had missed when she apparently tried to make herself look "presentable" before seeking a neighbor's help.

Bill did not want Rosey and me to get involved. He had compassion for the woman, but this was a domestic quarrel. Bill, in his prefeminist days, was like a lot of men and women. Somehow marriage gave a couple rights they might otherwise not have. A man could beat his girlfriend and everyone would side with the woman. But let a man hit his wife, and it was only a "domestic quarrel." They would eventually kiss and make up. And if they didn't? Well . . . that was what the divorce courts were for.

Besides, what if the husband came looking for *his* wife? He might strike out at the Pentland family. The children might be hurt. Rosey might be struck. Bill did not want his family involved.

Despite our discussions, Rosey did not stand up to Bill. She was an emerging feminist, but in that crisis, the desire to appease Bill was stronger than her sense of Sisterhood. As a result, I took the woman from the house into the car, not certain what to do but knowing I had to separate her from everyone.

"What are you going to do?" the woman asked, terrified. "Will you hurt me, too? Will you beat me?"

I was shocked. How could she think a Sister could do her harm. Hadn't I shown her how much I cared? Didn't she know that Sisters didn't hurt one another? Wasn't she at all enlightened in the ways of the world?

Eventually I took the woman to a McDonald's to get some food. As she calmed down, she was able to think more clearly. She came to my home, where I had a friend come by who had been through a similar situation with her ex-husband. After talking with her, my friend found the woman a battered women's shelter where she could stay.

I increased my resolve to educate and reassure women about the truth of who we were, where we had come from, and what we could achieve together. Certainly Rosey's neighbor was the perfect person to be educated, to come to the meetings at the bookstore. Instead, though, after spending a few days at the battered women's shelter, she returned to her husband. If there was a change, it was that they were both angry with me for causing them to be apart during those few days.

While still trying to understand how this could occur, I talked extensively with my friend Maxine Epstein, a social worker who had gone to Israel to conduct a study of the violence against married women. Jewish men battering Jewish women was a dirty little secret in Israel. It is a violation of the culture, the tradition, and even the Talmud. Yet it was taking place, and women were only beginning to come forward to complain publicly.

What made the study unusually interesting was that in Israel, all the laws governing the rights of women were interpreted by the rabbis. Most of them adopted the concept of *shalom bayit* – peace in the home. This means that the women were expected to return to their abusive husbands, not getting a divorce, for the sake of peace in the home. The perception of harmony that came from a couple staying married and living under one roof was more important than admitting that battering was taking place.

Even worse, Maxine found that many Israeli women came from Yemen, Ethiopia, and other areas where wives were routinely battered. The women did not like being victims, yet the violence was culturally acceptable. In addition, battering incidents increased during wartime. The stress of the community violence led the men to act out violently at home.

Through Maxine, I came to understand that Rosey's neighbor had no job skills, no way to earn enough money to meet her immediate needs. Just renting an apartment might require first and last month's rent, as well as a security deposit. A two-hundred-dollar-a-month apartment might cost five hundred dollars to get in, and that does not count the deposits for utilities. The battered housewife did not want to stay in the life she was living. She simply lacked the tools and the help to leave. It was better to try to avoid the physical attacks of an abusive man than to be on the streets after the short time a shelter might allow her to stay.

At first I had the attitude that perhaps women really did not want to change. They would rather shoot the messenger than consider the message. Then I realized that two points were critical – how the message was conveyed and whether or not the women could relate to the messenger.

Rosey and I talked about this. We were in agreement about the end and needed to see what common ground existed among women. Obviously we were strongly influenced by the feminist movement as we had been experiencing it in Denver. In fact, our group of women changed the name of the Woman To Woman Bookstore to the Rocky Mountains Women's Center, a name reflecting the fact that we wanted to speak for all women, regardless of their background. Then Rosey began performing with Black Orchid Productions, a guerrilla theater group connected with the bookstore. It was like being part of a sophisticated, directed version of the plays and dramatic performances we had done as children. Performances were in coffee houses and various feminist bookstores and meeting places though primarily in the nearby Unitarian church, which had a stage area the company used. Ironically, in one sense we had returned to our childhood and the outdoor stage of the Salt Lake City Baptist church, though this time there was importance in our productions.

Unfortunately, the audience was usually the same twenty-five to fifty women we saw all the time, though their enthusiasm was extremely nurturing for new talent.

One type of presentation had the performers giving speeches as different women from history. But we also found that humor was a good common ground, and Rosey was quite comfortable with this field.

The more Rosey developed what would become a comic act, the more we recognized the first important point of shaping our message. An idea presented in a joke is not rejected. If someone is not directly attacked, humor can help the person see the absurdity in his or her situation. Jokes about women in society, about male/female relationships, and about men were acceptable to the woman who worked as a janitor and the woman who worked as a professor. The message had to be clear, but it might be most effective when presented obliquely.

We also saw that our first audience would probably be women like Rosey – married, with three or four kids, a husband who felt himself more important because he earned the bigger paycheck, and a sense of frustration with life. Roseanne knew what it was like to be the blue-collar everywoman. She had lived in a trailer. She had struggled to buy a house that would always be a little less than her needs yet the largest place she would ever be able to afford. And the style of speaking used in her act was varied. Sometimes she deliberately made herself sound like a high school graduate, indifferent to advanced education yet with a Ph.D. in life. At other times she would sound as erudite as a Rhodes scholar. She might be a trailer park mama one minute, an intellectual the next.

By contrast, I was a single woman. I had known poverty. I had also known the frustrations of a large family, though my experience had been as a child and a sibling, not as a parent. Women would relate to Rosey easier than to me. And since we were both developing an act for Rosey, working together on some of the jokes she was telling, it was logical that we made Rosey the messenger for the message we were both working to convey.

We began working on a concept for an act that could be performed more widely. We were aware that the women's magazines were trying to find a way to redefine the roles of men and women in society. We had our own answers, and we wanted to provide them. We were on a crusade to save the world, and the production was one of the first steps toward that end. We had called what we were doing Funny Womaness, and initially the jokes were rather harsh, expressing more anger than humor.

Roseanne at first was rather strident, as we all could be. It was as though she was shouting constantly, preaching to the audience which, at first, shared our views. But we tempered this presentation as we both began to understand the "marketing" aspect of comedy. Subtlety was more subversive than open aggression, and she began honing her comments into an act that could be appreciated by both women and the men they brought with them to the performances.

Rosey had a gift for taking elaborate concepts, especially as they related to complex relationships, and phrase them so that they were universally understood. She could vary what she was saying for her audience, not leaving the stage until everyone understood her ideas. Humor was used for the presentation, but Rosey was more than a joke teller. She was able to touch the minds of people who thought they had closed themselves to radically different ideas. She likened it to a karate chop to the head. She called it making their gray matter concave, preventing them from ever being able to think the same narrowed way again. It was a side of her I loved. It was a side I admired. It was one reason why I wanted to work with her throughout our lives.

The act, for me, was a cause, a vision for our career, I would give her a premise, then bitch seemingly endlessly, discussing feminist philosophy. For example, I would talk about how women's bodies were dissected into parts, into objects used to sell products ranging from feminine hygiene ablutions to shaving lotion. Even automobile body shops have posters of half-naked women holding motor oil and calendars of totally naked women reminding you of the day of the month. Rosey would let the ideas lay dormant in her mind. Then, often at three in the morning, I would get a telephone call from an excited Roseanne, or she would get a call from me. Together we worked out a series of jokes based around the premise, perhaps beginning with "When I die, I'm going to donate my tits to Madison Avenue, because women's tits sell everything from cars to toothpaste."

Together Roseanne and I would not just create another funny little comic. Instead, we were going to create a product that would endure for a generation. Laughter would be a vehicle for social and political change. Ultimately we saw a day when there would be a women's political party.

Remember that this was long before there were many women in politics. Colorado had Pat Schroeder, of course. The late Frances P. Bolton had been a longtime congressional representative from the Cleveland, Ohio, area. But women were few in number at any meaningful level of politics. The idea that in a few years, there could be a woman running for Vice President was incomprehensible. None of us could imagine the future, yet all of us comprehended creating the groundwork on which that future, or some similar experience of female empowerment, would be based.

The real training I had came not from the comedy focus but from other areas I was learning. I had college level training in business and marketing, but I knew far less than I realized when we women began looking at the most important goals for the community.

It was fine to talk feminist theory. It was exciting to use the new buzzwords such as "empowerment." But the reality was that women could not change until they could be independent. A woman without a means to support herself could not get off welfare, leave an abusive husband, or otherwise begin changing her life. Some of this meant getting training for a type of work that was readily available. Some of this meant having businesses open their doors to women.

137

My education began in two ways. Perhaps my greatest mentor was Sharon Silvas, a single parent around fifty years of age. She was a media expert who was involved with both running her own enterprises and helping Hispanic women in the area. Sharon was an expert in public relations and had several small business accounts. She created magazines for corporations and other businesses. She was also concerned with helping women effectively lobby for political causes. She taught me how to think like the potential market for whatever I was selling, whether it was a product or Rosey's act. She also introduced me to the assistance that was available through the Small Business Administration.

There is an organization called the Service Corps of Retired Executives (SCORE) which is a volunteer program established to give business advice. SCORE exists throughout the United States and is comprised of former leading members in all phases of business and industry. They so loved the world of business that they volunteer their time to teach men and women how to be successful. They provide advice, forms, and everything needed to achieve your goals. They do not care what type of business you might wish to own. They show you how to determine if there is a market, how to create a business plan, and how to survive while growing to the level where you can be earning a fulltime living.

I don't think I ever left my meetings with people from the SBA and SCORE with fewer than fifty pamphlets. I learned how to create a business plan, how to analyze location, traffic patterns, service needs, overhead costs, and other areas of concern. I used the assistance as my postgraduate education, spending so much time with the men at SCORE that I always felt they were thinking, "Oh, Christ, it's the Barr girl again." Yet the truth seemed to be that they loved working with me. Not that I was special. They loved helping anyone going into business. And I never would have known any of this had it not been for Sharon.

Deborah Hampton, twenty years Sharon's junior, had a background in finance which complemented my training.

Using the knowledge we gained from Sharon and SCORE, we found that there was a market for a bookkeeping service focused on small businesses. We also realized that it would be possible to train others to handle all the non-specialized work. Special courses would be needed for certain types of taxes, for example. And there might be a need for additional consultants for certain types of expansion questions. But most of the day-to-day work that needed to be done could be handled by ourselves and other women we trained.

Our early customer base involved eight accounts, including flower shops, a café, an antique store, and even a successful Colorado Springs artist. We processed the businesses' payrolls, handled their tax records, prepared monthly financial accounts, and the like. In addition, we helped the artist plan the marketing of posters and similar mass-produced items to bookstores, galleries, and elsewhere outside Colorado.

Another business we created involved working with florists and corporations. Everyone needs to set a price for their time. If you're in business, you need all your employees doing work that justifies what they're paid and the overhead spent in keeping them (workmen's compensation, a desk, telephone, rented floor space for their cubicle or office, and the like). An employee who is generating income for the company is obviously more valuable doing that work than doing tasks that do not make money. But a support employee, such as a secretary, still should be doing work that helps generate as much income as possible. Every time a staff person has to do busywork unrelated to the focus of that business, the company loses money. That is why outside cleaning services are usually cheaper than having a staff custodian, for example.

We found that many corporations in the area liked to decorate with live plants. They are inexpensive, varied, beautiful, and provide a pleasant environment. They also needed to be watered, have the soil checked, fertilizer added, and similar concerns addressed to keep them from dying. Normally such tasks are handled by the lowest-paid secretaries, yet even at that level, the work is not cost-effective. Or so went our sales pitch as we created a plant maintenance business. The women in that business would go from corporation to corporation that had decorated with plants, caring for them for a fee. Although a seemingly simple task, it was still cheaper for the companies to pay a fair fee for the service than to use a staff person. And we were able to charge enough so that the women who performed the jobs could be self-supporting.

We weren't trying to get the women we helped rich. All we wanted to do was to get them into business where they could earn a living adequate for supporting themselves and their families without needing government assistance. Once they had the pride that came from doing something that had previously been impossible, we could help them advance in other fields.

Dee Galloway, a twenty-five-year old black woman, was a bookkeeper who worked for Kaiser. She was one of the driving forces in keeping me focused on the arts. She was also a violinist, and she arranged for me to join the Denver Community Orchestra, which I did in 1983. She had played with them for several years and felt I would gain from the experience.

The orchestra's rehearsals were in an area high school's music room. We were called upon to play a number of concerts, as well as special programs for holidays such as the Fourth of July. The only disappointment for me was that I was not able to be more involved with the group, since I quickly had to choose between working with Roseanne and performing with the orchestra.

Deborah Hampton and I also became involved with the business of selling supplemental insurance policies, which involved multilevel marketing. You could sell the insurance and take a percentage of the gross for your income. Or you could train people to work for you, taking a percentage not only of what you sold but also of what they sold.

Today this doesn't sound like it means very much. At the time, such multilevel marketing gave the women we were working with and other displaced homemakers both income and hope. They learned to present themselves professionally. They learned to be outgoing. They learned how to keep business hours, to become aggressive in pursuit of sales, and to be instantly rewarded for their achievements. For women who had been told they had too little education, that they were stupid, and that they couldn't function without a man to support them, and had otherwise been put down, this was a richly rewarding experience. More important, the cost of living was such that they could become independent through such work. And since it was sales, they could do the work part-time while taking another job, returning to school, or working out cooperative day care with other women who had jobs, kids and time when they couldn't be home with their children.

We also became involved with politics. I met with leaders of the League of Women Voters and other activist organizations, learning how to lobby and effectively work for a political cause. I went to the state legislature along with representatives of other women's groups. There I learned to speak effectively enough to help make an impact on the politicians. We were able to convince the state legislators to develop a program for raising money to support women entering the marketplace. State tax forms were printed with a check-off box that would provide a dollar of each person's tax money to support programs to help battered women's shelters. The allocation of these voluntary contributions including funding to train women for nontraditional, in-demand jobs as carpenters, mechanics, and the like.

We also utilized the talent from Black Orchid Productions to help Congresswoman Pat Schroeder's election campaign. We participated in working-women expositions, using performance to increase public awareness.

One of the more remarkable people in the nontraditional trades who also helped other women was Mary Gale. She was an educator who decided that she did not like the traditional school system. She loved to teach, though, so when she abruptly changed professions, becoming a self-taught cabinetmaker, she helped other women create products for sale.

141

Mary was modest about her success. She explained that the only reason she had gone into carpentry was because she wanted to have the perfect rocking chair for when she retired. The chair would have a seat that was designed to flawlessly support her own butt. To everyone's amusement, after a few months of turning out work for sale, her home/workshop suddenly had a magnificent bentwood rocker in one corner. It was never for sale, and if you looked closely at both the seat and at Mary, you'd see that it was perfectly constructed to fit her rear end.

And as I became more involved with Roseanne's career, Deborah Hampton continued helping the other women develop their businesses. My focus, I felt, had to be Roseanne. I had proven myself through the other ventures I had started, and I had the ongoing resource of SCORE for the few questions that remained. It was time to market the product that would be Roseanne as she would come to be known to millions.

My role model was comedian and social activist Dick Gregory. He knew that he wanted to influence the political arena, and his pain – the pain of being a brilliant black man who was denied opportunity because of his skin color – was very deep. Yet his jokes caught a universal nerve, and his anger only occasionally came to the surface. For example, his autobiography was entitled *Nigger*. In a dedication to his mother, he wrote that from that day forward, whenever she heard anyone use the foul term for blacks, she would know that the person saying "nigger" was only advertising his book.

Creating the Act

We knew that humor could be extraordinarily subversive, a tool for change, a means for education, a method for undermining authority. This was something Roseanne learned most blatantly around 1982 after she left her part-time job as a store window dresser because the forty-dollar-a-week pay was too little for the family's needs. She took a job at a night spot called Bennigan's. There she coordinated the cocktail lounge, acted as a hostess, and occasionally worked as a waitress when they were short-handed. The crowd was mostly men on the make, some single, some married. Some were verbally abusive, though never intending to hurt. Their humor was rough, crude, yet they delighted in a strong woman with tough comebacks, and Rosey usually gave better than she received.

Eventually Rosey obtained a following, men who would come just to verbally spar with her, then leave far larger than normal tips. Among them were those who suggested she go to the open mike at The Comedy Works on Larimer Street.

In the 1980s The Comedy Works was typical of what was happening in the entertainment business throughout the country. Every generation seems to have its own style of gathering place. The forties had dance halls and the big bands. The fifties and sixties had jazz clubs and coffee shops featuring poetry readings. By the time Rosey and I were getting started, comedy clubs were the gathering place. Each night that the club was open had a different type of act. The established talent, which might have appeared on the *Tonight Show*, in Las Vegas, on the Playboy Club circuit, or some other high-paying chain, would headline. There would be a cover charge and usually a minimum purchase in order to pay the bills. Then the headliner would either make one long appearance or perform three different times on the same night. When the latter occurred, the act would be tailored for three different audiences.

The first presentation was the most conservative, the most family-oriented. The jokes were meant for people who were sober, liked comedy, and listened closely to what was said. Some were dating. Some were married. And if the club allowed, the audience sometimes included families with older teenagers.

The second set of jokes was told at a time that attracted an older looser crowd. They had usually been out to dinner or seen a show before dropping by the club. They may have had something to drink, and they were either dating singles or couples who were either married or living together. Sex jokes were popular with them, along with biting political humor. Everything was sophisticated, and an occasional heckler was the price the comedian paid.

The third set was close to midnight. The audience was usually mildly intoxicated, though some were so drunk that they would have to take a taxi home. Some were going from the club to someone else's bed, getting laid as the high point of their evening. Others were still trying to make arrangements to score. And still others were talking about things their bodies were too inebriated to perform. It was considered normal for the audience to talk back to the comedians, trying to top the performers. And the jokes were crude body humor, the language liberally laced with "fuck," "fart," "stud," and other terms rarely heard in the earlier sets.

Monday night (or whatever was the first night of the week that the club was open) was frequently open mike night. This meant that both amateurs and professionals might appear, trying their hand for no money. Everyone present was either a humor buff willing to listen to anything in hope of a good laugh, a comic looking for ideas or checking the new competition, or a wanna-be who might get the nerve to go on stage. The cost for attending was next to nothing, usually a minimum food or drink order, a cover charge seldom being assessed. Unfortunately, most of the acts sounded like the midnight shows on weekends. It was as though they knew nothing but body humor.

Rosey and I went to the open mike Monday night show at The Comedy Works, where she tried out the humor she had been using with the guerrilla theater Black Orchid Productions. Some of the jokes were weak, of course. She was still learning. But other jokes were funny then and continue to get a laugh when repeated today. For example, one of the most universal stories that was part of her early work concerned her memories of ninth-grade health class.

Rosey first set the scene. An assembly was called, and only ninth-grade girls were permitted to go to the school auditorium. There they found a movie projector set up and the windows carefully taped over so boys could not peek inside and see what was being shown.

Finally a ninety-year-old, withered yet intimidating crone would stand in front of the group of nubile young teenagers and explain what they were about to experience. Rosey would announce the movie in a voice reminiscent of the announcers heard during a preview of a 1950s grade B science fiction movie. Her routine was something like the following:

"Experience your body going *out of your control!* Watch helplessly as your breasts grow like ripened melons, hair relentlessly fills your underarms, and every month blood flows from between your legs.

"Watch in horror as the body you've trusted begins *the transformation.*

"See innocent young girls mutated into horrible shrews."

Then, adopting the voice of the hysterical heroine of the movie trying to protect her boyfriend from the sight of her becoming an alien, she would scream, "Get away from me, *I'm bloated!*"

It was the type of routine to which women of all ages could relate. Teenage girls all experienced the very obvious physical transformations of puberty, and most women had an education that addressed such personal issues in a manner that, at best, might be called eccentric. For most females, early knowledge of sex and sexuality usually came incorrectly from the streets and older siblings, or from stern spinster educators who sounded like Marine Corps drill sergeants. The routine was funny because it touched the universal experience.

Several of the Bennigan's customers were in the audience to see her, and she was able to play off them. In a sense she had honed her skills handling the raunchier side of improv from their teasing her at the night spot, so she was happy to have them. They were much like Dad, whose style of humor was similar to much of Rosey's nightclub material. Naturally the Bennigan's customers were enthusiastic, and the result was a successful presentation. She was far from professional, yet she held her own.

Rosey was so buoyed by the success of her first open mike experience that she tried again the following week, and this time she was terrible. She had decided to try new and different material, and almost all of it bombed. Although I did not witness the reaction, Rosey remembered seeing one woman turn her chair around and her back to the stage so she could continue talking to her friends.

Roseanne had not yet learned the necessity of creating an act, then perfecting it. She wanted to use totally new material each time, a situation that did not let her refine anything. Some jokes were good, some bad, and you could have a completely off night where nothing worked.

I began noticing the politics of comedy during these open mike nights. At first Roseanne seemed to think that comedians were one big family. They had this special talent that separated them from society. They saw life differently from the average person. They worked nights while most others played. They were responsible for bringing pleasure to others no matter what they might feel like. They were a closed society and she was a dues-paying member of the group. Thus she felt quite comfortable verbally embracing them, effusively greeting them, thinking she would be made welcome. Instead, she was ignored.

Once Rosey began working regularly with the same acts every open mike night, her acceptance was determined by her success. The other comics were warm, friendly, and helpful every time her act bombed. If the audience loved her, none of the other comics would speak to her.

Then I began witnessing outrageous egos. The best and worst comics had the same attitude. A man could come on stage with a funny hat, a rubber chicken (yes, some did use them as props), and a series of dirty jokes everyone knew were stolen from back issues of *Playboy*, and no one would laugh. Yet he would be convinced that it was not the material or his delivery at fault. It was a bad house. It was too unsophisticated a crowd. They were all wanna-be comics overwhelmed by his genius. The excuses were endless, for he knew in his heart that he was a star people would recognize at any moment.

Later Rosey explained to me how hard it was to go on stage on a regular basis. You faced failure with every joke. Timing, a change in inflection, even the events of the day could influence how people responded. You had to develop blinders to the realities of life in order to keep going back.

I saw some comics who were terrible. Their jokes were about excrement, body noises, and other things only juveniles find funny. The audience either failed to laugh or laughed in embarrassment. Yet they came off the stage as happy as could be, certain that they had "killed." When I asked Rosey how they could be so bad and still have such egos, she told me that the ego was necessary. The work was intensely difficult, yet a handful of comics were regularly picked up for national tours, for television shows, for movie roles. The only way to go on, night after night, was to believe that you were as good as they were, that the next big break would be yours. Eventually the bad ones would either realize they did not have what it took, or play smaller and smaller clubs on their off nights. The good ones might get discouraged or they might actually achieve their dreams. But everyone initially had to believe with the same passion.

The real professionals had egos but were willing to write, rewrite, and refine their acts. They would tape-record what they were doing, listening not only to what they said but how they said it and how the audience reacted to it. They would use an objective listener to make notes during the performance. They would try variations. They would try to put together enough material so that they could refine their act according to the audience. Yet they always knew that their future was constantly determined by each night's show, and that was terrifying. You had to believe in yourself so completely that the jeers, the groans, and the awkward silences could never shatter your self-confidence. It was not a life for the modest, the self-effacing, and the insecure.

As would become my habit in the years ahead, I sat in the audience when Rosey performed, taking notes on the act. I mentally stepped back, listening critically, objectively to what was being said. I could tell which jokes did not work because they were not funny in a group not comprised of women with shared experiences. I could tell which jokes did not work only because the audience did not care for that type of humor. And I could tell which needed to be improved. I also realized that an open mike night was not the right venue for Rosey. Mostly there were bad comedians listening to bad comedians, and radically different approaches to humor would not work there.

Roseanne was hooked on comedy as a way of changing the thinking of women and as many men as possible. She did whatever she could to improve. She took any jobs we could find for her, because in those days I helped sell her act. I worked all day as manager of a chain mall shop called Things Remembered. Then I would spend evenings contacting clubs, coffee shops, and any other place where I thought Rosey could perform. I used whatever work she had done as proof that she was good, and ultimately some places let her perform.

The owner of a restaurant/club called Straite Johnson's let her do her act, though few in the audience listened. It was a delightfully eccentric business whose primary draws were its salad bar, which was placed in an ice-packed coffin, and the women who stripped to music. The comedian was not the principal attraction.

Rosey played at a macho, sometimes violent biker club where the patrons wore tattoos, leather, and beards. And their boyfriends were similarly dressed. (Okay. I'm just kidding about the patrons. But places like the Mercury Café catered to a rough blue-collar, straight, biker crowd that tested every comic, especially women. Rosey learned to both hold her own and gain their respect for her humor and professionalism. She was tougher and raunchier than she might be in quieter places, yet what she learned from the experience helped her in friendlier clubs.)

The way Rosey handled hecklers at such clubs was to

take the image of her life and throw it back at them so she proved she was tougher than they were, at the same time getting a laugh. She might say to a heckler, "I'm fat. I'm poor. I'm Jewish. I'm from Utah. Come on, fuck with me!"

She also performed at a lesbian club called Three Sisters. "I'm a heterosexual," she would say. "I don't know why I'm like this. I was just born this way." The act worked best with women, especially those who felt disenfranchised from mainstream Denver. The act was essentially the same as for the other clubs, though she did not have to worry about the sensibilities of the men who might be present. Thus she could limit the range of her jokes since she did not have to worry about losing part of her audience.

At all times, Rosey tried to get as much of an education in stand-up as she could. We listened to other comedians and she took a short course offered at The Comedy Works by Los Angeles-based professionals, including Dianne Ford.

Dianne became a mentor of sorts for Rosey. For example, she helped her to understand the importance of mastering one truly good set of jokes.

Dianne talked about trying the same good jokes in different ways, with different inflections and emphasis. Something could be mildly humorous told straight, then made extremely funny with a slight variation of voice, attitude, or some other minor deviation.

One problem Roseanne had was being allowed to appear on a day other than Monday at The Comedy Works. Other comics who were not as good were getting better time slots, being moved to days of the week when the crowds were better. She asked Dianne and anyone else who might have influence with the owner to help her get a better slot, since her work had improved. However, no matter how she improved, The Comedy Works kept her on Mondays. Finally we decided that the only way to make a change was to develop our own show where she could perform before a better house. We named the show "Take Back the Mike Night" and arranged to rent the Glen Miller Ballroom of the University of Colorado. It would not be just Rosey telling jokes, but a local talent show that ultimately took us nine months to prepare.

We used the same variety show approach we had used growing up, though this time we sought real local talent, not just someone with webbed toes. There were girl singers, dancers, and musicians. Some men were involved, including Bill Pentland, but it was primarily a showcase for local women, with Roseanne serving as both emcee and comedian.

The mix of talent was surprising. Some were barely competent, such as singers whose careers would never go beyond church choirs. Others were extraordinarily talented, able to hold their own with the best professionals. They were either at the start of their careers, had briefly been on stage before putting thoughts of a career on hold while going to school or having kids, or did not know how to break into show business. They stayed in the Denver area, appearing whenever and wherever they could, having no idea how to plan their futures.

Rosey and I were unusual in that we had no illusions about our tomorrows. We were going to be the Jewish sisters who took Hollywood by storm. Rosey needed a solid act, ever larger showcases, and skilled marketing following a clearly defined multiyear plan. The SBA men had taught me that with time frames, goals, and objectives, success was almost certain to be achieved. I kept that firmly in mind as the act was developed.

After the show, which was not reviewed by the local daily newspaper, we went to the alternative weekly. There are numerous such papers around the country. New York's *Village Voice* being the most famous. They are counterculture publications, devoted to the arts, printing what they perceive to be the important stories the daily papers underreport or never mention. Some are large and financially successful. Others lead a hand-to-mouth existence with extensive volunteer help and the constant juggling of payment to creditors. But the papers are delighted to have a good story about the "little guy' who finds a way to tweak the nose of the establishment.

I knew all this when I went to see the editor for *Westward*. I knew that "Take Back the Mike Night" had not been viewed by their reporters and freelancers. But I also knew that if I mentioned that the program was developed after Rosey was "censored" by The Comedy Works, we would get our article.

The newspaper was delighted to tell the story. The writer explained how difficult it is for women comics to get stage time anywhere. It explained what happened with The Comedy Works, assuming that Roseanne had been victimized when she was not given stage time at a better slot. It also told how successful the "Take Back the Mike Night" show had been, which actually was true. The performance had been a benefit for the bookstore, and there was money for the organization after all expenses had been met.

The owners of The Comedy Works were outraged by the publicity. They denied they had censored Roseanne. They resented the way she talked about them. However, the pressure worked in Rosey's favor.

Not only was Roseanne moved up to better nights with more sophisticated competition, the owners split up after a falling out, one staying with The Comedy Works, the other opening a new comedy club in the nearby suburb of Aurora, perhaps a fifteen-minute drive away. Both wanted Rosey, and both gave her jobs. It would not be the last time Rosey easily manipulated the press to her advantage.

Even with the new opportunities, Rosey felt she had to do more, to get still greater opportunities. She deliberately cultivated a friendship with someone who worked for The Comedy Works. What she did not expect was that they would fall in love. Rosey kept saying things to me about him, such as, "He's so cute. He really understands me." Soon one thing led to another, and I was being told that they were having an intense sexual affair. It was quite sordid, though so far as I know, Bill was unaware of what was taking place. Rosey was following her heart while trying not to lose her husband. She was no longer acting out of a desire for revenge. The Pentland marriage had ended emotionally. It would be a few years more before they physically separated.

The changes in Bill and Rosey's relationship during this period were not all bad. There had been tension ever since both of them were unfaithful. This kept him from suspecting later affairs, and Rosey still cared for him enough that he undoubtedly felt some lingering affection. Besides, she needed him to care for the kids, and Rosey was not ready to get a divorce, then try to survive on her own as a single parent.

In addition to the sexual tension, Bill was the type of man at whom Rosey was lashing out in her act. Later he told me that when he was living in the same house with Rosey, Stephanie, and me, he felt like a black man living with the Ku Klux Klan.

Rosey and I instinctively understood that there was a career to be had in comedy. Perhaps it was our father's influence, those many nights watching comedians on television. Perhaps it was the fact that Bobbe Mary talked of the time when she planned a career in the Yiddish theater. Whatever the case, we knew that Rosey was paying her dues. However, in the beginning Bill saw only a woman stepping out with her sister, ignoring her husband and children when she used to stay home with them in the evenings.

Once Rosey began getting paid, Bill saw the situation differently. I don't mean that he was excited by the money. If she received fifteen or twenty dollars, it was a good night. Rather it was the fact that there were comedy clubs, that people got paid for telling jokes, and that his wife was increasingly popular.

To his credit, Bill also listened to what Rosey was saying. He began to understand her anger and the anger of other women. He saw that it was not enough to be nonviolent, to love someone and not physically hurt them. The attitude of a man toward a woman could be negative in more subtle ways, and ultimately they were just as destructive. He became a feminist, and soon he was writing some of the jokes for the act. He could see the humor in both his own past actions and the actions of other men. In fact, as all of us mellowed a bit, Rosey and I named both Bill and my friend Rick to be honorary women.

As Rosey and I worked on the act, along with input from Bill and others who offered suggestions, we realized there were several important points to consider. First, the basic audience was going to be comprised of blue-collar women.

The women we saw as our primary audience were likely to be overweight, even obese. Certainly they did not have the figures of models, nor did they go to health clubs. A workout consisted of chasing after their children and picking up after husbands whose evenings were likely to be spent slumped in chairs, watching television, eating snack foods, and drinking beer.

Our target audience was often frustrated with their lifestyle. The women loved their children and usually loved their husbands. Yet they were victims of both, living in isolation, unable to explore the world. They hated the chores that kept them chained to the house, and often rebelled by just saying "to hell with it." The floors were not spotless. The dirty breakfast dishes might still be in the sink, unwashed, when it was time to make dinner. And if their husbands wanted to live like the stars of such shows as *Father Knows Best* or *Leave It to Beaver*, they had better get rich enough to hire a maid. The women in our target audience wanted something more than a pat on the head and a kiss on the cheek for spending the day cleaning and the night bringing beer and potato chips to spouses sitting in front of television.

Roseanne tried to do two things with her audience. The first was to help the women recognize that menial household tasks were important. They needed to be done and they were worthy of respect. They might be ridiculed by feminists wealthy enough to hire other women to do the chores for them, but there was dignity in all labor, in all roles in which women found themselves.

The other idea Rosey tried to get across was that there was a better future possible. Women could do more. Certainly they needed to recognize that they had the ability to do more if they chose. But if they stayed in an admittedly frequently boring situation, they were just as worthy of respect as the successful female executive.

We quickly came to understand another fact about performing. Our target audience came with men attached – casual dates, steady boyfriends, lovers, and spouses. We could not attack men without adding jokes that either also attacked women or somehow praised the men as well. There was a rhythm to a good comedy act, like that of a skilled prizefighter who combines a series of blows to the midsection with a carefully placed knockout punch. Rosey had to have an act that created the rhythm in such a manner that she scored a knockout punch the men never saw coming and were willing to experience again and again while she kept the women laughing.

Those early jokes give you a feel for this audience and some of the ways Rosey targeted her primary audience of females. Sometimes the jokes were funny only to women because they dealt with our world. For example: "Did you ever put those maxi-pads on adhesive side up? Makes you cranky, don't it?"

Over a two-year period of development, we created the concept of woman as Domestic Goddess. This actually came from a book that was popular with the women we knew in Salt Lake City. It was called *Fascinating Womanhood*, and in that book the idea for being a Domestic Goddess had to do with manipulating your husband. The author meant for the term to be applied to the woman who became the perfect wife. Rosey and I worked out the idea of using the term as the vehicle for rebellion. We thought women would relate to another woman announcing that she was not to be called a homemaker but a Domestic Goddess.

Actually such an explanation is too simplistic. The act was designed to work on several levels. Some of the jokes were just funny, but most of the humor evolved from consciousness-raising sessions at the bookstore.

We knew from experience that feminists could be classified as first-string, second-string, and third-string. A first-string feminist would say something such as, "I don't believe in the ERA (Equal Rights Amendment). I want to be treated like a lady. I want men to open the door for me."

Second-string feminists would say things like, "I still want a man to do things with me when I want them, like fucking me when I want to be fucked. But I want equal money for equal work. I don't care if I choose to be a housewife or a secretary or a business executive. I want to be paid what that job is worth, just like a man." They were economic feminists.

Third-string feminists, and that was what the core group at the bookstore considered themselves to be, had no intention of saying, "May I please have my rights?" We intended to take them. However, we did not wish to perpetuate the "us versus them?" mentality. We wanted to return to the societal structures where men and women could speak in synergy, where the word "we" meant partnership instead of one or the other sex being dominant.

We were using humor in a consciously subversive way. Not only could it result in getting across deeper messages than just the surface idea of a joke, we could use it to achieve financial success. With money we could have clout. And with that power, we could create social change using female language, art, and films. We wanted to have movies where women were central characters, strong achievers, not just male roles played by actors with vaginas and scripts that ended with their being rape victims, psychopaths, or dying.

We saw ourselves almost like double agents. We would be dumb women. We would be cute women. We would be charming, seemingly submissive women. Then, when the men in power had been lulled into a false sense of security while we made hundreds of millions of dollars, they would suddenly find that we were really smart and strategic. And if this worked as I envisioned, we could fundamentally change the way men and women related to each other. Power, money, and ideas would be shared. This was our plan, our ideal.

We knew that the wealthy get to influence society far more than people realize. With hundreds of millions of dollars, you get to endow things and take a tax write-off as you do it. The Ford family has long been doing this, as have the Rockefellers, the Carnegies, and others. When women did it, they would be in a position to tell the stories that have been ignored by many contemporary historians.

Having made the decision that Roseanne had to be the spokesperson for the act, I took upon myself the role of business planner and marketer. Many comics want to get rich, but they have no goals, no plans for how they will achieve the end they seek. I used my business and marketing training to put together a ten-year plan.

Having watched comedians with Dad while growing up, we had a sense of what it took to become successful. There were obviously different stages of exposure, the first important hurdle being Johnny Carson. Once you were a guest comic on *The Tonight Show*, everyone looked upon you as a skilled professional no matter how much previous experience you had. This meant that she had to have an act that was polished, that had a tempo which could carry the audience, and enough jokes in reserve to entertain for a prolonged period of time. Based on what we had seen, we felt this would take the first five years, at which time Rosey would be on the Carson show.

It did not always go smoothly. Jokes would bomb. An audience would sit on its hands, their faces plastered with dour expressions. We would see how little money was coming in. Rosey would need constant feedback from me in order to be certain we were heading where I claimed. And while I tried to reassure her, to keep her moving in what I was certain was the right direction, there was always the nagging question, what if I'm wrong? What if we were just plain nuts? What is this business plan is bull-shit? Yet we did keep advancing. If there was one faltering step backward, it both followed and preceded two steps forward. In hindsight, I also realized that in my moments of weakness, she had strength. And when she had nagging doubts, I had the certainty that pulled her through. We willed it!

In theory there was no reason for us to believe our evolving plan might have a chance for success. Yet we had no doubts about what we were doing. It was as though we instinctively understood the business of comedy, our biggest hurdle being the packaging of the act we would sell.

We allowed five years for the Carson show, and as it turned out, we were ahead of our projection. The first two years were spent working on the act. Rosey went from jokes told specifically for the women in the bookstore, to jokes with broader appeal, to a properly paced act. We learned that in a mixed audience the first two jokes would be a harsh slam against men. Then, as the males in the audience were still listening but obviously becoming a little defensive and uncomfortable about the act, the third joke would be a slam against women. The females in the audience were slightly taken aback, the men relaxed, smiling and laughing, and the fourth gag was what I called a "nice Mommy" joke. Everyone could relate. Everyone enjoyed it. And then, when the entire audience was with her, again there would be a women's joke, a slam at men, a slam at women, and the nice Mommy gag. The first two jokes began making the points of social commentary we wanted to get across. The third might or might not relate to our political agenda. And the fourth was a nice transition. It is doubtful that anyone other than another professional understood what we were doing, but the end result was success growing so rapidly that, after two years, we had changed to Domestic Goddess, the concept that Roseanne continues to this day.

We felt that somewhere around the fourth or fifth year, we would be in the national introductory phase of the career. Rosey would have Carson. She would have one or more television specials. She would play the major clubs. She would become a household name in the field of comedy.

Around years six and seven, Rosey would be in the growth phase. We expected her to have her own television show. We expected her to be making movies. We expected her to be accumulating large sums of money to form the production company I would run, to finance other women in the arts.

By the tenth year, everything would be in place, with what I was certain we both believed would be joint ownership between us. She would generate the income from the act. I would run the businesses, acting as producer and manager, since by then, we would understand the intricacies of the Hollywood system.

Again based on what we had learned from watching the rise and fall of other comics, we expected a further growth and maturation phase lasting approximately fifteen years following the original ten. Rosey and I would write. Rosey would star. I would manage and develop properties. We would become a corporate entity. Our role models for the business side (though not their personal lives) were people like Woody Allen and Barbra Streisand. The latter was not a comedian, but she had used the fame from her singing to become an actress/director/producer and successful entertainment business professional.

There was one other possibility, though. We never questioned our plans to have a production company I would run. However, Rosey thought that when the money was in place, she might quit show business and go into politics. She had a strong interest in making a change in the world, and the popularity from her act would give her a recognition factor. Other acts had entered politics over the years, Ronald Reagan having become governor of California, George Murphy, a former song-and-dance man, having gone to the Senate, and other show business people entering one or another office.

We were still in a period of great idealism, and politics fit that image. I would be helping women through the arts. We could create a foundation that would fund historians who were writing the full story of humanity, a story that showed the truth about women rather than the one-sided view of the sex currently dominating politics. We would underwrite educators, entertainers, and others. We would give opportunity to the disenfranchised, changing society through the steady tide of feminists whose voices would no longer be suppressed. It was an exciting concept for me, an exciting time. And during those heady, early days when Roseanne went from feeling herself to be the drudge of Bill and the kids to being a star of ever increasing magnitude, Rosey and I shared the hopes and dreams. And all would come as a result of the ten-year plan.

Obviously this was constantly fine-tuned as Rosey gained experience and a positive reputation in the field. But out goals remained constant, and the steps we knew we needed to take were ultimately the ones we did take. From the time Rosey branched out from the bookstore, there was never a setback, never a reason to doubt her eventual success as we planned it.

Much of the political influence on Roseanne came from eleven of us women in the bookstore, some heterosexual, some of us having come to recognize that we were lesbians. In my case, I had enjoyed intense relationships with men and women, though even as a little girl I was emotionally and sexually drawn to other females. However, it was only as an adult that I chose to act on the feelings I had known for so long.

Looking back, I can see that in my relationships with most men, I had enjoyed sex more than intellectual intimacy. Ultimately I realized that my deepest feelings of love and commitment were with one woman, Maxine. And ultimately I chose to spend my life with her, facing whatever societal consequences that might mean.

This self-awareness was what drove me to become involved with the lesbians and other women in the bookstore who also were trying to raise their consciousness about their lives and their work. The eleven of us would regularly meet in the basement, Rosey staying upstairs to answer the telephone. However, she would regularly get bored, turn on the answering machine, come downstairs, and ask if she could be a lesbian for a while. We not only included her in our conversation, we made her an honorary lesbian.

It was during these sessions that we began exploring feminist theory expressed as humor. We worked on this the entire time we were both in Denver, hanging out in the bookstore and in coffee shops, drinking endless cups of coffee and smoking thousands of cigarettes. Our conversations and evolving philosophy was the basis for the act Roseanne was developing. She, in turn, would present the jokes to a core group of fifteen of us, the original eleven and four additional heterosexuals with whom we all became close. Thus there was an excellent mix expressing criticism, finding what worked, improving good ideas that were still weak in their execution, and determining which jokes needed to be dropped.

Refining the Act and Defining Ourselves

I remember one conversation during which we were talking about many men we knew who were the subject of complaints by straight women. Some of these wives and lovers said that their men wanted to fuck them only so they could go back to their male friends and brag that they had scored. Such men were not interested in a relationship. They were not concerned with the personality of the women. Fucking was the end in itself.

As the conversation continued, I mentioned to Rosey and some of the lesbians in the group that what was weird for me was listening to what I considered similar behavior in the way straight women talked. Many straight women say that lesbians are man hating, yet I found straight women to be far worse.

Why do women stay with the men they put down so much? I asked. I didn't mean the men who were physically or emotionally abusive. I meant men their wives considered to be normal, decent, and hard working, yet who they still viciously attacked.

I talked of listening to these women complain that their husbands couldn't satisfy them sexually. Rosey talked about how she could not get enough sex. She had the desire, and the men she had known were the ones to quit before she was done, turn over, and go to sleep. She said she wanted to be like the image of Mae West if she ever got

rich. She wanted a horde of carefully chosen males to service her.

Other women I was listening to said that their men
didn't make enough money or they didn't have a prestigious enough job. It was an aspect of heterosexual
relationships I could not fathom.

"I don't understand why lesbians are supposed to be
man hating," I continue, "because I've never known a lesbian who would talk about a man that way. Straight
women can be really hateful."

From that conversation came the joke that Roseanne
would deliver to an uproar of laughter: "They say lesbians
hate men. How can they? They don't have to fuck them."

Although it became obvious that many blue-collar
women responded to Rosey's way of thinking, their lives
were such that they dared not discuss that viewpoint, even
with their friends. The only women who were comfortable
saying such things publicly were usually lesbians. Straight
women feared they would be called dykes and ball busters,
language so uncomfortable that they often found it easier
to be silent. Thus, when women heard these so-called lesbian ideas coming out of a straight woman's mouth, they
were fascinated and delighted. Although Roseanne focused
on the stardom she was receiving, if only in a minor way
back then, I was delighted that our plan was working. The
ideas for which we rarely found an audience when lectur-
ing were becoming part of mainstream, straight-woman
thinking through the humor Roseanne was performing.

When Roseanne took this concept to the stage, it was different from what the audiences had heard before.
Professional stand-up comedy had any number of variations. There were magicians telling jokes while doing
tricks. There were comics using props. There were comedy
teams. But no matter how a comic worked, most of the
clubs had men who made crude jokes about their sex lives
and their body parts. They had the attitude, "I'm up here
to tell some jokes, then we'll go have a few beers, pick up
some broads, and see if we can score."

Rosey addressed the women who had endured such humor as well as the men who enjoyed it. She spoke to both marrieds and singles. She said things in ways that were not being heard in the clubs very often if at all:

> My husband says, "God, Roseanne, I can't remember the last time we had sex." Well, I can, and that is why we ain't doing it.

> Here is my personal opinion about prostitution. If men knew how to do it, they wouldn't have to pay for it.

> My best friend Linda is leaving her husband just because he is unfaithful to her. That is no reason to leave the person. I feel like after that, you should stay with them and make sure that the rest of their life is sheer hell.

Then there were the soft jokes to keep the men from becoming defensive while their wives and girlfriends were laughing at the images Rosey was creating in their minds: For example:

> Me and my husband just found a new method of birth control that really works. Every night before we go to bed, we spend an hour with our kids.

Roseanne took on motherhood and domestic chores in the casual way of the overburdened housewife. These women did not read *Town & Country* or any of the magazines devoted to domestic perfection. None of them would ever hire a maid, though some might work cleaning houses:

> The day I worry about cleaning my house is the day Sears comes out with a riding vacuum cleaner.

> I figure when my husband comes home at night, if those kids are still alive, hey, I've done a good job.

You may marry the man of your dreams, ladies, but fifteen years later you are married to a reclining chair that burps.

Being a mom is rewarding. You've got all these little people and you could really mess up their heads forever. Only moms can say stuff like, "Don't talk with your mouth full. Answer me!"

Roseanne also addressed the weight issue. Even when she was thin, she understood that her audience was not. Thus they liked someone who shared their pain without suggesting they diet:

People get all the wrong ideas about why you are fat. I think people just have sex because they can't afford good food.

People are so rude to the fat. I go in this dress shop and I ask this broad, "You got anything to make me look thinner?" She says, "Yeah. What about a month in Bangladesh."

And then Roseanne would add one of those outrageous jokes that skewer everything and create an image everyone can laugh at, such as:

I'm on the mirror diet. You eat all your food in front of a mirror in the nude. It works pretty good, though some of the fancier restaurants don't go for it.

Of course the jokes were developed over a number of years. But we were refining the concept, working out the rhythm, finding what would reach our target audience without alienating the people who came with them. The core group at the bookstore was serving as Rosey's sounding board and advisory council. And Rosey was getting more and more work.

163

The Laff-Offs

As Roseanne began earning pay from The Comedy Works,
she also began traveling around the state. The Comedy
Works had a person who acted as a booking agent. Once
you reached a certain level of professionalism, the comedian no longer had to rely on personal calls, family, and
friends to find places to perform. The network of comedy
clubs relied on the owners or bookers to find new talent for
the circuit. Suddenly Rosey was traveling to Colorado
Springs, to Aspen, and anywhere else in the state where a
new act or a female comic was wanted. Then, when she
was liked, she was routinely asked to return. She was
becoming a middle act, not ready to headline but earning
steady money.

The real change in Roseanne's career came when she
won the Denver Laff-Off. This was the most important
step in Rosey's promotion at the time, and yet it was an
odd event.

The idea behind the Laff-Off was to find the best comics
in the city of Denver, then make them compete against
each other. The contest increased the crowd coming to one
of the two major comedy clubs, and that meant that the
high-profit drink consumption was on the rise. Thus the
owner of the club was always delighted.

The down side was that this was still Denver, Colorado.
Johnny Carson was never going to fly out to Denver in
search of new talent. When comics think of where they
ultimately hope to perform, Denver is not the city where
they plan to get rich. After all, the Laff-Off competitors
were seldom paid more than thirty-five dollars per night.
Big time it wasn't.

The advantage to winning the Laff-Off is that it would
broaden a comic's exposure. A Denver comic was welcomed in clubs throughout the state provided he or she was
booked through The Comedy Works or a similar facility.
The winner of the Denver Laff-Off would start traveling to
clubs out of state. Thirty-five dollars a night became a
hundred dollars. A club booking you by the week might

pay you five hundred dollars. There were expenses that came out of that, yet the net was still more than any of the comics were skilled enough to earn in a real job. The win would free Rosey from the need to focus solely on supplementing Bill's income. It would expose her to a broader audience. And it would assure her that she had mastered the art of putting together an effective act.

That was the theory. In practice, the fate of the Laff-Off's seventeen contestants was decided on the vote of a mostly drunken audience whose preference was for raunchy.

Rosey was easily the most popular performer, and I noticed that as a comic was eliminated, he or she began cheering Rosey. Her material was good, but she had a defiant attitude that was rare among women comics doing the local circuit. However, the last joke she used was the one that won the audience, and she had planned to use it no matter what. But as luck would have it, a drunken woman in the audience added to the setup. "People say you are not very feminine," Roseanne commented about herself. That was when the woman heckled, "Well, you are *not* very feminine."

Suddenly the audience was with her, waiting to see her comeback. Everyone knew that hecklers could be your best friend or your worst enemy. They didn't know if the joke Rosey wanted to perform next was one that might be destroyed by the heckler. However, instead of doing it as planned, she varied it slightly. Right after the heckler repeated the fact that Roseanne wasn't very feminine, Rosey turned to her, fixed her with a cold stare, and said, "Suck my dick!"

No matter what the reaction to the other material that night, the comeback won.

I looked upon the Denver Laff-Off as Rosey's college graduation. There was nothing more for her to learn in Denver. She was valedictorian of her class, and that could be parlayed into the big time, which in those years meant Los Angeles.

Making the move took more time than we would have

liked, but there were many concerns. First was the fact that Rosey was making more money than she had ever made in her life. Five hundred dollars a week in Louisville, Kentucky. Five hundred dollars a week in Kansas City. She was working unfamiliar crowds with different backgrounds, discovering how to fine-tune her stand-up act. At the same time, she was also learning the similarities of women's interests that kept her material exciting for the audience. Blue-collar women shared the same attitudes towards their husbands no matter where they lived, how they survived, or what their ethnic and racial origins. I saw this when I accompanied her to Boulder, Aspen, Colorado Springs, and similar locations to which we could drive fairly easily. She went alone to most of the other cities, calling me each day and discussing the reactions.

Bill was also becoming a problem Rosey could not ignore. She would say she did not want to be married. She loved her kids and was ambivalent about what to do with them if she and Bill split. She also saw the intact family, especially the existence of a real, live husband, as helping her image. Maybe a Phyllis Diller could be accepted talking about her "husband" between marriages, but Rosey didn't think she could get away with it. She expressed to me the belief that her audience would be accepting of her anti-husband jokes only is she shared married life with them. There was no one else whom she wanted to marry, even though she had periodic, very intense affairs. Thus she was staying together with Bill because she still felt she might work out the relationship. Or so she said at times.

At other times Rosey changed her tune. Bill would be making an effort to improve himself and his relationship with Roseanne, and she would talk about how much better things were becoming. She no longer wanted a divorce, yet she continued having affairs, her actions never quite matching her words.

Perhaps the most important aspect of Rosey's new fame was her relationship with Lannie Garrett, a popular local singer. She and her band needed an opening act when they played in the Denver area. She heard Roseanne, liked what she heard, and talked with her about opening. This meant a solid twenty minutes of material, well rehearsed, much the way Dianne Ford had taught her.

Lannie exposed Roseanne to different audiences than she had known when strictly working the comedy clubs. Lannie could sing just about anything in the popular music field, though she often specialized in torch songs and love songs. These were popular in upscale clubs and other locations where the audience was quieter than the traditional comedy fans. Many of the clubs had never had a comic before Roseanne, and she had to learn to play off a more sober group of people who preferred listening to ballads rather than the raunchy jokes of the typical nightclub comic. Thus Rosey had to learn to modify some of her language as she learned what would be most effective.

Lannie also introduced Roseanne to her manager Alanna Rothstein, a wonderful woman who would later move to Los Angeles where I hired her to be Roseanne's publicist.

Because of Roseanne's success in Denver, it was suggested that she go to San Francisco to participate in that city's Laff-Off. While the principle was the same, San Francisco was an important city for comedy. Such performers as Dana Carvey and Robin Williams were alumni of the San Francisco contest. Many of the stars of *Saturday Night Live* had appeared there.

Roseanne and I only knew that her act was strong, and we felt she should take on the competition. Lannie Garrett was extremely supportive, to the point where she arranged with a friend to provide us with a place to stay.

The trip to San Francisco was decidedly low budget. Rosey and I traveled together the cheapest way possible. We pooled the few dollars we had with a loan of one hundred dollars from Mom, twenty-five dollars from the bookstore, and another seventy-five dollars from various friends.

We had two options as the result of both Lannie's and Alanna's help. The first and most exciting was the chance to stay in a condominium there. One of them had a friend who was a Jewish yuppie who agreed to let us crash at his place. However, we arrived too late to go there, so we spent the first night at the YMCA, where we rented a room with two cots for twenty-two dollars. It was spartan but not terrible – until we went to the bathroom. The toilets were enclosed by stalls but were generally filthy. The shower was a large open room with several showerheads. No privacy was possible, and the facility was used by both residents and street people, including derelicts, the mildly crazy, and other disreputables. There were disgusting-looking stains and odd smells we did not want to think about. We hoped everything had been cleaned and disinfected, and we stayed the night, but the next day we went to see the yuppie.

The second night was as much of a fiasco as the first. This time the condominium was spotless, but the Barr sisters were not what the yuppie had envisioned. The impression we had was that he thought he was being sent a couple of "chicks" he could screw in exchange for letting them stay. We would be gorgeous and loose-moraled like "all" people in show business and make our gratitude known. We would appear in the club and do whatever we had to do during the day. But he would have a few days of wild, uninhibited sex.

We stayed one night and the yuppie would not even give us a spare key so we could both go out at the same time. We had a good shower in a clean bathroom, and he did allow us to leave our bags while going to see about the other possible living arrangement. So much for him.

Our saviour came in what was the strangest experience of all. Following the directions we had been given, we walked two miles to a gas station where an aged hippie worked. He had mastered all manner of survival skills, including carpentry. And the proof of his abilities was the love of his life, the home Rosey and I would be sharing for the next few days – a bread truck.

The Laff-Off was an odd one. There was some excellent talent, and there was one man with a rubber chicken which became both the prop and the subject for most of his body

168

function humor. One female comedian felt Rosey would win, in part, she confided, because she had an inside track with one of the judges, a local disk jockey with whom she had been having an affair. She mentioned this the day after she lost and Rosey won one of the preliminary rounds. There had apparently been pillow talk concerning the contestants that night, and the woman wanted to encourage Roseanne.

Round after round was waged, the crowd an unusual one. I later found that the San Francisco entertainment scene was basically controlled by one promoter. It was also extremely conservative, no one wanting to embarrass anyone else. And the crowd, even when drunk, was so "hip," they didn't want to embarrass themselves by laughing at anything.

Strange as it was, and with Rosey apparently breaking all the local, unspoken, unwritten taboos for comics, she still managed to be among the finalists. She did not win, though, nor did that honor go to the new Robin Williams or Dana Carvey. Instead it went to the comedian who used the rubber chicken in his act.

Normally the winner went on to achieve at least some fame and fortune, if not a spot on *Saturday Night Live*. That year, though, my understanding is that despite the boost the contest gave his career, it was like jump-starting a truly dead battery. The comic sparked for just a moment, then died. However, rumor has it that during the year following the win, the rubber chicken headlined at clubs throughout the city.

Rosey returned to Denver and continued to test material with the core group of women at the bookstore, to travel outside the state to as many clubs as possible, and to refine her act.

Bill, now more supportive of the new career, began writing material for Rosey's act. He had his consciousness raised by living with her, listening to her, and listening to our friends. He also thought that he might have a future in stand-up and was himself planning to try open mike nights.

Along the way, Roseanne became as self-centered in many ways as the rest of the comics. Performing was like a drug for Rosey. She got to tell her story. She got to improve her jokes. She was enjoying being propositioned by men in the audience. At the same time, she spent her days so intensely involved with the kids that the night was an escape. It was Mommy's time to be the center of attention, to be adored, to not have to satisfy anyone else's needs.

Nothing was more important to Rosey than herself. She genuinely loved her three children, but after her hippie earth mother phase, they were never as important to her as performing. She did not so much neglect them as spend most of her nurturing time developing the act. She was physically present with them, but they lacked what some people called "quality time." They would watch television while Rosey would take me into the kitchen, where we'd sit at the table and write jokes. That drive of Rosey's, that focus, as destructive as it would become to those closest to her (all three of her children have since required intensive therapy), was the quintessential element necessary for Roseanne to become a star.

5 Rosey's Family Crisis

It was in 1985, several months after the San Francisco Laff-Off, that Rosey made her first trip to Mitzi Shore's Comedy Store. She borrowed three hundred dollars from Mom to make the trip and arranged for the kids to spend four weeks with their grandparents in Salt Lake City.

Mom had been a secretary for eight and a half years. When the job ended, she stayed at home because, with her kids no longer in the house, our parents could get by on Dad's salary.

During this period when Mom was being a housewife, friends of our brother Ben had a baby. They needed day care and had not found a place they trusted when Ben suggested that Mom might want to take care of the infant. The couple offered her ten dollars a day, two dollars more than the going rate for licensed group day care. It was not much money, but the price seemed fair. Besides, Mon always loved babies and little children, and she could not resist.

Dad could, though. Babies to him, meant messy diapers and endless demands. He didn't think she should sit. He figured Mom deserved some free time after raising four children of her own, and he also looked forward to more quiet at home than a baby would bring.

The baby, nicknamed "Boo," became a major part of my parents' lives. Five days a week, for nine or ten hours a day, Boo was their responsibility. Wherever Mom went, alone or with Dad, Boo was along. Both of them fell in love with Boo, but after approximately nine months, it became obvious that they couldn't quite get by on Dad's pay alone, and the money Mom received for sitting was inadequate to meet the additional needs. Mom decided to tell Boo's parents they would have to quickly find a day care center because she couldn't sit any longer.

Dad exploded. Boo had become the love of his life. He told Mom that she could not stop caring for the baby, because he feared Boo might accidentally be placed in a less loving environment. He told her to find some more babies and open a real day care center so they could pay the bills and still care for Boo.

Mom was thrilled. Soon she was caring for five kids, three of whom needed all-day care and two of whom were part-time. The babies began arriving at the Barr family home at seven A.M. and did not leave until five P.M. Mom adjusted her hours to the parents' needs, looking upon the ten-hour days (plus cleaning and preparing for the next day) as a service she delighted in performing.

Mom took training in day care, became licensed by the state, and eventually hired assistants. She had found the career I think she was born to enjoy.

"It was a sacred trust to have those people's children," my mom, Helen Barr, said when discussing that period.

"I made good money. I have to tell you, they paid me . . . I was licensed and I went to meetings, and the going rate at that time for people who babysat or day-cared in their home was like eight dollars a day, and they paid me fifteen dollars to twenty dollars and bonuses. I did well, and I could be at home, and I had fun.

"You have to know, that was very, very, very important to me that a child didn't get hurt physically or mentally in any way. And I felt, hey, that's a pretty awesome responsibility to have someone else's child. And that they were all . . . the strange thing was all those kids were from professional parents, and they were all only children. And so their parents checked me out. Their parents could come in and out [of the day care] any time they wanted.

"I felt . . . It was just the most marvelous thing I'd ever done. It was pretty sacred to have people entrust that to you, to feel that you were worthy of it."

Mom told about the different children and the loving relationship that developed with them. She spent more time with them than their parents did during the week, and it was with mixed pride and surprise that she discovered one little child who was happy and active in the morning, then cried when her mother came to pick her up after school. They child was from a good, loving home, and the tears were not of fear. Just as some children don't want to leave their mommies to go with a teacher, this little girl didn't want to leave my mom to go with her own. There was no fear. She just loved my mother, and because more waking hours were spent in my mother's home, that was where she developed some very strong, positive emotional attachments.

Rosey knew of Mom's day care and its success. She thought it would be easiest for all involved if Mom could take in her three grandchildren for the four weeks Rosey had to be away, Bill agreed, and Mom was delighted. Jessica was ten, Jenny nine, and Jake was seven. They were old enough to dress and bathe themselves, to work together to help around the house when appropriate, and even to help with the day care children. At the same time, they were young enough to delight in playing with Grandma, whether that meant going for a walk or, in Jake's case especially, playing basketball. Jake was becoming the sports nut in the family among the new generation, a fact that delighted Dad. He and Jake would watch basketball, baseball and football together, depending upon the season, and Jake was learning the names, teams, uniform numbers and statistics of all of the players. None of Dad's children had been sports enthusiasts, and Dad had been closest to Rosey because of their shared love of comedy. Now he had a grandson with whom he could share his other great love – TV sports.

Mom instantly discovered what I had seen but overlooked once I stopped living with the Pentlands. The kids were like animals. Bill and Rosey had no idea how to instill the ideas of boundaries, of limits, of appropriate and inappropriate behavior.

The first problem was personal hygiene. Rosey was not the greatest in that regard during this period, and the kids were rather disgusting. Normal acts of cleanliness had not been consistently enforced enough for them to have become habit. As a result, they occasionally soiled themselves and failed to wash up after themselves. It was nothing weird. They were like any kids would be with less than adequate discipline.

More shocking to me was their rudeness. I still remember when Mom told Jessica to do something in the house, and Jessica, refusing, said, "Fuck you, Grandma! Go fuck yourself!"

Mom did not know what to do, but she did know who to call. She had a friend named Shirley Backles who heads a nationally respected organization called the Children's Center. It is a business that evolved from her own past and a series of unfortunate circumstances.

Shirley had been raised in a troubled home. While in school she discovered she loved children, loved the field of education, and wanted to give kids the greatest opportunities for success in life she could. She also adopted two children before her marriage ended in divorce when she was in her early thirties.

The divorce was a shattering experience that caused Shirley to reevaluate her life. She realized that she lacked self-esteem. She realized that it was extremely important for children to have a positive sense of self-worth to avoid growing up as she had, lacking in a firm belief in their God-given abilities.

The end result of all this was that Shirley had the courage to go back to school for additional training, then take advantage of all the money available to her. She even cashed in her teacher retirement fund, money she would desperately need in retirement if her business venture failed. Then she opened the Children's Center to counsel children and their parents, and to find new ways to give a child self-esteem.

Shirley found that by changing a child's attitude toward himself or herself, grades improve, relationships improve, and the child can grow into an adult capable of reaching full potential for both success and happiness.

Mom felt that something had to be done to get her

grandchildren back in control. She called Shirley and asked if she would make a house call. There was no time to bring her grandchildren to Shirley's place of business. To Mom's relief, Shirley agreed.

"Shirley gave me some advice which was called 'time out,'" Mom later explained. "What time out meant was, if they were doing something I didn't think they should be doing, I would say to them, 'Time out.' I had a little rug in front of my kitchen, and they would go sit on that rug and I set a timer up on my stove for one minute. I told them, 'When Grandma says "Time out," you go sit on that rug. You stop what you're doing. Grandma will be okay and not lose her temper or be mad at you. You then decide what we can talk about at a later time.' We couldn't talk about it right then because of the babies at day care.

"So what it was, when Grandma said 'Time out,' you went to the rug for one minute. Sometimes Jenny, I gave her two minutes. And you thought about it, and you went back to what you were doing. Nobody said a mean word. You went back to what you were doing, and later in the day, when the babies were sleeping or we had a chance to talk, we'd talk about what you were doing and how we could do it better. And that would then give us both an opportunity to get through this without hurting anybody or saying a mean word."

(Actually Mom didn't remember that she had tried a form of time out with me. When I did something wrong, she would sit me on a small chair in the front room. She would set an egg timer for ten minutes, telling me I was not to dare to get out of that chair until the timer went off. I was to think about what I had done, apparently either to repent or to become so filled with remorse that I did not do whatever it was again.

(But Mom was not really prepared for the type of kids she had. I picked up the chair, holding it tight against my butt, and walked into the kitchen. "Hi, Mom," I said. "I sure miss you. I'm sure lonely in the front room, but I'm not out of my chair." Then I walked around the house, holding tight to the chair. She said I couldn't get off the chair, but she never said I couldn't walk around with it.

(Child rearing had not been so easy with the four of us.)

Rosey's kids were hardly instantly obedient, perfectly mannered, and adorable. The first time Mom and Shirley tried the approach with Jessica, the first words out of her mouth were, "You're a fuckin' bitch and I'm not going." Mom did the only appropriate thing she could do at that moment, giving her a swat on the rear. There would be other swats that first day, but by the second, Jessica got the point. When told to take a time out, she gave Mom the finger, then sat down for her minute.

Mom was quickly able to talk with the kids about their behavior. She worked with them to understand values, respect, and what was important. She worked to instill in them a willingness to tell the truth if they did something wrong. She explained to Jenny, for example, that she could not lie about eating some flavored cough drops that had been left out on a tray earlier in the day. The cough drops were gone, the wrappers left on the tray, and none of the other children had been near them. Mom worked with Jenny to understand that eating the cough drops was not the problem. They could be replaced. What mattered was honesty. Mom made it clear that she would love Jenny and the others unconditionally, but she did care if they were honest. That was important for them to understand.

When Rosey and Bill picked them up, they were both surprised and delighted with the change in the children. They had also been bothered by the bad habits that the kids had, by their rudeness and verbal violence. In the four weeks there was enough difference for them to be thrilled with both Mom and Shirley Backles. In fact, Rosey and Bill were so delighted with the change that they asked Mom to keep the kids two more weeks. My parents agreed, but before Rosey and Bill left, Jessica caused a small disaster.

"I don't remember what happened or what was said, but Jessica lost her temper," my mother later commented. "We were all sitting there [on the deck] and Jessica was mad. And the next thing we know we hear the glass bust and glass came flying down on the deck.

"I ran upstairs and Jessica had put her fist through the

window. And I told her, 'You are very angry. Shirley Backles said you can hit pillows, you can run round the block. And Shirley told me to buy you a punching bag and I'll buy you a punching bag. You cannot punch the window. You could have cut the arteries in your hand. You could have bled to death."

Fortunately, Jessica was not hurt. However, Mom insisted that she understand that her actions carried responsibility. A friend of the family replaced the window for fourteen dollars. For the next seven weeks, Jessica dutifully paid Mom two dollars from her allowance until the total amount had been reimbursed.

From the Sally Jessy Raphael show of October 10, 1991:

> MRS. ARNOLD. *When I came out here to do* The Tonight Show, *I left my kids at my parents' house, because I didn't have my memories [of sexual abuse] yet. And my father cracked both of my daughters' heads together. And then they locked them in an attic, where they wouldn't let them out all day. And my one daughter broke out a window with her fist, when they were 8 and 9, so that they could breathe. And the way I heard the story from my parents was that she was a bad little girl and broke their window and they wanted her to pay for it. And, of course, I believed that.*

I suspect that, for the first time, Roseanne truly understood the need for loving structure, not anarchy. In fact, after she was settled in her home in Los Angeles, beginning to make big money, she flew Shirley Backles to her residence. There Ms. Backles lived with the family for several days, teaching Rosey and Bill the methods for helping their children that she and Mom had developed so successfully.

Roseanne also realized that the children had to take a more important role in her life. She never again was Supermom. She also never found a balance with the children and her chaotic existence. But she did learn to respect them. I

177

remember when we would go on the road, she blocked out time to call her children. For example, when we went to New York together, she scheduled two hours during which she talked with Jessica, Jennifer, and Jake, giving each individual time on the telephone with her. Maybe it wasn't ideal, but at least they knew that no matter what had happened during that difficult period in Denver, their Mom did love them.

Despite all this, the girls became frustrated and rebellious. Part of this may have had to do with periodic bouts of low self-esteem. They were frequently sent to fat camps to lose weight in a guided program. And when they returned and talked with me, they always felt better about themselves, in part from weight loss and in part from the physical activities at the camp.

By 1988, with Jessica in the throes of puberty, Rosey began putting her daughters in one treatment center after another, in California, Idaho, and Utah. They were all expensive, some costing as much as $1,500 per day. In interviews with Rosey and Tom Arnold, they usually refer to these places as boarding schools. While the quotes may have been deliberately misleading to protect Jessica and Jennifer, I suspect that, to some degree, that was how Rosey viewed where she sent the girls. (Only Jake lived at home.) Later Rosey claimed to me that the girls were involved with drugs and alcohol, and, like all teenagers, they might have been.

Ironically, the majority of the patients in the expensive adolescent treatment centers to which Rosey's girls were sent were the children of wealthy, very successful parents. The kids had all been victims of driven adults whose goals had not always included meeting the nurturing needs of their children.

I felt the repeated institutionalization was terrible. She had committed herself to Provo and later decided it was awful. Then she turned around and put her kids in what I saw as the same circumstances. However, I have to admit that such facilities at least provided a consistent structure for Jessica, and, later, Jennifer, something Rosey seldom was able to give them. The one time I talked with her about this, I said to her, "After what you've been through, how can you justify doing this to your daughters?" And I remember her replying, "The difference between where I went and where they're going is that it costs a lot [*sic*] of money to send them there."

In hindsight, given Rosey's work schedule, her being tired from the pressures she was under, and the other factors in her life, the institutions were probably a good choice. At least the kids got consistent care. Relative to their home life, they undoubtedly benefited greatly. What is sad is that her priorities, her parenting skills, and other aspects of her character prevented her from being the mother the kids needed.

6 I'm a Dumb Woman, But . . .

It had finally happened. Dad had been sitting at home, waiting for the theme song for *The Tonight Show* starring Johnny Carson. His announcer and straight man, Ed McMahon, had given the standard opening, then said the familiar "Heeeeeere's Johnny!" There had followed the usual thunderous applause, the opening monologue, and the opening commercials.

The taping had been earlier in the day. *The Tonight Show* ruled the late-night ratings, but Johnny was no longer a creature of the night. He was as content to get home early as most people, and so the taping was in the late afternoon, when both he and his audience were fresh. No one was drunk, as they might be at the eleven-thirty P.M. Eastern Standard Time slot in which he appeared. No one was half-asleep. No one was worrying about getting home to relieve the babysitter. The earlier audience was hip, loose, happy to be in the presence of the master, ready for a good time.

That was why Rosey already knew the evening had gone well when Dad shouted "Comedian!" and Mom rushed to sit by his side. The exact words of introduction are faded from my memory. Even Roseanne has forgotten how Johnny Carson spoke of the exciting new talent he was introducing. Most of what was remembered was the cheese tray in the Green Room, the waiting areas for the performers appearing on the show, and the fact that Dad was bursting with pride when he knew that the person to make him laugh that night was his firstborn daughter, Roseanne.

I later learned that there had been shouts of triumph mixed with tears of joy when Roseanne got the first of many laughs during her routine. Mum and Dad had long worried about Rosey's eccentric rush through life. They had always just wanted us kids to be happy, yet they were never certain what Rosey wanted, where she would truly find direction and happiness. The only consistent interest in her life had been humor, and now that love had paid off. That night, when Roseanne was on Johnny Carson, when she was even asked to come by his desk, to sit in his presence for the thirty seconds remaining before the commercial break, they knew she had succeeded. Thirty seconds wasn't very long, but only the best of the comics were allowed to share that time with Johnny. Rosey's invitation meant that she was among the best.

Only Ben had been able to be at the taping with Rosey. He had gone to Los Angeles, taking the large diamond ring Bobbe Mary had worn during the later years of her life. My mother had inherited it, and she thought Roseanne should have it for luck. As Rosey sat on the couch near Johnny, moving her hand, the overhead lights occasionally flashed against the stone, the sudden burst of color making me feel as though our grandmother was still in our midst.

I was in Denver, preparing for my move to join Roseanne, when she first appeared on Carson. Several of us from Woman To Woman had gathered in Sharon Silvas's home to watch the show, eat, drink, and celebrate her success. We were thrilled for her, as a friend and as a Sister.

The first change to affect Rosey was the money she was paid. "As seen on Johnny Carson" placed in an advertisement for a comic increased the audience for that performer in every comedy club in the country. They usually filled to capacity because of Rosey's new credentials. Some places charged a little extra for the right to see her.

The Tonight Show appearance also meant that it was time to increase the amount of writing we were doing. Rosey and I each had microcassette recorders we took everywhere. I would tape the act each time I attended wherever she was playing, then she would play it back, listening to the response. Did a new joke go over? If it did, should she change the pacing? Change the inflection in her voice? Vary the wording slightly? And if it didn't, was it the joke or the timing? Did she talk so fast that she stepped on her own punch line before the audience could laugh? Did she pause too long, letting her audience laugh themselves into silence so she had to work them back into the right mood? Were there too many jokes specifically for women before she had one the men would enjoy?

We also made notes with the recorders. Everything we did, everything we read, everything we discussed became a possible joke. A joke used in a club can be used again and again throughout the country. A good joke that is based on a timeless premise, such as the relationship between men and women, can be retold for months. But use that same joke on television and you can never use it again. Instantly it is heard by millions, and the next day the late-night enthusiasts have told their early-to-bed friends the punch line. By week's end, if the comic who told the joke in the first places uses it in a comedy club, the audience is so familiar with it that they think it is old. Some routines are popular enough that the audience wants to hear them again. Some routines are altered, either by modifying existing jokes or by adding new material. Thus each television appearance instantly added the need to reevaluate the use of several minutes of Roseanne's best material. The search for fresh ideas became endless, using up hundreds of batteries and dozens of cassette tapes as we worked.

The change also meant that we could afford to move into a small, functional, poorly built, ugly apartment in "beautiful" West Hollywood. It was no more than three blocks to two different comedy clubs, a deli, restaurants, a theater, and a swinging singles club scene. It was a ten-minute drive to the agents in Century City. It cost almost three times what the same size apartment would have cost in the best neighborhoods of Denver. However, for the money we paid, we got to look over a garden courtyard. Mere mortals in Los Angeles have to rent suites with a view of either the next building or a smog-covered street of nearly hopelessly gridlocked traffic. Success meant we could see colorful flowers peeking at us through the low-level smog.

Had Rosey been able to perform every week, her increased pay-checks would have meant we could afford other "luxuries," such as furniture. As it was, between her income and the money I was making working for National Medical Home Care near Century City as a junior accountant, we felt it best to rent furniture. The apartment was temporary, Rosey needed to consider where Bill and the kids would live. And I knew Maxine would be returning to the United States to start a life with me. This was a step up from living on the floors of other comics' apartments or sleeping in bread trucks.

That first night, as we lay together in bed, we talked about how far we had come. Just as we had schemed and planned, Roseanne went from reaching an audience that might not be more than a hundred or so people in a club to reaching millions on nationwide television. We had gone from Denver, Colorado, to Hollywood, California. We had gone from having separate beds and enough room to move about our homes without falling over each other to having to share a bed, something we had not had to do back in Salt Lake City. We had gone from open skies to crowded skyscrapers. Finally, realizing the incongruity of it all, I looked at her and said in my best hillbilly accent, "I be so poor, I have to sleep with my sister till I be thirty."

We both laughed at my comment, then settled down to sleep. And that was when our neighbor farted.

He was in the privacy of his own supposedly soundproofed suite next door. His door was closed, as was ours. The ventilation system for the building did not connect the suites in any way. Instead, despite what had been claimed when we signed the lease, the walls proved to be paper thin. We lay together on our bed, listening to a round of flatulence that sounded like a primitive form of experimental music until our laughter about our success overcame all other sounds in the building.

Rosey and I spent the next few weeks trying to sort out the pieces of our lives and her career.

When Roseanne was working the major clubs, she began

making from $1,500 to $2,000 per week. However, she was traveling, the expenses often coming out of her pocket. She had to pay a percentage of her earnings as the fee for the booking agent. And she was not working every week. What mattered was that by pooling our time and money, Roseanne could have her kids join her in Hollywood.

The Pentland marriage was over for all practical purposes. Sometimes she would talk with me about no longer wanting Bill for a husband. We talked of having Stephanie come up to live with us, bringing out the kids, and the three sisters working together for Rosey's family and career.

I felt a little sad about all this, though I planned my work around helping Rosey achieve her ends. I liked Bill. I considered him somewhat selfish at times, but he had a wicked sense of humor and the maturity to change. When Rosey first married him, he liked his television, his beer, and his creature comforts. By the time Roseanne had arrived in Los Angeles, he had taken the time to read, to talk with us and our friends, to begin to change. When I first met him, he was a firm believer in UFOs, space aliens, and other dangers to American society. He transformed into an ardent feminist and became extremely supportive of his wife simply because he believed it was the right thing to do. Her growing income was enjoyable, but that was not a primary concern.

Bill's sense of humor came out at times when others lacked the nerve to express what were often quite similar observations. For example, while Bill was raised a Lutheran, the Jewish faith is passed through the women in a family, and Rosey wanted her children raised in a Jewish home. That meant that when the Pentlands' son Jake, was born, he had to be circumcised.

I have never fully understood the traditional ritual of circumcision in contemporary American society. Not long after the birth of a male, the rabbi and the family gather for the ritual removal of the foreskin. The baby is awake, alert, and quite outraged by the experience. It is rather disgusting to view, and I am further troubled by the social ritual that follows, where food is served, including raw herring.

There was a time when the circumcision was believed to have strong health implications. Tradition holds that all Jewish males must be circumcised after birth, and Rosey was insistent that Jake would have the ritual performed in the usual manner.

The foreskin was removed, the penis was wrapped in a clean bandage for healing, and the infant Jake went home with Bill and Rosey. The next morning, though, all was not well. When the bandage was removed as the doctor had told them to do, a broken blood vessel or some similar minor injury resulted in blood spurting into the air. Rosey flipped out. Bill held his newborn son and called the doctor, who told him to hold the penis, letting the pressure stop the bleeding.

I had been visiting, and I ran into the room as Rosey was screaming and Bill was fixing the problem as the doctor told him to do. Bill glanced at his wife, glanced at the penis he was gently grasping in order to stop the flow of blood, then looked at his crying son. "So, son," Bill said, a wry smile on his face. "How does it feel to be Jewish?"

Somehow I guess I felt that a man like Bill Pentland deserved to have some importance in Roseanne's life even when the love was gone. When we were all still in Denver, working on the act, Rosey would talk with me several times a day. If she went out of town to perform, she would telephone me to discuss the audience, the jokes, the reactions, and where she was going. If I had a job, she would often call me at work. We probably talked a hundred times a month, both of us fixated on the same goal for her, working together, sisters beginning their path to the conquest of Hollywood.

A husband should have been almost as important to Roseanne. At the very least he should have been someone she wanted to contact every day, if only to hear his voice. Two emotionally committed people leading independent lives still have a link they want to nurture when separated. Unfortunately for Bill, Rosey did not see it that way.

Roseanne missed her children, not Bill. Once she knew that Hollywood was going to be her home, she approached

Stephanie to join us, taking care of the kids while we developed the act and worked toward our goals. She agreed, and Roseanne sent for her children at once. Soon it was impossible to hear our neighbor's flatulence or anything else. Three adult women and three growing children made their home in the one-bedroom apartment.

To appreciate what was taking place, you have to understand that in West Hollywood the majority of people want nothing to do with children. The building in which we were renting banned children, something it was still legal to do.

Although there were some families in West Hollywood — there are families everywhere — they were in the minority. This was because West Hollywood was then a community dominated by two main groups — the elderly and homosexual couples. Old people who liked to walk, go out to eat, gawk at celebrities, and spend hours talking, and who did not wish to be reminded that they had grandchildren in Cleveland, Pittsburgh, Detroit, or Chicago, lived happily in West Hollywood. Young people with the same-sex life partners who wanted a good life without being hassled by kids or bigoted straights also lived there. Rosey, Stephanie, three kids and me, all sharing a one-bedroom apartment, were not appreciated. And when the kids began decorating the apartment's garage with spray paint, we all knew it was time to move.

Mitzi Shore came to Rosey's aid by loaning her the condominium she maintained in La Jolla. Then, after a little searching, I found a home for Rosey in North Hollywood. There was a carriage house in the rear where Stephanie lived for a short period of time. But the big house was adequate for the Pentland family, and Rosey had Bill sell the Denver home and move out to California.

Rosey almost didn't get the house, though. Bill had created some credit problems in Denver, and Rosey's credit application showed that her work could only guarantee her $2,500 a weekend — up to $5,000 for two weekends a month. This meant that she was guaranteed between $30,000 and $60,000 a year, not a stable income according to the landlord. However, the problem was solved when Herbie Nannas, a man she had met on the Carson show, cosigned the lease in exchange for Rosey signing on with him as her manager.

Rosey was now a Superwoman "having it all" – career, family, and community respect. Such women, no matter how much help they had from their husbands, were always overtired, always overstressed. And many of them would say, "I need a wife."

Rosey needed a wife, and since she was earning better money than she and Bill had lived on in Denver, she felt Bill could serve that role. She continued their marital relationship in order to have the help she needed with the kids.

Only someone wealthy can succeed in Hollywood without help, and if they were wealthy, they probably would not have had the drive to get there. Neither Rosey nor I had any money. We were both doing just fine by the standards of the average person, but an entertainer's expenses and needs are not average. Even the first stage outfit Rosey wore after reaching Hollywood – styled coveralls meant to remind the audience of her Midwest Mom image – cost approximately two hundred dollars. When she needed to look more glamorous, she needed clothes such as the silk blouse that set her back almost as much money, as well as skirts, slacks, and accessories.

There are other expenses as well. Entertainers need head shots and press kits. The more you are featured in newspapers and magazines, the more the public want to see you perform. But somebody has to obtain the clippings, arrange for photocopying, pull quotes, and create an information package that provides club owners and others with information. The press kit is also sent to writers to help them with their stories. Some interviewers are lazy, and they will pull quotes and other information from the press kit for their stories. You can control what is in some of the media this way, guaranteeing more favorable press.

We were also aware that there was much we did not know about the business of Hollywood. From my business training, I knew that Rosey was a product to be sold, but I did not yet understand the language of Hollywood, or the politics of the entertainment business. But I knew how to listen, to learn, and to interpret what I learned to Roseanne.

The night Rosey first appeared on Carson, Herbie Nannas approached her about representation. He was a partner with Stan Moress in a management company that was primarily known for handling some fairly important stars. He was also a friend of Jim McCawley, but Jim would not recommend him because he felt that the friendship created a conflict and prevented him from getting involved.

A star's manager is like a star's mother. The manager, at personal expense, develops press kits and promotional material. The manager might also act as producer and put together a variety of talent to create a special show, plan a movie, or anything else to showcase a client's talent.

A good manager would handle every aspect of the career other than what the agent would do. This might mean hiring the business manager, who would plan investments, work out a budget for living, plan an estate, deal with tax obligations, and coordinate career movement. The manager might arrange for a media coach to help an entertainer come across more effectively during interviews with the press. The manager might help the client find a house, buy a car, or even get a divorce. The manager might go so far as to hire a publicist to handle mechanical problems. This became increasingly important when AIDS began taking some of the hottest names in show business, who needed to be seen as healthy in order to get work until their dying was too obvious.

The star creates a corporation. The star is the product and wants to be Chief Executive Officer, a title the manager also covets. Usually the manager becomes the equivalent of the corporate employee handling research and development, strategic planning, and day-to-day managerial functions that might include marketing. The publicist handles advertising and acts as the front person

for the product (star). The business manager is the equivalent of the corporate Chief Financial Officer, handling
accounting and payroll.

Ideally the business manager and other professionals act
as a check and balance on the manager. In Hollywood,
though, one hand washes the other as much as possible.
Family members, close friends, and those anxious enough
for work to give kickbacks usually get first choice at the
special jobs. And since the performer relies on the reputation of the manager, an undeserved trust arises for all.

In earlier times, a Hollywood manager might arrange for
an abortion either for the star or for a lover if the star was
male. The manager might pay off police, help hide drug
and/or alcohol addiction treatment (this was before the
Betty Ford Clinic made stars who were not addicted to
anything other than achieving fame feel like there was
something lacking on their resumé), and sometimes even
plant stories in the tabloids when the client's image was
becoming less sought after

The men we interviewed varied in their appearance and
actions, though even the best of them had a bit of the
Hollywood pretentiousness to them. They always dressed
well – though in Beverly Hills you can receive a citation
from the police if caught on Rodeo Drive wearing any
clothing that is off the rack. Most of the men liked Hollywood formal – good slacks with properly pressed crease, a
tailored shirt, boots made from the hides of creatures from
exotic lands, an expensive sports jacket, and no necktie.
Even the vegetarians often wore leather, and gold chains
were as common on men as earrings were on women. The
cigar smokers had New York accents and tough guy attitudes. Most were lean, and many looked as though they
worked out.

For our first meeting with the agency and management
people, we dressed as expected. I borrowed a striped silk
blouse from Rosey that had cost her two hundred dollars. I
wore black pants and sandals. Rosey also wore black,
though her style was different, more effective than mine.
What mattered was that we looked good, and while we

weren't wearing the requisite one thousand dollars in clothing, we were close enough to be taken seriously.

Oddly, in Hollywood the livelihood of the moguls is dependent upon how well the television shows and movies they create will play in "heartland America." Yet these same executives, both male and female, hold any place east of Los Angeles as areas lacking in "hip." They are intensely condescending about the Midwest and even the East Coast. That was why Rosey and I chose to adopt the attitude that in their condescension, they ignored the reality that the Midwest was in the vanguard of American society. Our act represented everywoman, and the Midwest was aware of what was happening, while Los Angeles was too busy preening in the mirror to see the world starting to pass them by.

Rosey and I understood that the act was reflective of society. We took all of our family shit and turned it into a performance. That was why the act was successful and would become even more successful. But since the potential managers had blinders about the working-class world of America, we decided, at first, to put them on. First we expressed surprised delight with the menus, which we noted were color-coordinated with the napkins, the tablecloths, and all other decorations. Then we commented on the food when it was served, saying things like:

"Oh, look, Geraldine. They cut the radish just like a pretty flower. I wonder how they did that."

"And the tomato, Rosey. It looks just like one of Bobbe Mary's roses. Somebody sure went to a lot of trouble to learn how to do that. Never seen anything like it before."

Whatever we ate, we'd find something to comment about. We didn't play totally dumb. We'd always notice what mattered – the delicate blending of flavors, an unusual seasoning, a beautifully decorated petit four, or something similar. We obviously understood that we were experiencing quality, yet it seemed equally obvious to the people trying to bullshit us that we were doing so for the first time.

Herbie Nannas was our first effort at seriously playing

the Hollywood game. His office was in Santa Monica, but he and his partner wanted to impress us when Rosey and I agreed to meet with them in September 1985. They drove us in Herbie's Jaguar to a restaurant called The Ivy. The Ivy was in Santa Monica, a long enough drive from Los Angeles so that we were supposed to be impressed that they knew about it. In Los Angeles, the mentality is that no restaurant close to where you work or live is sophisticated. The real test of the knowledgeable diner is being aware of restaurants many miles away. Thus everyone is busy driving somewhere else to eat when they want to impress a client, even though superior restaurants might be closer at hand. This point was emphasized on the way when we were informed that the restaurant was extremely hard to get into but the men were well known to the staff. We would be, and were, given preferential treatment.

It was typical of Hollywood pretentiousness, including the paisley motif used for everything from the napkins to the tablecloths, the menus, and the wall coverings. But even before you could go inside, your car was met by a valet, who would park it for you according to the tip you gave him.

I was still filled with working-class righteousness, and the idea of servants bothered me. Valets reminded me of houseboys on some plantation back before the Civil War. I wasn't about to play the Hollywood power game, lording it over fawning sycophants. Instead, as the valet opened the car door, then extended his hand to help me alight, I moved out fast, took his hand, shook it, introduced myself, and told him I was pleased to meet him. Herbie Nannas undoubtedly thought he was with a couple of hicks, and that was fine with us. We only planned to learn the business from him, take advantage of what he might have to offer, then create our own production company and produce our own work. "We will need him for two years until we can become our own producer," Rosey and I had earlier reasoned together.

Herbie and his partner seemed to understand what we were trying to do. He called Rosey and me "the Dolly

Sisters," a reference to a famous sister act in the vaudeville era. He was married and had been raised in a family dominated by women – sisters, a mother and a grandmother. He would use encouraging phrases like "Honey, it'll be great!" Yet he was not condescending when Roseanne told him, "I want to be as big as Barbra Streisand."

Herbie was reassuring. He started by making it clear that Rosey could achieve her dream, then began talking with me about any personal goals I might have. I explained about our working together, but Herbie did not care. He was amused by our closeness, though he didn't quite know what to do with me. When the conversation came around to music and he learned I was moderately skilled with the violin, he began talking about the possibility of my recording. It was all bullshit, though. Not only had I never considered such a career, we weren't there for me. What mattered was Rosey, and Herbie really did understand her act. He knew that Roseanne had the potential to reach the top, and he genuinely wanted to represent her.

Herbie then did what everyone we would meet did. He put me down, not for my knowledge or ability, but because I was a sister. In Hollywood, I was informed, no one takes seriously the sibling, parent, spouse, or adult child of a star. Everyone wants to deal with professionals, he explained, a fact we accepted yet suspected was not true.

Next we went to Triad Artists. The people involved with versatile entertainers are highly specialized. Hiring the necessary representation is a little like being a general contractor. Officially the general contractor is in charge of building a house, office building, or other structure. However, most general contractors work with specialists – electricians, plumbers, drywall installers, architects, and the like. They understand all the trades. They oversee the trades. But there is only a portion of the work that they will handle themselves.

The "subcontractors" working with the manager are usually selected by the client based on the manager's suggestions. People beginning their careers seldom know to whom they should be going for specialized support. They usually hire on the basis of the manager's recommendation, a fact that gives Herbie Nannas and people like him tremendous power. Not only do they essentially control who controls your career, they can actually reward you for the referral.

The power situation is one where you are buying access to the system that is Hollywood. In the early stages of your career, there is no free lunch. A rising star will ultimately pay as much as 75 percent of earnings just to enter the world where real fame and fortune can be achieved. If the star were a box of cereal, she would be buying shelf space in supermarkets and advertising in newspapers. In Hollywood, you buy the people who can put you in the position you need for success.

No one wanted me around because I was Rosey's trusted confidante. Rosey wanted me to stand between the talent and the management. I was given power because she knew I was thinking of the agenda we had planned together. But the management team wanted that power, that access, and that trust. I wasn't going away. They weren't going away. And the combination resulted in constant tension, which in my mind was well worth the struggle because Rosey was protected. Only later, when we really knew the business, we found that many spouses, parents, siblings, and lovers act as very successful managers because they uniquely care about the talent.

We eventually decided to hire Herbie when he assured Rosey he would find her a place to live. He was thus our first manager in Los Angeles. And though I never told him, Rosey and I saw my involvement as an apprenticeship during which I would learn Hollywood before taking over. We were in year six of our ten-year plan, and this was the next stage for me. The only frustration I had was in having to keep quiet about what we were doing.

Hollywood is a put-down capital. We came with an established talent, a proven act, and a future that was certain. Yet many of the agency people acted as though we had just stepped on to the planet. It was as though no one paid their dues. The agency said, "Let there be a star," and you were a star. You received no respect for your hard work, your business acumen and the success you had achieved that made you a desirable client, a product that would make them large sums of money. Yet I knew I had to shut up, work behind the scenes, and mark time until we could show them that the Barr sisters were their equal. We, like so many of them, would be the producers, the one credit line that speaks of ultimate power.

The truth is that in Hollywood, certain positions provide power and control. Your name is only on the television screen for a few seconds, and most people never read the credits. Within the industry, though, having a "created by" credit can enhance both your career and your residual share. Having a "producer" credit gives you power. You can control scripts, shooting schedules, the acting, and may other aspects of a project. You also can share in the bulk of the income from the project. It is extremely important.

We also quickly discovered that if you are making large sums of money, the networks, the studios, and everyone else will negotiate with your dead, freeze-dried parakeet if that's what you want. Success generates power, money, and control. Rosey was new enough that we would not argue, especially since Herbie's days were numbered from the start. But we instinctively knew better, and today there are examples of family-member management from the father of a child actor Macaulay Culkin to Roseanne's second husband, Tom Arnold. Spouses, parents, and adult children all have been involved in careers of stars, but we were naive back then. We accepted what we heard, not knowing what else to do other than to change the situation when we took power.

The managers we came to know tried to find a way to have themselves and as many of their friends as possible on the payroll. One lawyer who currently works for Roseanne is an officer in her corporations, has a son-in-law working as a business manager, a daughter in his law firm, and another daughter who works for the insurance company with which Rosey does business. They are undoubtedly all quite competent or she would never allow them to have so much power, yet the family involvement with a single successful client is typical Hollywood. The more credits they took, the greater their power position and the greater their future within the industry.

Soon we were working with a staff that included people such as Tracy Kramer, who worked with Nicole David as the agent who essentially handled career development. Bill Gross coordinated personal appearances and comedy concert dates. Russ Garrison was the agent for commercials. And on and on it went. A lawyer was always available to review contracts. An accountant had to help determine which aspects of Rosey's work were deductible, such as the clothing worn solely while performing.

Everyone took either a salary or a percentage. We couldn't afford to place anyone on retainer at that stage in Rosey's career, so her gross income *before* taxes were paid was being divided into percentages. Depending upon the project, the manager might take 15 percent, the agent 10 percent, the business manager and accountant would demand 5 percent each, and the lawyer usually wanted 5 percent. This meant that as much as 40 percent of the gross was paid out to others before Rosey could begin to benefit.

We knew it would be cheaper to consolidate some of the jobs, and we gradually learned that the more powerful someone became, the fewer people they employed. Still, even when you were successful enough to cut your staff to the minimum, there could be situations that were proper in Hollywood though they were suspect elsewhere. For example, we found that many agents are trained in the law and are perfectly capable of checking the fine print of a contract. They may also be able to coordinate several career aspects without using specialists. But Hollywood is a make-work town where nepotism is a way of life. We were learning, though we had no illusions that we would even consider long-term relationships with the first people we hired.

The number of people with whom we were involved did not eliminate the need for me to be working. Even more than in the past, Rosey was in a world that required some-one who was willing to help with the writing, provide emotional support, and coordinate all aspects of the growing enterprise. Ultimately we both expected that I would take over several of the jobs for which we were paying others. For the moment, we were both learning, combining our skills to move her to the top.

In the early days, much of our time was spent hanging around many of the comedians who were friends of Mitzi's. We'd spend time with Pam Madison, Caroline Simpson, Dianne Ford, Karen Haber, Carrie Snow, and others. They were an odd lot, as comics seem to be. But they could be intensely loving and generous. In the earliest days in Hollywood, we knew we could count on them for a place to crash for a night or a week. Those who could afford an apartment shared space with those who couldn't. Those who could afford food often fed those who were on a tight budget. They might be cutthroat when it came to their egos and their self-perceived status on stage, but personally they were generous.

We spent many nights listening to the comics, and I was usually intensely bored. They all seemed self-centered to a great degree during the nights they were working. Each would compliment the other on their set, sometimes meaning the compliment, usually just waiting for you to say something nice in return. They were like a supermarket checkout cashier who, when ordered to be more friendly, would briefly flash a look shaped like a smile, announce "Have a nice day" in a flat, monotone voice, and then handle the next customer's order. The actions had all the warmth of one of the old happy-face buttons – superficially friendly yet with no depth underneath.

My primary job, when not working with Rosey on the act, was what in a normal business would be considered strategic planning. I was the liaison among the various agents and business people. I would receive the various offers coming in, weigh their relative value, then discuss them with Rosey in light of what she wanted to achieve. There is a finite life to every act. Sometimes comics get lucky, succeeding for more than a few years. Most of the ones who truly triumph are able to move along different fields. George Burns and Gracie Allen's work went from vaudeville to radio to television, movies, nightclubs, and other fields. Bob Hope, Jack Benny, Lucille Ball, and numerous others all reinvented themselves in whatever way would please their audience.

We knew that many people wanted to use Rosey as a domineering housewife, a fat woman with an attitude, and in similar roles that would not advance her career. We felt that the type of commercials she made, the types of appearances she made other than when doing her act, even the movie ideas she accepted had to all move her career in the direction we originally planned for her. I was regularly on the telephone, fielding information from the various agents and businesspeople, analyzing projects with Rosey, and keeping an eye on what could move her career forward.

My role in all this was becoming recognized by others as well. NBC Television sent a camera crew to record a day in our lives. We were followed everywhere, including to the NBC Burbank studios, where the videographer taped from the backseat of the car as we drove past the security checkpoint. It was all great fun, combining some of Rosey's stage work with the work we did together. Unfortunately, she was not quite so big as she became in a matter of weeks. The material was never aired. But the other network show, George Schlatter's "Funny," did go on, giving Roseanne her first major television showcase after *The Tonight Show*.

My personal life was very important to me, even though in many ways it was secondary to our mission. I think the reason I functioned effectively was because I lacked the narcissism of the power people. I didn't need to cultivate the contacts necessary to drop the right names before the right power players in the right restaurants. I didn't need an image to imply substance. I needed to have the substance, to be the "worker bee" that is such a common metaphor in Utah, which is, after all, the Beehive State. And because of this, because I kept focused on family, music, and what really mattered, I did not become another Hollywood crazy desperate to climb the ladder of success.

The business plan I had developed for Roseanne had worked. We clearly saw where we needed to head, though in Hollywood we needed insiders to teach us the business, to give us a chance to control our own destiny. We had to enter the phase we called "I'm just a dumb woman, but . . ."

Roseanne and Geraldine Do Hollywood

Despite the glitz and glamour, the first thing you have to know about Hollywood is that much of it is bullshit and boring. If you are a star, you have enough money to pay people to act in a manner many would never do otherwise. Some people are what are known as "star fuckers." They desperately seek the excitement of celebrity. They will do anything, say anything, to try to be a part of a star's inner circle, a part of the person's life or work. It is not the money they might earn being in what they consider a glamorous industry that motivates them. It is the vicarious thrill of their associations.

Ironically, many of the stars feel the same way. The new stars like to mingle with the longer-established stars. Their lives are often empty, their conversations boring, their minds filled with schemes for getting close to the next person who will help them achieve a yet higher level of status in the entertainment gossip columns and the trades.

Other people have real goals. They want to pay the rent, buy food, and provide an education for their children. They use a star's vanity to earn enough money to eventually escape from the bullshit. But the stars don't care. In Hollywood, when you're afraid of the truth and rich enough to buy only the lies you want to hear, you are usually willing to pay someone to kiss your ass.

We were in an unusual position in those early days of living in Hollywood. Rosey was a comer, and everyone knew it. The only questions were when she would make it and how big she would be. I already knew that she would earn the money to be completely in control of her work, to

My big sister and I sit for a formal portrait.

My protector.

Roseanne was my first
friend.

She always made me laugh.

Rosey and me and Dad at home.

Dad and his girls at Disneyland.

Roseanne and me in 1987 in Los Angeles during happier, earlier days.

Livin' large: Louie Anderson accompanied Roseanne on her "Vast Waistline" comedy club tour.

From Denver clubs to HBO specials, Roseanne carved a whole
new role for women in stand-up comedy.

Rosey at Desert Inn. Her nose-picking bit never failed to get a
laugh.

Roseanne's "Domestic Goddess" character spoke to millions of women that TV had previously ignored.

Mom and Dad at Caesars Palace.

Roseanne's Conner family proved that being less than middle class and pretty didn't mean you had to be dumb.

Rosey at the Utah AIDS Foundation Benefit. Utah—home of big hair gals.

Roseanne Conner, working-class hero.

In her first movie, *She-Devil*, Roseanne got to star opposite
Meryl Streep. They're seen here with Ed Begley, Jr.

Here, Tom and Rosey seem to be attached at the shoulder.

Most people had a hard time believing Tom and Rosey's lovey-dovey act. In the end, I guess they stopped believing it too.

be able to use the role of producer to change the thoughts of society as we had developed in our ten-year plan. But the agents and managers who wanted to sign her figured she was little more than a hillbilly who could still be impressed with the image they had bought for themselves. They began courting the two of us, including taking us to restaurants where the staff had been sufficiently bribed to treat them as if they were as important as they claimed when trying to get her to sign contracts with them.

It is important to admit one minor personal embarrassment at this point. We may have been professional feminists, but when someone drives you to a restaurant in a car that is more expensive than the biggest house you ever saw as a kid growing up in Salt Lake City, you've got to be impressed. We planned to use our money in quieter, more meaningful ways. But we loved zipping through the streets of Beverly Hills while pimply-faced Beverly Hills High School boys gawked in awe from behind the wheel of their "staid" little Corvettes that Daddy and Mommy had given them when they turned sixteen without getting their girlfriends pregnant. Occasionally they'd try and drag race us, but they were soon left in the dust of our driver's thousand-dollar-per-wheel custom racing tires. Like I say, it was a kick.

Admittedly, nothing was quite the kick of a limousine when Rosey became popular enough so that the club arranged one for her transportation. If you've ever rented a limousine for a senior prom, you probably think you know what they're all about. They're all long, either black or white, and come with a small refrigerator stocked with whatever drinks the driver thinks the customer for the evening is old enough to consume.

Star limousines are different, as Rosey and I quickly discovered. For example, there was one in which we rode while she worked in a club in Milwaukee. She and Louie Anderson toured together, sharing the stage, usually arguing over who got to go first. They had the same agent, though Louie had earned national success sooner than Roseanne. He had also been extremely encouraging to

Roseanne whenever he was playing Denver. He was a comic whose humor focused on the fact that he came from a dysfunctional family with alcoholic parents. It was deeply moving, the type of stand-up act where there are tears streaming down your face from both laughter and compassion for the world in which he was raised.

Louie is an extremely sensitive and compassionate man who is a brilliant, dedicated writer. He works hard every day developing new material and refining the old. His best work remains stand-up, and he has played to large crowds in Las Vegas for more than a decade.

We frequently talked about how the public had difficulty focusing on Louie's and Rosey's material rather than their appearance. Both were heavy, and Rosey taught me that in the first three seconds of an act, you have to talk about the first thing the audience sees. You have to address your baldness, your big nose, your unusual appearance, or with Rosey and Louie, the weight. Thus they would both usually open with a joke about being fat, then get on to the material that made them successful. However, recognizing the realities of the business, we called the tour the "Vast Waistland Tour" and the "When Do We Eat? Tour."

Some of the limo's furnishings were expected – leather seats, wall and ceiling covering, plush carpeting, and high-intensity reading lights set to meet the needs of as many as five passengers who could comfortably ride in the back. Actually, with Louie and Rosey sitting on the big bench-style seat meant for three, there was no room for anyone else. I sat on one of two fold-down seats positioned with their back to the driver so I faced Rosey and Louie.

A color television was set on a small platform on each of the back two doors, allowing the passengers to watch two different programs. The rear entrance doors served as part of the bar, each side stocked with different items. One side held soft drinks and Perrier. The other side held expensive liquor. The small refrigerator held ice, lemons, limes, and similar items. There were flawlessly designed glasses so clean and clear that they were almost invisible. Privacy was made possible by a blackened, soundproof partition that blocked the passengers from the driver and could be raised and lowered only from the passenger section. There was also a combination telephone and intercom so that you could talk with the driver or telephone friends in China if you wanted. In addition there was an expensive stereo on which Rosey played tapes of her favorite songs by Barbra Streisand and Patti Smith, especially Smith's hit "People Have the Power."

There was also a tablelike working area on which Rosey could place the mountain of magazines – *Cosmopolitan*, *People*, *Vanity Fair*, trade journals like the *Hollywood Reporter*, the tabloids, and others. Some were read in search of fresh material. Some were read to see if her name was in them, and if it wasn't, to consider what she could do to get mentioned. And some were read to learn about the business. No matter why she had them, as soon as she finished whatever she wanted from one, she would toss it on the floor, then start on another. If the ride was a long one, we'd have a "rug" of slick paper, newsprint, and trampled photographs the limo driver would have to clean before he drove anyone else. Rosey was a slob in the way she lived and the way she traveled, but in the limousine the driver acted as though her trashing the floor was expected, the cleanup a privilege.

I luxuriated at first. Then, as I became more accustomed to the experience, I came to see the limousines as offices on wheels for us. However, Roseanne and her second husband, Tom Arnold, used them extensively. And while Rosey and I disagree about how to spend money, she occasionally uses the limousine to touch lives unexpectedly. Although she gradually abandoned our idea to change society through the productions and art grants we would arrange for women, her heart is frequently touched on a one-to-one basis. It has not been unusual for Rosey to be riding in a limo, see people obviously in need, and stop to help them. I remember one time when there was an aged woman in an alley, obviously either homeless or in dire poverty. She had the driver stop, then rolled down the window and handed the woman five hundred dollars, about what she would later spend on dinner. Over the years, it was common for her to hand out two hundred to five hundred dollars to people.

I always both respected and was troubled by the form of her generosity. My studies of Jewish philosophy kept bringing me back to the idea of giving anonymously, that the greatest gifts are the ones that go unhonored in the giver's lifetime. Certainly this was the case with the way we planned our corporate philosophy for the production company we would create. Yet I felt that Rosey had reached a point where she needed the immediate gratification of the face-to-face giving, avoiding the importance of larger planning to reach the goals we had long set for ourselves. Admittedly, that may say more about me than her. The fact is that most people, including those with her growing wealth, would have turned away. Her kindness gave someone an extra few days of eating, of being able to get off the street.

"Doing lunch" is a high art in Hollywood, an event of near religious significance. Nothing could be a greater thrill for two Jewish sisters raised in a culture where food had layers of meaning beyond mere nourishment. We could put up with a lot of bullshit for a disgustingly opulent meal in one of those thoroughly pretentious restaurants for which Hollywood is deservedly famous. But first we had to learn to lie. The first "lie" you have to learn to do lunch in LA is to wear outrageously expensive outfits as if they were casual clothes. Hollywood women had to wear at least a thousand dollars in clothing on their backs. It also had to be properly coordinated, something I never understood. Roseanne fortunately had a sense of style. She and I had begun putting on weight again, a fact that meant that attractive clothing was difficult to find.

Every woman knows that the fashion world lies. Over the years, there are three basic types of female fashion models who move in and out of popularity with designers. Sometimes these are very tall and boyishly slim – no hips, no breasts, and a shape that seems to indicate that any time she might get pregnant, she will have to let some other woman carry her child. At other times the look of the jitterbug era is in — full breasts, small waist, and slightly wide hips. And still other times, the woman is somewhere in between. She has breasts that protrude more than her navel. She has hips that indicate she is capable of giving birth. And her waist does not allow her to take her skirt and substitute her watchband for a belt.

None of them are real.

No artist airbrushes the lines from a real woman's face. Real women bag and sag. They protrude where the models recede. They are flabby where the models are taut. They have thighs they dare not reveal in shorts, breasts that fall no matter how cantilevered their uplifting bras, and enough chins to mock the camouflage efforts of the most expensive makeup products.

Rosey and I were real women with a vengeance. All we had been doing was eating, sleeping, eating, working, eating, and developing Roseanne's act. We had abandoned "svelte" for "cute." Then we abandoned "cute" for "you really should lose a few pounds, ladies," and were heading towards obese, just like millions of other women. It was the recognition of this that helped make Roseanne's comedy work. It was also the reason we had trouble finding the right clothes to wear.

The big lie for fat women, regardless of where they live, has always been that if you see a dress that looks great on one of the anorexic models, the same design in a size ten times larger will look just as wonderful. Thinking that the same fabric, albeit in far more massive quantities, makes the image work is like thinking that a pickup truck looks like a sports car because they're both made from the same type of steel.

Roseanne had a great sense of style and was able to find ways to look reasonably attractive with the clothing we could afford. I lacked that sense and felt that the oversized racks always made me look as though I was buying an overnight tent for two from L. L. Bean, then adding head and arm holes.

Still, we had to try to match the pretentiousness of the restaurants where we were being wined and dined. It was part of the lie of Los Angeles culture. Only later, when Roseanne was rich, famous, and could take a legitimate tax deduction for the glamorous outfits she wore in her act, was she able to afford custom designs. Stores such as The Forgotten Woman offered clothing created specifically for the overweight, and the fit made everyone appear attractive. We shopped there all the time. But their prices were high, ranging from $100 for a simple blouse to $3,000 for an elaborate "working wardrobe," to $10,000 for the type of gown you would wear to the Academy Awards. The clothing was worth every cent, but it was mostly beyond our reach when Rosey first began making her move to the top in Los Angeles and we were attending some of the more pretentious restaurants. Still we did our best.

The interiors of the restaurants seemed as though someone had watched all the 1930s movies about the disgustingly rich, then created numerous reproductions of old sets inside eateries through Beverly Hills. Since racist Hollywood had to look liberal, the valets were invariably Vietnamese, Thai, Cambodian, Salvadoran, or similar refugees instead of being black as in days gone by. The kitchen staff was usually Hispanic, often legal immigrants, and one step in income ahead of the nervous valets who were frightened of government agents stopping and asking for their green cards. The few black restaurant employees seemed to be given largely invisible jobs behind the scenes.

Women seldom waited on tables in the luxury places. Their employment was reserved for locations such as the Hamburger Hamlet chain. Instead, we were served solely by white European males with highly pretentious accents and tuxedolike uniforms. They were all somber, serious, and deferential enough to get tips that put their children through college.

The best of the waiters had the type of nondescript accent once taught in the various studio schools for young actors. You knew they weren't quite American, but you couldn't quite place their country of origin. In that way they could pretend to be of Italian extraction in one movie, French in another, and German in a third, all without changing their inflections. They were proud, proper, and always delighted to see whichever men accompanied us, since those men had invariably established the proper fawning status by overtipping, clipping their business cards to the paper money they passed.

The table position within the restaurant was also part of the power game. The ideal seat was usually in the center of the restaurant by a window, your chair angled by the waiter so you could see everyone coming and going and they could see you. In a restaurant without windows, the power position required the dominant male in the party to also have his back to a booth or a wall so that no one could sneak up behind him.

This need to cover one's back had nothing to do with the cutthroat nature of the film industry. Instead, I later realized, it resulted from the fact that Rosey and I were being feted at a time when gangster movies and television shows were popular. Hollywood men often create their vision of reality, then try to live in the fantasy they think is truth. Powerful male characters in the stories they filmed were in danger, and so the moguls thought real life held the same threats. If the Mafia don, the western hero, or anyone else was so powerful, so hated, or so feared that others were gunning for them, they had to protect their backs. And the moguls who bought into the myths they created fantasized living the same lives, forcing them to take the same precautions. When the public taste changed to favor horror pictures, dinosaurs, and love stories, the same moguls stopped watching their backs. Image and fantasy were everything for the movers and shakers of Hollywood.

The worst seats were near the kitchen. These were reserved for tourists, wanna-bes dining alone, all women unaccompanied by men, and lousy tippers. Ironically, you sometimes got the best service in such locations, if only because you were in a position to trip the waiters as they started to rush past, trying to ignore you.

Everyone arriving at the better restaurants checked to

see both who was sitting in the power positions and who was sitting in "Siberia" near the kitchen. They wanted to know who was in and who was out. Sometimes this determined whose calls they would take on the telephone the rest of the week. At other times it determined which former friends they would have to stop speaking to.

The meals in such places were designed to allow you to spend an obscene amount of money in order to flash a big tip and make the waiters very, very happy. Instead of admitting that they were serving portions that were too small and charging too much money, they claimed they were serving "nouvelle cuisine."

The food lacked fat, cholesterol, and rich sauces. Instead, it was heavily laden with green things Bobbe Mary would have discarded from her garden as too disgusting to consider even looking at. There were also light-colored things, equally nondescript, served raw, poached, or baked, and everything was beautifully arranged on the plate by a chef who had studied interior decorating. The more artistic members of the kitchen staff would skilfully carve radishes and even tomatoes into a variety of flowers to adorn your plate. Servings were very small, perhaps half the amount you would be provided for less money and far less pretentiousness in a normal restaurant.

Because the portions were so tiny, and because men determined to prove their coolness dare not admit they were shocked by the bill, we learned that overordering was expected. You host would order more than one entrée per person (entrées began at a price that was usually as great as the entire meal, including coffee and dessert, at a lesser establishment), then share the variety. Salads were ordered individually, but appetizers were sometimes created by request (pheasant pâté and beluga caviar on toast points, with a side of marinated calamari, for example).

Desserts, which were always small and always magnificent, were generally ordered in quantity. Why ogle an elaborate dessert tray when you can have one each of everything, then taste all the delights?

Wine was critical to the meal. It had to be something no

one could pronounce, of course. Something vaguely French, or perhaps from one of the private wineries in California that had recently won an international competition. Sometimes the agent or manager would order for us, the wine steward bowing, scraping, and saying, "An excellent year, an excellent vintage, such exquisite taste, Mr. More-important-than-I'll-ever-be, sir." At other times there would be the ritual of sniffing the cork, then tasting a little, swishing the liquid around in the mouth, and, often as not, ordering a different bottle. House wines could easily start at fifty dollars or more a bottle, and the "good stuff" could be several times that amount.

Sometimes the menus given the guests were without prices, an added touch of what passes for class in California. Usually the prices were obvious and a little like looking at the price sticker on the window of a new car. Several times I totaled the charges in my head for the three or four of us who had gathered to talk over a thoroughly hedonistic meal. The price was rarely under three hundred dollars, and with the tip usually 20 percent of the bill, the total was more than Rosey and Bill's combined weekly pay in Denver.

Ironically, the real joy of eating out came during the Vast Waistland Tour. I loved eating my way across the country in the great local restaurants that dot small towns and mid-sized cities throughout America. Everywhere we went we would ask what the best restaurants were where the locals regularly eat. We were invariably sent to unpretentious locations with moderate prices and great food. But better than the menu was the attitude of the chefs when they or the managers recognized Rosey. Special meals would be prepared for us, the chef fixing what he or she loved to serve, no matter what the usual fare of the restaurant might be. We could not use the menus, and we rarely had a meal that was not excellent.

I also found that people loved to feed Roseanne. They were as excited about bringing her food as we were about eating it. I remember one really incredible night in Florida in a restaurant in an Embassy Suites Hotel. The chef came out and said, "Don't even look at your menu. I will make you the most wonderful food. You will eat like we eat in Italy." It came family-style in massive bowls, the chef bringing course after course out to us, then standing to make certain we enjoyed his creation. And he was right. It was the most incredible food we ever ate, and Rosey, Louie, and I stayed up much of the night trying to figure the cost of opening a restaurant in California with this man as the chef.

We quickly understood that there were several ways a newcomer could handle the pretentious games that are played in Hollywood. One was the we're-more-full-of-shit-than-you-are approach:

"Oh, look, Sister, they scoop out each snow pea and stuff it with a caviar egg before inserting it in the head of the baby octopus that forms the sauce for the truffle-filled lobster. Wasn't it Grandma Hattie's sister Bernice who used to make that same recipe for all the church socials? Of course, it was never as tasty as the fantastic ways she used to prepare her endangered species soufflés, but with all the social consciousness out here, I suppose eating endangered species is out of style."

Another approach is to play the gourmet, savoring each bite and suggesting the seasonings that should have been used. "A touch more anise and fennel would have nicely accented the salade à bête noir, but this is Los Angeles, isn't it? And I suppose the really fine restaurants will start copying them. No one has proper standards anymore. That's why I grow my own herbs in the greenhouse Daddy is tending back home. Perhaps I should send the chef here some appropriate cuttings. He wouldn't have to settle for his food just getting three stars in the Michelin Guide anymore."

A third approach is to just ignore it all, especially if the bill is going to total at least one hundred dollars per person, for lunch, without wine. You order, eat, and drink with the same attitude you might have in a McDonald's. "So as soon as we get the catsup, relish, salsa, horseradish, and mustard, we can get started. It's just the same old crap we always get when we don't feel like putting on airs, so we don't really have to think about what we're eating. That's what we like about you guys. No pretension. You take us to a place where the food is so familiar, we can concentrate on the serious business that brought us here in the first place."

And the fourth approach, the one Rosey and I adopted with Herbie Nannas, was one Roseanne named the "I'm a dumb woman, but..." style of "taking a meeting." The agents and managers knew we were from Salt Lake City, the only other place we had lived being in Denver. By Hollywood reasoning, we were hicks. We decided to let them retain their condescending attitudes until it was appropriate to shatter them with our sophistication in business, the real reason we were meeting.

I had essentially handled the role of manager for Roseanne prior to our moving to Los Angeles. However, once we arrived we both understood the areas in which we were lacking. Roseanne had gone from small time to big time through her good fortune with Mitzi Shore. She was given the chance to do concert tours, opening for either a comic or a name singer. The money was steadier than the clubs. The heckling was relatively nonexistent. And the exposure took her to the level just below the big leagues.

That was the "I'm just a dumb woman" part of our sister act. Then, after making all the small talk that mattered, including our comments about the meal, we would begin the "but..."

For example, Rosey said quite seriously that she wanted to be a star as big as Barbra Streisand. The men were not shocked. In fact, during that lunch at The Ivy with Herbie Nannas, he had commented, "You do everything I tell you and you will be, honey." It was obvious that they wanted to represent Roseanne, that they believed in her, that they saw her as a money machine for themselves.

We let the men make their sales pitches, describing the things they would do and the money that would come in. Each time, Rosey would turn to me for clarification. I would then put the matter in simple, direct terms. "What they're saying is . . ." I might begin. "The projections should be . . ." And Roseanne would support me, explaining. "My sister translates all this business shit for me."

They'd throw something out and I'd say, "Are we talking net or gross? And how will you define net?" And then they'd answer, and I'd say, "Well, Sis, they're going to do this and take the expense from that." I'd be figuring on paper. "Sis, after you pay commissions and taxes, you're going to keep 25 percent of everything you earn, and they want you to feel really good about that."

Then she'd say, "Oh all right. So long as we know what they're talking about."

The reaction on one level was respect for what we understood. On the other level, we were seen as the Bitches From Hell. We were unknown entities in Hollywood, playing the game and not playing the game simultaneously. We kept the vultures off balance, yet we were respecting what they had to offer us. It was not something with which they were comfortable, yet the fact is that Roseanne was and is a solid professional. She understood that comedy is a business, and the person who masters the business will come out on top. Between us, we could handle anything, and we were willing to do whatever it took.

All of this stemmed from decisions we had made in the bookstore days about how we would handle business and the fact that we would talk in what others saw as "girl" terms. Part of this was reinforced by a story we had been told about one of the old black blues singers. I don't recall her name anymore, but I have never forgotten how she handled her money. She would get paid in cash, then put the pile of money and a stack of brown paper bags next to each other on a table. After counting the money, she would divide it according to the expenses she had. Ten per cent might go into one bag, 15 percent in another, 5 percent in a third, and so forth. Then she would gather all her staff in front of her and hand her agent, her manager, her accountant, and everyone else the appropriate bag. Each time, she would tell the person the exact percentage owed, and always the cash amount would be correct. One bag would be set aside to pay taxes, and the last bag, containing 40 percent, she would reserve for her own pay.

We just loved that story. The singer handled her business in brown paper bags, something the men probably thought was a "girl way" to see to her financial affairs. Yet she was in control, as we intended to be. She was in control of her life, her money, and the people she paid to handle specialized affairs.

While we had our role models clearly in mind, and while we were able to gain respect by the way we handled ourselves, we were frightened of what we did not know about the business. We were frightened by our growing awareness that in the entertainment business as practiced in Hollywood, no one wants you to have information. No one wants to tell you how anything is done. No one wants to tell you the breakdowns. They want to play a game with you so you are kept naive and dependent upon them so that they can produce your work. Yet producing our own work was our stated goal.

The business of Hollywood actually proved quite simple. The attitude we encountered implied that there was something complex to the business, something that would take years to learn and more years to master. In truth, it was a closed system; gaining access was all that really mattered. When someone talks about needing to hang out in the Polo Lounge in order to make deals, what they're really saying is that they have so little work to do, they can talk, drink, and play cards. The men and women representing the big-money stars can get away with the game. The small players try to do so.

Talent is product. In many instances, it is interchangeable product. You need a short, well-endowed woman between twenty and twenty-five for a role. There are three lines of dialogue. There are perhaps a thousand actresses who could fill the part adequately. The agent whose client gets the part is often the one who is best connected to the producer.

In many instances, bribes still exist in the business. One television network executive was found to be "selling" a week's work on an episode of a popular though brainless situation comedy that used a large, ever-changing cast. He would have sex with the women seeking parts. He made sure they were always appropriate. He made certain they got that week's assignment. Their pay was something over two thousand dollars for the work. He got to play around. And his superiors said nothing because they were having one-night stands with the hired help (actresses and, in some instances, the actors).

The executive was eventually fired. His superiors claimed to be morally outraged by his actions, and they were. However, it wasn't because he was quietly using the casting couch, but because they had discovered that he was also having an intense, long-term affair with a woman who was neither his wife nor his mistress. Cheating on your wife was expected at his level in Hollywood. Casual affairs – whether lunch-hour sex, a one-night stand when out of town, or a long weekend when one's spouse was away – were common. In addition, a single, long-term mistress was an accepted perk of success. But only a heel would cheat on his mistress, and this man made the mistake of letting others know he was doing just that. Fortunately, when he divorced his wife and his mistress dumped him, he had the good sense to marry the woman with whom he had been cheating. That resulted in his being forgiven and led to a new job, this time as a film studio executive instead of with the networks.

Cash bribes were known to occur, and drugs were frequently a commodity of choice for many. But none of these were really necessary. It was a matter of understanding what and how to package a product.

Talent agents and publicists use techniques to get jobs and special attention for their clients. For example, suppose a columnist knows that having an insider story about a famous star will boost interest in her writing. The publicist for that star will promise the columnist an exclusive if she will also use items about several lesser individuals also handled by that publicist.

The same can be true with an agent. If the agent represents a name star very much in demand, the price to a producer for having the name value of that star may be the hiring of a half dozen lesser-known talents also on the agent's client list.

This is the way it is in Hollywood, but it is also typical of business everywhere. Such actions happen in Washington, where the price for having a political connection may be giving a job to that person's spouse or child. Likewise in the business world, a company that has a large corporation for a client may also eventually have a family member of the CEO, the chief buyer, or some other power player on their employee roles. It is the subtlest form of kickback, but it is one that happens daily throughout America. And when it is not about family, it might be about free meals in fancy restaurants, favoritism when awarding contracts, or even hiring old college classmates.

The best agents were concerned with the career development of the talent they represented. They were constantly seeking to stretch the performers, writers, and other professionals they represented. They wanted the person to gain an ever-increasing amount of money, of course, but they also were concerned with positioning them for advancement. Instead of asking Roseanne to play in clubs that were the equivalent of the ones she had played from her Denver base, they helped her gain exposure. She was booked to headline the major clubs, to open for acts playing major cities, to go to Las Vegas, to become exposed to the HBO cable audience. They genuinely wanted her to be in commercials, television, and movies. They wanted her in demand in as many ways as possible, and they worked hard to help her achieve the plans that she and I had developed.

But as I watched what was involved, I realized that anyone could do this work. It was necessary to knock on a lot of doors, but in Hollywood, it was not difficult to know who was going to need what. There are always all manner of information sources for each profession, from their own newsletter or magazine to the trade journals *Variety* and the *Hollywood Reporter*. The latter two tell which producers and directors are putting together the different projects.

If you knew the right people, a little reading and a few telephone calls and it is often possible to get work even before casting officially begins.

But what really bothered me, coming from the Beehive State, where everyone is expected to be competent in several areas, was the make-work attitude. For example, a writer can't take a script to the buyer at a production company. He has to take it to an agent who takes it to the buyer. The agent may not bother reading the script. The agent can't vouch for the competence of the script or even if the material is original. But the writer has to go through the agent.

A person who uses more than one skill is often looked upon with disdain. Hollywood calls a multitalented person a "hyphenate." They talk of producer-writers or director-writers or producer-director-writers. These people are involved with the total control of their product. Oliver Stone, for example, has fantastic wealth from the success he made himself. Yet though he has won many honors, he is still considered suspect because he is competent in more than one area.

Despite all this, I met wonderful people in Hollywood who were willing to share their knowledge and their connections and do anything else they could do to help those in whom they believed. They were as helpful as the men from SCORE and others who had mentored me over the years. They were honorable, earning respect through their integrity, not through favors granted.

There was nothing we could do about the negative side of the system in the short term. Ultimately, the person who had the money had the real power. That was why our plan to create a production company was so important. Our theory that there were hundreds of millions of dollars to be made in the Domestic Goddess idea would ultimately prove correct. What mattered to me was how the money would then be used, and so far as I knew, Rosey shared my goals.

There was also a corporate philosophy we envisioned for the future. First, after we were on top in Hollywood, we would be concerned with economically empowering work-ing-class women. Nothing happens for such women until they can feed themselves and their children. Once they have basic independence through their efforts, they need the help, often in the form of seed money for an entrepre-neurial enterprise, to truly succeed.

I was about to have the opportunity to handle vast sums of money. I felt that I could do it wisely, using it as seed money for others, giving back as we had gained, and letting it grow through nurturing the women who were tradi-tionally ignored in society's economic hierarchy. This stemmed from all our beliefs, including seeing the money in spiritual terms where, if you take vast sums from the uni-verse, you must return vast sums in kind.

This is especially important for women. My generation had the chance to regain the type of freedom through en-trepreneurial enterprises that my mother's generation lacked. In those self-created businesses, women routinely excel because, more than men, they are accustomed to wearing many hats, doing many jobs, in the course of the day. They are willing to make executive decisions, handle sales and marketing, answer the telephone, and clean the corporate toilets if that is what it takes to succeed. More important, they build businesses based on shared power, not the attempt to gain power over another. They succeed in their willingness to work with their staff, with their customers, and others. They do not measure success by who and what they dominate in life.

As much as I knock the eccentricities of some of the agents and managers, the stars are equally eccentric in their demands and perks. Every contract has what is known as a rider attached. This is a personalized addition that details special needs for the star.

Roseanne was usually too professional to take advan-tage of the rider other than for the act. She would specify the type of lighting gels, for example, or the type of drum set that needed to be rented for the musicians. The latter saved the drummer from risking the destruction of bulky equipment as it was toted from city to city. The former referred to a special translucent color material that was placed in front of a spotlight. It would alter the star's appearance just enough to make her look more attractive or a little like a clown, depending upon which type she used. Rosey knew what worked best for her complexion and the clothing she wore. The gels she requested, all commonly available, assured she looked her best on stage.

The only other request Rosey made concerned food. She had learned that the eating habits that we both enjoyed, diets that were loaded with sweets, would not enable her to sustain her energy. She needed to use better judgment in her meals and her exercise. Eventually she hired a personal trainer to help her build endurance, and she requested that the clubs have Diet Coke, popcorn, and a fruit tray for her. Nothing elaborate. Just snacks that would be healthy when she got hungry. (There was one exception. Periodically she would develop cravings where she insisted upon having two types of special food combinations. One was brown rice and strawberries. She also insisted upon having bowls of popcorn and containers of mild green salad peppers. She would cut the ends off the peppers and squeeze their juice on the popcorn before eating it.)

Other stars had extremely eccentric riders that sometimes revealed more of their personality than the public ever got to see. For example, my favorite was the rider for a major beloved comic. This comic had an image as a loving father, a devoted husband, and a humanitarian. He also portrayed himself as being easygoing and laid back.

During one of the times I was in a club office, I happened to see his contract rider. Curious, I read it, discovering that he expected to have, among other things, twelve bottles of Perrier water, fresh limes sliced for use in the Perrier, a cheeseboard, assorted soft drinks, and an espresso machine and a person whose sole job was to run it, along with young women for sex. The young women had to be of legal age, but not much beyond. He wanted consenting adults, and he wanted them of the opposite race. At the same time, he was officially protecting his home life, his beloved wife, his wonderful children, all of whom were supposed to be the focal point of his existence.

One of the major singers loved Life Savers. His rider specified the number of packages of each flavor, as well as the order in which the flavors were to be arrayed when he reached his room.

The one perk we got when making a major tour was a luxury hotel suite. A club might pay $100 to put us up in a suite that officially cost $1,500. Naturally such luxury arrangements were made only during a hotel's down time, when business was slow and occupancy was off. The management needed that room rented at full price, if possible, more than they needed the publicity of having a star for a guest.

We first experienced the joys of special perks when Roseanne was beginning to earn money, big money. She bought a house in a neighborhood where a half-million-dollar home might be considered a modest "fixed-upper special." Bill Pentland was buying expensive cars as a hobby. And she put me on a full-time salary because of the volume of work I was doing. We knew where we were heading (or at least I thought "we" did). The plan all along was to deliver a saleable product to the networks. I was willing to defer credit, title, and money until we achieved that goal.

The salary was modest because of Bill, or so Rosey explained it to me. She kept telling me that Bill Pentland was jealous of anything she paid me, feeling that all the money should remain Rosey's and, because he was her husband, his. He knew I was filling several major roles in the ongoing development of her career, including the continued refinement of her act. However, I think he remembered that I had done that for free back in Denver when we got started. He did not realize that if I was not involved, someone else would have to be paid large sums of money for the same work.

In hindsight, I know that how I handled all this was a mistake. I trusted Rosey. Producing the show, getting a proper credit on the Roseanne Show, co-owning with

Roseanne a production company that would control spin-offs from the show such as cartoons and a line of women's clothes, were subjects Roseanne and I discussed every day. It was part of the ongoing dream we had been building since Denver. Perhaps not formally playing the power game diminished me in the eyes of other businesspeople. Certainly it allowed me to be demeaned by Rosey a few years later, or so I believe. An appropriate title, a job description, and the other aspects of corporate employment would have shown the outside world where I stood. I was naive enough to think that we would be "Sisters" for the rest of our lives, with Rosey performing and me producing. I wanted no title except producer, and that meant that only the people working directly with Rosey ever gave me credit for my efforts. To the outside world, I would eventually be an enigma.

I also did not benefit from Rosey's ever-growing income. I was not the one helping Roseanne to spend the big bucks. Because I worked with her behind the scenes, my expenses were considered "cost of goods sold" on the long tours such as the one with Louie Anderson. My plane flight, my hotel room (usually a shared two-bedroom suite), my meals and ground transportation needs were all paid for. My salary was kept to seventy thousand dollars despite the fact that the work I did, if done for some other star at Rosey's level, would have been a flat percentage fee. Based on that, my income could have been in the low six figures. However, I saw myself as deferring income during the early years of our work together.

What we were doing was a gradually evolving process, no different from what many product businesses experience. There are steps which must be accomplished and secured, one success leading logically to the next, with the ultimate target always in mind. Just as many business managers defer income from the new businesses with which they are involved, so I was doing that with Rosey. I made enough money so I was obviously respected, but I was concerned with where we were heading, not trying to match income with other men and women doing similar

218

work in the industry. In my business training, this was called building the owner's equity account.

It is necessary to remember that I have always viewed Roseanne and her act in many ways. There were important components relating to politics, feminism, the empowerment of working-class women, spiritual connections, and the like. But where I knew I was of greatest value was in analyzing the comics as product, seeing why they did not succeed more frequently than they did. Many comics were brilliant and could have made careers on television and in films. While I think Roseanne's phenomenal success has to do with many factors unrelated to business, the fact that she received the opportunities she did was no accident. And that was the difference I made.

I learned that in any business you analyze your competition. What are their strengths and what are their weaknesses? In addition, when dealing with a product that has to be marketed, what about the marketing of rival products that either works or seems to fail?

Our timing in launching Roseanne, the product, was flawless. The mass media was not yet saturated with issues relating to the roles of men and women in work, in sex, and in raising children. Thus Rosey was almost a first, a strong feminist, working-class voice with ideas and observations to which many men and women could relate. She was new, she was different, and she was one step ahead of the society at large when she first hit the stage in Denver.

By the time Roseanne reached Los Angeles, men and women were reevaluating their roles and relationships. The popular culture was filled with articles and television discussions about these problems. Radio call-in shows were swamped with people expressing opinions or seeking advice. Rosey's voice, having been a pioneer in this type of observational comedy, was increasingly respected, increasingly in demand. What went unnoticed except by those who had worked with us in the formative years was that her evolution from regional comic to national star had been carefully orchestrated by me.

I had seen that most comics waited to be discovered.

They developed an act, they went on stage, and so long as they seemed to be playing ever larger cities and receiving ever larger paychecks, they felt on their way to success. One day they would be discovered. One day they would be offered the television series or the movie role of their dreams. Yet most never made it, regardless of talent.

I knew better. The idea of waiting to be discovered was hilarious to me. A product, including a comic, required the careful short-term and long-term planning for its introduction into the marketplace.

Business courses teach that marketing success involves having a product someone will desire, a price they can afford, effective placement in the marketplace, and promotion to make people aware of them. This is called "the Four P's."

In Denver, we developed that product through the constant refinement of her humor and the development of a stage presence. Sometimes she would try to be like Joan Rivers, taking a chair to the edge of the stage and rapping with the audience. At other times she put on jewels and furs, trying a glamorous image. She was looking for what would fit her best, what would fit the material we were writing, rewriting, tossing, or refining.

Roseanne was nothing more than a raw joke-telling emcee during that first "Take Back the Mike Night." The comedy she was doing was the radical feminist material we discussed at the bookstore. However, we listened when the owner of one of the comedy clubs told us that if Rosey wanted a soapbox, she should get one. Nobody wanted to hear it. But we wanted to say it. We knew that if we wanted a soapbox, we would have to build it. We needed a popular program, a forum that would allow us to say what we wanted to say in a format that made sense on TV. Within five years we created *Roseanne* to do just that.

The problem was that we wanted to continue getting across the same message – that mothers and working class women were not idiots. Women's work has value. Women see the world differently from men, and that vision is equally as valid as the male perspective. We are not powerless. We are not victims. We are not lacking in ability. And to get across the message, we made the conscious decision for Rosey to retool the edge to her material and become more of a mainstream comic. In the context of the times, she stopped sounding like what was then called "Lezzies" (lesbians) in order to gain a far larger market share than just radical, profeminist audiences.

There were several results, going back to the Four P's concept. Promotion was the most important. Suddenly Rosey was being interviewed by the mainstream press. There she could make serious statements and open meaningful discussions. She was able to say during interviews that, as a woman, she had no country. There was no justice for women in the world. She talked about how justice serves only them who serve themselves. She explained to men and to the wealthy that when you don't look personally powerless, they world doesn't look unfair.

The process was logical. First find what we wanted to say. Then refine the act so mainstream audiences would hear her. And with that came the press, making Roseanne ever more important, ever more of a national figure through the interviews they published. The product was created. The placement had moved horizontally across the country, from the first club to the Laff-Off to Mitzi Shore, HBO, the tour with Louie Anderson, the movie and the series that would make national news.

I focused on the process, knowing it would achieve our goals. Others focused only on the goal. Even the most successful were likely to stumble along the way because the process was not thought real.

My excitement comes from getting an idea and making it real. I love putting together a map that leads to the success of what had once only been a concept. And when I chose to do such work with Rosey's comedy career, I provided a map to success that did not require magical discovery by some "big name" who just might drop into a club in Denver, Kansas City, or St. Louis. That was why Rosey took Hollywood on time and as scheduled while most other comics only reach Hollywood in their dreams.

The Rosey/Louie Anderson tour, which lasted nine months

from the end of 1986 through the start of 1987, was planned around weekends. Thursday was spent traveling to the city where they would play in. Friday and Saturday would involve from one to three shows each night, and Sunday we would return home to Los Angeles. Rosey traveled with as many as ten changes of clothing in three large suitcases, making certain she always had something that looked and felt right to her on stage. I stayed both backstage and in the audience, my tape recorder always present to monitor the act and make notes.

7 The Roseanne Barr Show

By the end of 1987, Roseanne Barr was the most important comedian in the United States. There was reason
for some in the media to dislike her, of course. Contemporary wisdom in the entertainment industry found her too
fat, too mouthy, and too controversial. Many industry
executives were convinced that the American public
wanted its television stars to be glamorous and the portrayal of family life to be uplifting. They ignored the fact
that most women were overtired and overweight, and that
despite loving their husbands and kids, they experienced
times when they were fed up with having them underfoot.
When the network executives claimed they were programming for men who liked watching sexy women, they
ignored the fact that, in real life, those same men were
making love to women closer in appearance to Roseanne
than Vanna White. They also did not see that a large number of men were changing, were attempting to at least
understand the women's movement, and thus could relate
to much of Rosey's humor.

Some of Rosey's jokes had become classics, lines the
public wanted to hear delivered in her slightly whiny manner. Magazine and newspaper writers were constantly
quoting such jokes as "I've been married fifteen years. I
have three kids because I breed well in captivity." Or "My
husband says, 'Roseanne, don't you think we ought to talk
about our sexual problems?' Like I'm gonna turn off
Wheel of Fortune for that."

Rosey was quoted on everything from her sex life, which
she described as a normal bodily function, like an aneu-
rysm or a heart attack, to her mixed marriage. She
explained that there is a Jewish tradition in which the
groom crushes a glass under his foot as a symbol of the

scattering of Israel. However, as Roseanne was telling it, "for the sake of my family, he [Bill, a Gentile] crushed a beer can under his heel. For his folks, I pretended I was a virgin."

She was interviewed for everything from the regional publication *Utah Holiday* to *Vogue*. *Playboy* did its first interview with her in May of that year. She was featured in *People* weekly and in *Adweek* because of television commercials for the giant supermarket chain in California and the national Pizza Hut commercials.

The quotes used varied with the publication. Sophisticated urban papers like the *Los Angeles Times* delighted in perpetuating the "hick" image of Roseanne. They mentioned her jokes about being insulted in a local clothing shop in the blue-collar neighborhood where she supposedly lived – "I slammed the door so hard, the trailer fell off the cinder blocks" – and her comments about small-town gourmet dining, such as the restaurant resting high atop the Texaco station where she enjoyed "Linguine Boy-Ar-Dee."

But everyone loved her stories about contemporary culture, such as the bit about *The Phil Donahue Show*. "You can really learn from *Donahue*. I didn't know you could be a woman in a man's body." She would pause, then explain how you could tell the difference. "You go out and you can't parallel park."

I knew that some members of the press could be gullible, and they were the ones on whom I counted for generating the publicity that would move Rosey's career to the next stage we had planned. Rosey was a star, and many reporters jumped at the chance to get an exclusive story from a star in order to win the respect of their editors. After all, the entertainment beat is not the most prestigious. A reporter on the beat spends much of his or her time watching television, going to movies, watching plays, and attending press conferences with the hunk and bimbo of the moment. Compared with the men and women who cover hard news – wars, the social issues affecting the cities, and the like – they have little chance to gain respect. That's why they like the opportunity to be seen as a celebrity insider, as someone who is so skilled that he or she has developed exclusive contacts with the stars.

Rosey and I understood this, and many times we would arrange for private interviews where Rosey would often say outrageous things as though they were the truth. She delighted in manipulating them, and they were thrilled to have a story no one else could get. Checking to see if it was true might have hurt their new "friend," and they were not about to do that. It was better to print what might be a lie, quoting Rosey without editing to protect themselves from libel, than to do the digging that would have revealed the truth.

I was always fascinated with the fact that such manipulation was common to both coasts and both glamour professions – entertainment and politics. Hollywood agents also represented many politicians. For example, I believe the publicist for the company that backed the creation of Rosey's television show also represented former President Gerald Ford.

Not all of this was bad. The media was where Rosey could reveal her intelligence, could bring out the ideas we had discussed for so many years. And when the reporters realized that she had substance, she was not just some overweight, raging, raving bitch who knew how to read a script, they were even more smitten by her. Yet that respect was another reason they did not dig deeper, did not discover that Rosey believed she must always keep private feelings from being revealed in public statements.

Ironically, the politicians followed the same procedure. A politician could reveal compassion for controversial issues in private interviews. The press would reveal a side of the politician that gained the respect of one or another special interest group, and the reporter seldom would dig deeply enough to realize that the voting record of that same politician proved he worked against what he publicly seemed to support.

Our brother, Ben, has said that he believes that once Rosey learned how easy it was for a celebrity to manipulate some members of the media, she became a junkie. He feels that her drug of choice is power, and that the media is her enabler.

I was thrilled with Rosey's ability to manipulate the press as I guided her. I just had no idea that one day she would use the skills she learned to shatter her own family.

Rosey's base of fans was probably composed of the same blue-collar women we tried to reach through the bookstore in Denver. But her jokes were increasingly quoted by sophisticated newspaper columnists, corporate executives taking a break at the water cooler, small business owners, and others.

Commercial offers came in on a regular basis, though Rosey avoided most of them, especially if they focused on her weight rather than the character she had developed. For example, M. Susan Blake, of the advertising firm Ogilvy & Mather, contacted Russ Garrison about having Roseanne handle the NutraSweet account. The agreement showed how important she was perceived to be. According to the terms of the contract for the humorous commercial that also attacked NutraSweet competitor Sweet'n Low, there were to be four payments. The first was for $33,500 and involved the shooting of the commercial through the end of 1987. The other payments, which were optional and based on airing the commercials in three different regions of the United States, would pay her $70,000 split equally for the southeastern and eastern regions, and $55,000 for airing the rest of the country. The only restrictions were that she could not represent other artificial or natural sweeteners (corn syrup, fructose, honey, sugar, saccharine, and the like), or products that used competing artificial sweeteners.

I respected Rosey for another reason during this period. It seemed that everyone wanted her for products that ranged from toilet bowl cleaners to prepackaged desserts. I know she could have made millions of dollars if she was willing to grab at every offer. But Rosey had integrity and refused to endorse anything she did not believe in. Of course, Rosey, being Rosey, did not refuse companies out of political correctness. She did not check a firm's record on the rain forest destruction, release of gases into the ozone layer, or willingness to fund inner-city Head Start programs. The two endorsements I remember her accepting involved a grocery store chain where she loved to shop and a fur company – Rosey loved to wear glamorous coats made from expensive leather and mink.

Rosey had approval of the storyboards, the series of annotated sketches that form a rough draft of the ad. And the large sums of money and the enthusiasm of the advertising agencies are proof that she had become important to American consumers.

I was thrilled. Not only was Rosey entertaining, but increasingly some of the messages we had been trying to spread were getting across. Paul Swenson, writing for the August 1987 issue of *Utah Holiday*, quoted her as saying: "A few years ago we would not have imagined Danny DeVito or Rodney Dangerfield as a leading man. I think Oprah is sexy. Maybe people are becoming just a little more sophisticated [about different body styles]. Maybe we're opening up as a culture. There will always be the Neanderthal element, but nobody really talks much about the fact that we're a spiritual country. Maybe some of the barriers between spirituality and sensuality are being broken down. If it's happening, it's because of the women's movement. Do you know what 'erotic' means? It means 'with spirit,' and that's what it's always meant."

The money was also coming in. Rosey had become enough of a star so that she was paid a guaranteed income of several thousand dollars a performance plus a percentage of the gross. For example, one place might offer her $7,000 or $8,000 and have in the contract that the promoter's costs were such that perhaps $35,000 was needed to begin making any money. Then the contract might call for Rosey to get her guaranteed money plus 40 per cent of every dollar in excess of that $35,00 minimum.

It was in the midst of this success that Home Box Office contacted Triad Artists, Roseanne's agents, about a special. HBO was actively pursuing the best newer comedians in the country for a series of one-person specials. They were traditionally filmed in a club, a re-creation of the act being performed wherever the person was appearing. Such work was relatively inexpensive to produce, and the response was so strong that everyone profited.

The HBO special was right on schedule, much like the Carson appearance eighteen months earlier. We had been planning for such a showcase to launch what would be our first production and Roseanne's television show. This was the "pilot" for showing what we could do, where we could introduce concepts that would be the basis for a regular network show. As such, it was one of the critical building blocks in the process of structuring her career. I knew I was a step closer to becoming a producer. We both knew that we had to do it right or the opportunity would be wasted.

We decided to subtly take control of the program by doing more than HBO expected, and by doing it in a way that would prove that the concept for the Roseanne show would work. Rosey had to do stand-up, of course. The specials HBO was backing all revolved around a stand-up comic. But we also included segments in what was supposed to be Rosey's trailer home. We cut to the kitchen in the home where Rosey and her family supposedly lived. Unlike her glamor look on the stage, nothing was "right" in the home. The kitchen was cluttered with dirty dishes, food in various stages of preparation, and the turmoil known to all hardworking families. It was actually the model for what would become the Conner family home on the series, but by using it for humor on the special, we proved that Americans loved the mirror of their own real lives.

We created a show within a show. Roseanne combined segments in her "home" with her stage performance. We broke things down to a 75 percent/25 percent ratio, with the bulk of the time she would be given spent doing her stand-up. But the other 25 percent was with her "real" family at home, preparing for the special and hearing their reaction to it. Toward this end we used two husbands, one as an on-stage foil and the other at "home."

We had no intention of dragging Jessica, Jennifer and Jake into the show. Instead, we hired three actors to play the children, who were called upon to quarrel with each other, whine, and never understand why their mom has to keep leaving to go to work. The kid actors met my nieces and nephews to get a feel for the family. In addition, since Bill was interested in stand-up and was actually writing some of Rosey's material, we recruited him to be her husband in the segments done in their home, the large house trailer. This fit her image at home of the struggling housewife in a blue-collar world.

The man we hired for her on-stage husband was a comic named Tom Arnold, a man who, according to Dad, had performed as Rosey's opening act in a Minneapolis club, among other places. Rosey was comfortable with him, and comfortable with his understanding of her character. At the time, Rosey told me that Tom was her really good friend, that he "got the joke." He would do anything to make her laugh, no matter how mean spirited or outrageous. For example, when I picked him up at the airport for the HBO special, we were waiting for luggage along with a woman and her toddler son, who was attached to one of those tether devices for little kids.

Tom looked at the kid and the leashlike device. Then he walked over to the woman and said, "Has it had its shots yet?" The woman was outraged. Others who overheard looked at the child, the leash device, and the mother, then began laughing. It was in-your-face comedy, hilarious, at its best, hurtful to the person who takes the brunt of the joke at times, but always an area where he was at his funniest on and off the stage.

I came to realize that when Rosey said, "He gets the joke," she meant that Tom, like Rosey, saw life as a world filled with comedy. There were no limits to what they would do – no floor, no ceiling, no walls. If they saw something as funny, they would not edit themselves. They would not think of the pain their jokes might cause, nor would they consider the propriety of the remark. They would do anything, say anything, to amuse themselves and whatever audience found the moment as funny as they did.

Despite this relationship at the time, I don't remember Tom being very involved with the writing of the show, if he did any at all. Instead, Bill Pentland was a major contributor of jokes. He had learned to put a mirror to his former self, then to create jokes about that time in a manner that would seem natural to Rosey. He received equal credit with Rosey and a writer named Rocco Urbisci when the show was aired.

Making the special was a learning process for all of us. The various television guilds have ways of determining credits, and those credits not only identify what you did, they also help you sell yourself later in your career. While I wanted to produce, I could not be the executive producer. The executive producer not only coordinates everything, he or she puts up the money. There was no way I could underwrite the show, but I was hoping to apprentice, to learn through watching and handling whatever work matched my existing skills.

Herbie Nannas was Rosey's manager and the man who arranged for Syd Vinnedge to provide the money and get the credit for producing the HBO special. In exchange, Herbie was also given a producer credit, something Herbie believed he deserved for making the telephone calls to put it together. After all, we only created the concept, developed the act, developed the broader concept for the HBO special, found the talent, wrote the special, and ... You get the idea. It was his power play. It was also a primary reason why he was soon to be fired.

I later came to realize that Herbie and all the others like him with whom we had to work at HBO, at the Carsey-Werner Company that underwrote the Roseanne show, and elsewhere, thought they deserved the credit they claimed. We were nothing. It was as though they put up the money for Rosey and me to design a house, build the house, furnish it with exquisite furniture and appointments, and turn it into a major tourist attraction, after which they would come by and say to the visitors, "Do you like my creation?"

At the time, learning about the credits and what they

might mean in the long run did not seem critical. I was intensely driven back then, constantly thinking ahead. As much as I thrilled to each new achievement, I was also aware that once the contract was signed, I had to be thinking about the next step. Rosey's contract signing for the HOB special, which was completed in July 1987, and which gave them the right to a second show, accomplished part of our ten-year plan. Even as we were preparing for that special, part of my mind was working on the television show, the production company, and the other projects that were finally obviously within reach.

Ultimately the project was packaged by Syd and John Vinnedge of Scotti Brothers/Syd Vinnedge Television. They had been working to promote Roseanne with the networks, syndicators, buyers of pay cable, and the like. They had made contact with HBO and coordinated the program as well as the personnel. These included Rocco Urbisci, a delightful, understanding man who acted as both a writer, working with the rest of us, and director.

Rocco met with us in our suite in the Las Vegas Desert Inn where Rosey was performing while preparing for the special. Rosey and I were tired from being on the road, tense about the upcoming special, and concerned about antagonism she was encountering with her career nearing the top. Hostile telegrams were being sent by someone, presumably a female comic who considered my sister her rival. They read "Stop stealing from Judy" and "Stop stealing from the world." Because of the name, we had a suspicion who was involved. Yet they could just as easily have come from some other comic's fans. We never knew for certain, and there was no way to narrow our suspicions or stop the messages. For me, they were a nuisance. Rosey, by contrast, was so outraged that she obsessed on the problem, often weeping and having trouble focusing on her work.

We closed all the drapes to darken the room. We drank tea and water. We ran cold water up and down our arms. I had several white Sabbath candles with me which we lit for illumination and ritual significance. We were trying to relax, to regain our focus. We lit incense to fill the room with familiar aromas, to overcome the smells of past visitors, the sensations that would detract from our purpose. Then we took out a deck of tarot cards and did a reading, something we had done in the past in order to give ourselves clarity. Ever since the bookstore days when she was first exposed to the cards, she always had a deck and read them frequently, especially when she felt uncertain about where her immediate focus should be. Then, as we finished the reading, Rocco came in to talk. Whether it was the intensity of the energy in the room, which he said he felt, or his inherent honesty, he decided to be our friend. In addition to working on the material, he tried to explain more about the way the industry functioned – the producer credit, the budget, and the business of control. We knew that after the HBO special we would have to make some changes, one of which was the firing of Herbie Nannas and his partner, Rosey's manager. But for the moment there was nothing we could do beyond what we were doing – trying to create the best show possible, and trying to learn the business to assure the success of our future plans.

The Vinnedges were responsible for budgeting the show and making certain that all personnel functioned as contracted. They were paid $25,000 though they also assumed the risk of an over-budget production. Had the program cost more than they agreed to take from HBO, they would have had to cover the difference. Naturally they had insurance towards this end, but their insurance had a $25,000 deductible as an incentive to keep within the allocated money.

While this was an important time for us, it was not a happy time. We were green in Hollywood. We knew we could get fucked. That's the favorite pastime of Hollywood business professionals. What we didn't understand was where the problems would come from or what we could do to cover ourselves. Rocco was the first one to break the insider's code, yet even his knowledge was less than we eventually found we needed.

We were also exhausted. Everything was process, and

there was little time to assimilate, to analyze, to seek alternatives. There was never a moment for celebration, because there was just too much to do.

Everyone was nervous as the Home Box Office special approached. Roseanne was having trouble with focus. Bill was somewhat paranoid. Everybody was writing, and everybody wanted to try something different. Not all of it was good, but the main point was to experiment, to reach beyond the act and the usual HBO fare.

For example, during the opening of the show, Roseanne, Bill, and their two "daughters" are in the trailer home with a woman identified as Aunt Grace. Rosey is trying out jokes for the act when it opens, and her husband and daughters are delighted in her work. At the same time, Aunt Grace is interrupting with questions about a carryout pizza delivery and mention of Bill's cousin Don. Bill explains that he has no cousin Don as Rosey resents Aunt Grace's interruptions while she prepares to appear on stage.

Aunt Grace gets mad and starts criticizing Rosey, insisting she change her jokes to ones like those that had been used in vaudeville – "My girlfriend is always melancholy. She had a head like a melon and a face like a collie." Rosie tries to be nice, but Aunt Grace finally realizes that her interruptions are not appreciated, leaving the room. That is when the truth is learned.

Bill says, "You know, your aunt is a pain in the ass."

Roseanne says, "My ... I don't even have an aunt, it's your aunt – what are you talking about?"

This is followed by a news show where the newscaster says: ". . . and on a lighter note . . . Grace 'the Aunt' Plotsky has escaped once again from Sunnydale sanatorium. Police are warning people to be on the look out for Plotsky, who is well known for slipping into people's homes, stealing their food, criticizing them unmercifully . . . generally behaving like a member of the family."

There is also a commercial for a product called "Fem-Rage, for that one time of the month when you're allowed to be yourself."

Then Roseanne appears on the show itself. It was taped in the Mayfair Theater in Santa Monica, California, and though it is supposedly live, she keeps getting interrupted by her children. She is periodically forced to return to the trailer in which they live, a trailer near the theater, so she can handle a domestic crisis.

In the stand-up portion, every topic was covered, from being Jewish in Salt Lake City – "For a synagogue we had to sublet space out of a Fotomat booth" – to crude bodily functions – "My son is into that nose-picking stuff. . . . I tell him if you're going to pick in public, at least do it like an adult." Then she did a bit about adults who subtly pick their noses while driving in their cars, stopped at traffic lights.

There was something to offend everyone. At the same time, the special broadened her audience and established her in a manner that had previously been impossible. No one would turn off the show with their reactions in neutral. Roseanne was going to make the impact on television that she had been making in the nightclubs and large auditoriums.

The problem we were facing when planning the HBO special was not so much with the material and the structure of the show, but the location. Rosey needed the right audience to perform most effectively.

Like many comics, Rosey feeds off the audience, and the audience she wanted was in our old hometown, Salt Lake City. Rosey had left Salt Lake City when the population was 80 per cent Mormon. But there had been an influx of new people to the community, mostly non-Mormon. They had experienced the aggressiveness of the Mormon missionaries and their evangelical zeal. Among these newcomers were several thousand who wanted to see a local girl who had broken out of the mold, become successful, and now was talking back to the establishment.

We took Rocco, Herbie, and representatives from Syd Vinnedge to Salt Lake City, renting a van to give them a tour of the community. We showed them the architecture, the layout of the community, the beauty of the surrounding land, and the inadvertent humor that was there. For example, the Mormon church in the heart of the city took on a very odd appearance from the air. I always found it to be the ultimate phallic symbol – penis-shaped with two globelike smaller structures on each side. From the air, fliers would see what to me was obviously an erection.

Rosey and I wanted to have a helicopter-mounted camera take an aerial panoramic look at the city. We would show the beautiful and the humorous, giving a feel for the land we loved and hated. Then we would hold the concert in one of the beautifully renovated nineteenth-century buildings whose meeting halls would be adequate for the camera crew, sound crew, and other technical people, as well as the several hundred people for whom Rosey would perform.

Roseanne's manager did not want to use Salt Lake City. We were told this was a budget issue, though we were not allowed to learn what the budget might be. We didn't know if some of the people involved, including her manager, might be able to take a bigger personal slice if the costs were kept unusually low, or if there might be real concerns. I kept asking for the figures so we could decide what was best, but these were denied us.

The manager said that the audience was not all that important. Instead of listening to his client, he wanted to buy an audience and bus them to a theater in San Diego.

Most people don't realize that many shows buy audiences. They will send marketing people to popular tourist entertainment attractions in Hollywood. Questions are asked, and the people who respond in a way that seems appropriate will be given free passes to a show that is going to be taped. Sometimes the people are invited to just show up, since the taping is near where they are being interviewed. In the case of the HBO special, the idea was to tape in San Diego and bus the selected viewers.

The problem with a bought audience was that there was no way to tell their attitude toward Roseanne. The crowd you can find inside a movie theater, for example, does not necessarily include the type of people who would be strong supporters of Rosey. We knew that no one but fans would turn out in Salt Lake City. San Diego offered us no control.

Finally a compromise of sorts was reached. There would be no taping in either San Diego or Salt Lake City. Instead, the work would be done in the Mayflower Theatre in Santa Monica. The theater was an older one with the grandeur we had been seeking in Salt Lake City. And the director decided to go with our idea of using an aerial view of the area as a lead-in.

I was allowed to control the selection of a portion of the people who were in the audience. We couldn't dominate the theater with people who were pro-Rosey, though we could control those who would sit in the first few rows, the only ones whom Rosey could see. She would be partially blinded by the spotlights, like all stage entertainers. And she would not be able to draw the energy of a house full of wildly enthusiastic fans as she would have done in Salt Lake City. However, the compromise helped.

There would be three parts to the audience. The most important were Rosey's friends, especially comics who truly supported her. They would cheer and laugh and generally have a wonderful time with her. I arranged for them to be as close to the front as possible, allowing for the camera setups which, of course, got priority placement in order to most effectively film the show.

We also use some loyal fans. There had been a publicity contest earlier where you had to explain why you were willing to help clean Rosey's house. The twenty-five lucky fans who won the contest never actually saw Roseanne's home. She wouldn't allow that. Instead, they got to go to the taping of the HBO special and the party afterward, and they received autographed photographs showing each of them with Rosey.

Next I passed out tickets in much the same way the marketing people would have done in order to buy the house. I did it differently, though. I went to the area around Sunset Boulevard where there was a strong counterculture. The street, and the side streets running off it, had everything from conservative hotels, such as the Sunset Hyatt where people such as the late Broadway producer Joseph Papp often stayed when visiting California, to the La Cage aux Folles club on La Cienega. I went there as well as to other nightclubs in West Hollywood. I knew the patrons would appreciate both Roseanne's act and the free passes.

The third portion of the audience was comprised of production people, management people, and their friends. These were the industry insiders quite separate from the talent. They were professionally jaded, more interested in being seen than seeing the show. Some were high-level executives an agent or manager was trying to impress by showing off the rising new talent. Others were has-beens, still-important people on their way down in the industry.

Ultimately there were only a couple hundred people in the audience, and the bulk of the house was outside our control. The front four rows of people were enthusiastic enough to help bolster her act, though it was not the house we would have liked. However, the program went well enough that we soon heard from the two most important people in television comedy shows in the 1980s, Marcy Carsey and Tom Werner.

Had Carsey-Werner, their production company, produced only their one most famous show, *The Cosby Show*, they would have made television history. The long-running story of the Huxtable family, headed by Cosby, dominated American television ratings in the 1980s. There were many parts of the country where water consumption dramatically increased from flushing during *The Cosby Show* commercials because that was when so many Americans took a break to go to the bathroom. So when Carsey-Werner approached Roseanne about developing a television pilot, we were excited. We knew that Carsey-Werner had just syndicated Bill Cosby for more money than had ever been earned before. Everyone involved in a meaningful way with *The Cosby Show* was instantly rich almost beyond greed (by 1993, Cosby was so rich that he, along with a few partners, was able to make a serious bid to buy the NBC television network). Even better, they had developed a way to spin off one of the Huxtable children into the series *A Different World*. While the show was not nearly so profitable as *The Cosby Show*, it easily held its own in the ratings.

But Carsey-Werner had other successes, and would continue developing product based, in part, on a formula. The shows were original, and in the case of *The Cosby Show*, the casting was nontraditional for the generally racist networks. But the idea was the same. So far as I could tell, Carsey-Werner took comics with an established name and following, then built a show around them. A base audience was guaranteed, and if the product was effective, the show would become successful much faster than normal. Roseanne was to be their next success.

Yet for all of the feel-goodness of *Cosby*, I quickly learned that television is all about power. It is seldom about quality product. It is not about vision. It is rarely about social change.

Television can have an impact on the viewer, of course. A good story, well told, can change a life. Books are more effective because there is more time to create images in the minds of the readers, but someone watching television does not have to feel he or she is wasting time. The way a show is cast, the way characters are portrayed, the image of family presented, and the type of behavior of the characters can all have an influence on the viewer. This can be positive, as in *The Cosby Show*'s opening up the reality of the successful urban black family. Or it can be negative, such as the much more usual portrayal of black males as villains on crime shows.

We wanted to show a normal family, and by that I mean one that is lovingly dysfunctional. The shows of the 1950s created flawless family units with everyone having a special place and delighting in their role. Real life has frustration, seemingly endless bickering among parents and children, yet an intense and highly protective love that ultimately lets them triumph in life.

Roseanne's having her own television series was part of our plan and fit a very definite timetable. We knew the characters we wanted, and that the show would be a mix of fantasy and Roseanne's real life.

For example, there would be Jackie, Roseanne's TV sister, who would be better educated, independent, single, and happy with her life and work. Jackie was me, just as Roseanne Conner was Roseanne Barr. And this meant that, in approximately two years, it would become obvious that Jackie was a lesbian.

It is important to note, based on publicity stunts Roseanne and her second husband, Tom Arnold, have pulled since then, that the lesbian character would not be defined sexually. There is a bias in television writing that says there are only two ways to show gay and lesbian people. One is to show them according to stereotype – the limp-wristed man who speaks with a hint of a lisp, and the bull dyke female with close-cropped hair and the personality of a Marine Corps drill instructor. The other is to shock the audience by stressing sex. Until the episode of *Roseanne* that featured the kiss between Mariel Hemingway and Roseanne, there seemed to be a race to see who could find a plot where two men or two women kissed on screen. Hinting at nudity in bed would be even better according to such thinking.

There may be nothing wrong with sexuality in context, but if you think about the vast numbers of hours of television featuring heterosexuals, most programs do not show couples having sex. Even today, when the production companies are trying to stretch the limits of moral acceptability, most shows do not have nudity or sex to stress the heterosexual nature of their stars.

We wanted to show a woman – Jackie – having a full, rich, rewarding life with both men and women. The only difference would be that if she dated someone, if she lived with someone, it would be a woman. After all, for the vast majority of gays and lesbians, the only way anyone knows their sexual orientation is if they try to invade their private lives. The people who look like the stereotype "queer" are actually in the minority. Thus Jackie would become the first whole person on television whose sexual orientation would not be heterosexual and whose story would not re-volve around stereotypes or heroically dying from AIDS. (Actually, much of the historical literature with lesbian characters has them falling into what one writer called a "well of loneliness," so emotionally isolated that they had to kill themselves. The "necessity" of suicide by insane les-bians became a joke among my friends, a stereotype with no basis in reality.)

We also planned to spin off Jackie so she could have her own show. The character of Jackie was radically different from the character of Roseanne. Each had her own strengths, as we envisioned it, and each could ultimately carry their own program. We planned to use the show's scripts to make statements that just might cause people to think differently than they had in the past.

I cannot stress enough my feelings about the Jackie character spinoff. It became my mission, my passion. It was what I thought about for part of every single day, just like the Mormon missionary boys on their bicycles riding endless miles and talking to countless people with an in-tensity that never diminished. The Conner family of Roseanne would create the context from which *Jackie's World* could be spun off just as *A Different World* was spun off from *The Cosby Show*.

I knew in the beginning that I couldn't pitch a lesbian sit-com called *Jackie's World*. Instead, we put the seeds of it in *Roseanne*, something that could be nurtured along with the viewers until it blossomed into acceptance like any other spin-off.

From the inception of Roseanne, over what seemed like thousands of discussions with Rosey about the creation and development of the Jackie character, I thought we had the same goal. With the success of the show, we would have the power and the clout to do what had never been done before, giving a lesbian character her own program. Yet instead of making it the in-your-face kind of program people assume gays and lesbians desire, we would expand the viewing audience's comfort level. The viewer would embrace Jackie because he or she had already embraced the diversity of the Conners in their everyday lives.

240

Jackie's relationship with Dan, Roseanne's television husband, would be the same as mine with Bill Pentland, the man who was still her real-life husband. He would be jealous of the close friendship between Roseanne and Jackie. He would resent the time the two women and their friends spent together. Yet in a crisis, there would be a real love and respect for each other.

Likewise there would be tension between Bill and the women with whom Roseanne worked. The factory work and the friendships there would be as important in the storytelling as the family. The workplace is a home for blue-collar women. It is a place of close friendship, a support system that would help Roseanne with all aspects of her life. This also would let us develop material from more than just the home, and to bring in friends such as Crystal. There would be bitch sessions, and while they might include men, they would also be about men.

Historically what I jokingly called bitch sessions have actually been very important activities for women staying at home. They are isolated from others. Their primary focus involves children too young to participate in meaningful conversations and men who are either away or see themselves as too tired to talk. Women sharing over coffee, like women talking over the back fence in the suburban housing tracts of post-World War II America, provide a greater context to life. Together they combat loneliness, they resolve trauma, they empower one another to live happier lives. These sessions are support groups, though never formally defined as such.

If all this sounds familiar, it was very much based on what we encountered in the Woman To Woman Bookstore in Denver. That was a world to which many women could relate. That was a world where home, work, and issues concerning what it meant to be a woman, to be a unique person, were handled.

There were two problems I could not anticipate. First, the show's writers did not understand the relationship of sisters, whether biological or the extended sisterhood of female friends. Male bonding and the emotional relationships of brothers have been themes in popular culture for years. One brother must avenge the death of the other. One brother fights to replace the other at the front lines in battle. One brother gives up a kidney for the other who is dying from renal failure.

Westerns, gangster movies, and other art forms have long dealt with brothers. But the culture of women's relationships has only been lived, it has not been reflected by popular culture. And the writers did not know how to research what they had neither lived, nor read, nor witnessed. Even worse, they had so much trouble defining characters that they kept confusing Jackie and Roseanne when writing for the two quite different sisters.

The second problem, unrelated to the show, was what would happen when Rosey and I had a falling out. We never thought about this for the show, but the reality of sisters is that there can be a negative side, a world with few controls. When girls fight in a schoolyard, more people are drawn to watch than when boys go at it, because girl fights are vicious. They have fewer limits when riled. They want to hurt in ways that boys do not consider. Perhaps testosterone makes boys more prone to violent behavior, but once girls cross over the line, they stretch the boundaries to almost terrifying limits. And eventually I was to discover this dimension after the relationship with my older sister, which I had spent so long in cultivating, was shattered by Rosey's actions.

The show would be funny. Classic situation comedies like *The Donna Reed Show* used to have the children love and mutually support each other by the end of each episode. *The Cosby Show* had his children plotting to get to college. The three kids who played Roseanne's children would be normal. That meant that they were always plotting to kill each other. They would be bratty, rebellious, and real. They would be loved. There would also be times when Mom would be sick of them and want them to just go away for a few hours of peace.

Most important, the show would reveal that working-class people were not dumb. They had aspirations. They just lacked money.

The program would also be a mirror to real life. The Conners could become frustrated, tired, irritable, and unable to even think about looking their best. They could hurt each other with their words. They could want to walk away from their children and each other when the stress of daily living seemed almost overwhelming. And there was nothing wrong with that. Everyone tends to experience such feelings in life, but the other programs on television only allowed viewers to see an idealized world no family could attain.

The show's messages would be subtle, such as when Darlene, the youngest daughter, got her period. To those of us in the women's movement in Denver, there was something exciting about the menses. Women have a twenty-eight day cycle like the moon, a fact that has all manner of goddess connections from ancient times. But more important, it is a constant reminder of a woman's strength. Once a month a woman bleeds without dying, without becoming anemic. She has eggs that can become new life. The cycle is life-affirming. It is about the creation of new life, not destruction. It is to be celebrated. In fact, we often talk about why there weren't greeting cards congratulating a young woman on her first period.

This may sound odd to men, but it is something women can understand. It is also a topic normally not handled on television, or handled in a very trite way, as we quickly discovered.

Matt Williams, the man placed in charge of the *Roseanne* show after she signed with Carsey-Werner, was a well-established writer who earned an Emmy for one of his *Cosby* scripts. Carsey-Werner saw him as reliable, trustworthy, and able to put together the kind of program *they* wanted. He was in full charge of the writing staff, and he was also a man who had been raised in a motherless home. His father had reared him, and that made him perhaps the worst possible choice for understanding a woman's comedy, especially a segment on menstruation.

The script that was originally created for that particular episode had Darlene becoming very upset. She was twelve years old and had long been quite athletic. With the first menstruation, she reluctantly put away her sports equipment in order to enter womanhood. Then the show ended with her taking two aspirins and lying down. It was disgusting.

Roseanne did not play the show as originally written. Instead, I rewrote parts of the script in Rosey's dressing room so the Roseanne character explained how menstruation was proof of her strength. In our version, she asks Darlene. "Do you think Jackie Joyner quit running when *she* got her first period?" The thought of a strong female role model just never seemed to occur to Matt and the other writers.

But until they were fired, Matt Williams and his staff just did not get it. They accepted some of the changes to their story lines, yet they did not truly understand Roseanne. It was a power struggle from the very beginning. Matt was protecting his turf and we were protecting our vision.

The writing staff was hardly blue-collar. They did not understand the value system that prized the stability of the family over the cleanliness of the home. By many standards, the Roseanne character was a bit of a slob. But she and her husband were trying to raise the children with limited money and endless hope for better times. What they had was proportionately what they might always have. Yet they fought, they schemed, they worked constantly to give their children a better tomorrow.

The writers did not understand women who worked for Avon, Tupperware, and Mary Kay, who get hooked into any scheme that looks as though they can get a few dollars ahead without losing what little they have. These are small-scale entrepreneurs, gamblers for a cause, delighted with even a few extra dollars because they can be so beneficial in helping the family.

Roseanne and Jackie would follow this idea, as we envisioned it. Jackie's line was "See it and be it," which came from me. This came from a saying which I have frequently discussed with others — "If you will it, it is no dream."

Even though they were radically different from each other, they still came from a background where scheming for the future, for the next generation's success, was important.

We wanted to show blue-collar people, especially the women, as brave, honorable, and aggressive for a good cause. Prior to this, television had portrayed the poor as being dumb and wives as being dependent helpmates. There was a saying that "behind every great man is a woman," and my question was, "What if she steps forward?" We were trying to create characters who were as different from the stereotyped images of the poor as Bill Cosby's character was different from the 1930s black move star Stepin Fetchit.

Ultimately, though, television *is* about power. Carsey-Werner had the power. Tom and Marcy wanted Matt Williams to be in charge, and Matt Williams filled the writing staff with old friends, many of whom had gone to college with him. They came with their own ideas, and very different backgrounds from what we wanted to portray.

We tried to make clear that our concept was the reason Roseanne had been offered the show in the first place. We tried to get through to Tom and Marcy that the Roseanne character had a following, that we had a vision we knew how to make work. Again this was most frustrating to me because I knew we were in year six of our business plan and they acted as though they were responsible for all we had previously created.

But television is about power, and we didn't have it . . . yet. For the moment, all we could do was fight for the best possible scripts, and the best possible changes in scripts that we could not fully challenge. We also knew that if Rosey could be a success, our power would increase. A successful show built around a star resulted in that star's gradually taking control. If enough money comes in, the network executives and other power players will do whatever is necessary to keep the source of the money happy.

There was also a political part of our schemes. The show was to be entertainment, the messages subtle. But the success of the show would give Rosey a major media forum.

And it was from this position, with reporters from news-papers and magazines constantly seeking interviews, that she would gain a voice. There was a need to change the perceptions of the American public, and the press would be willing to quote anything she had to say, just because she had a hit television show. Likewise, the successful show created a platform. It would mean that people would listen to what she had to say.

What I did not think about, did not realize I needed to consider, was that the press could be equally manipulated for good or evil. A celebrity in America does not have to be honest, intelligent, or knowledgeable in order to be given a forum. *People, Vanity Fair,* the *National Enquirer, Time, Newsweek, Entertainment Weekly,* and so many more would give a television star editorial space. The editors and reporters might or might not believe what the person had to say, but they would quote them until such time as the person's name and photograph stopped selling additional copies. I assumed that we would use Rosey's new position for powerful political statements that could help streng-then people previously disenfranchised. I never thought that she would use the position for what I now see as an unhealthy, destructive personal agenda.

The fact is that celebrities become beloved icons. The love people have for the character is translated into love for a person who may be radically different from the character portrayed. In real life, Roseanne Conner does not exist. My older sister, the actress, is a very different person. Yet because people love Roseanne Conner, because she is regularly in their homes via their television sets, they think the real-life Roseanne is their friend. They think they know her. They make of her something she is not and almost cer-tainly never will be.

There were many personal business mistakes on that first show. For example, Rosey and I created it, along with Bill's input. Yet Matt Williams was given the "created by" credit for the series. He claimed he wrote the pilot, yet it was really her act, as many of her stand-up comedy fans noticed. We protested, but apparently the way Triad Artists sold the show prevented Roseanne from getting either a producer credit or a "created by" credit. What she received was money and fame, and in Hollywood, for a first-time star, those are supposed to be the goals that everyone is perceived as wanting to achieve.

We were different. We were looking ahead in ways that new talent previously had not done. We arrived with a sound concept that we had been perfecting since Denver. But now, "Roseanne" was considered a Carsey-Werner "creation." So this was how Hollywood worked. Unfortunately, we did not know all the different ways you could get credit in Hollywood, relying upon the agents and managers to do the right thing for the client. We thought our interests would come first.

The day we met for the first time with Triad Artists, Roseanne said, "I want a production company for me and my sister." We wanted all our deals structured in a manner that would assure that reality as fast and as effectively as possible. And they claimed they understood. They claimed they would handle things with that in mind.

It was only when we saw the pilot that we learned that credits we should have had were given to others. Rosey went ballistic, and I was outraged. I made an appointment to have lunch with Tracy Kramer of Triad to discuss what had happened, what should have happened, and where we were heading now that we felt he had "sold the store" from under us.

I met Tracy at Triad and we walked around the corner to a restaurant in Century City. It was just me and Tracy, a person with whom I thought I had developed a solid working relationship, a man I thought was a pretty good guy.

"Tracy," I said. "We saw the pilot. We saw the 'created by' credit going to someone who did not create the show. We didn't see any producer credit for Roseanne or me. How did this happen? I don't think this is a good deal for us."

Tracy was not at all upset by my reaction. He treated me like someone who was naive, who would be as happy as he

247

was when I understood the facts. "Geraldine, this is a great deal!" he said, enthusiastically. "This is a great deal for two women who have never worked in television. You have no track record as a producer. Besides, if it works, you get a chance to renegotiate your contract a couple of times a year."

And then he threw in the standard Hollywood clincher. Roseanne's percentage from the show was going to be a lot of money. Again it was the familiar: If you're rich enough, who needs morals, ethics, principles, or goals. What he did not understand was that creative control was all that I was ever after. Money was just a by-product.

Knowing there was nothing we could do at the moment, and understanding that at least some portion of the contract could be changed if the show was a success, we decided to learn if we could regain the "created by" credit that was rightfully Roseanne's. That was when we did get to add "Based on a character created by Roseanne Barr." Matt Williams still retained the "created by" credit for the entire show. But the point had been made: The only person looking out for your ass is yourself. Unfortunately, only Rosey heeded the advice completely. I was still trying to protect the dream we had nurtured since Denver.

The series had its official beginning on October 18, 1988, but the pilot, aired several months earlier, was meant to introduce the concept, the characters, and the feel of the show. There were three sections to that pilot program, each designed to show a different segment of her life. A portion took place in the plastic factory where Rosey, Jackie, and their friends all worked. A second portion took place at home, where she had to deal with her husband and a leaking sink. And the third segment had her son receive a bad report card. Roseanne was forced to go to his school to stand up for her son before his teacher, showing a parent as advocate for her child. However, the teacher obviously held her in disdain, even to the point of making her sit on one of the child-size chairs while they discussed the problem.

The situations were all common to the working-class wife, something that had not been seen before. The audience reaction was strong, though we knew from the moment we signed the contract for the pilot that it would be successful.

Part of our confidence came from the same intense belief we had always had in the Domestic Goddess persona that we had created. Part of the confidence came from the fact that there was time to build the show. ABC had committed to running the pilot and six episodes before deciding whether or not to renew. We were certain we would be renewed with that type of commitment, since it was not unusual to shoot a pilot, bury it in a bad time slot, then re-run it during the summer months when nobody cared. With the order for six additional episodes from the start, the show would build, be promoted, find an audience, and secure the future.

The fact that this was a Carsey-Werner production also helped, of course. They had network clout. Carsey had been involved with the successful series *Mork and Mindy*. Their *Cosby Show* was legend. Both had been around long enough to have the right contacts and a solid track record. ABC was willing to give their new shows more of a chance than might otherwise be possible.

We had no fear of failure, and therefore no reason to believe that the network would have to "give us a break" in order to succeed. We knew that our unique point of view would find its audience. We knew that once we had the pilot, the rest would come. We understood what we were trying to do. We understood our audience. We had no doubts whatever.

Oddly, while I vividly remember the HBO special, I don't recall that first ABC show with any intense emotion. Probably this was because, once the contract was signed, we were moving quickly. Glancing through the memos that Triad Artists sent me, I can see appointments for numerous meetings as Roseanne and I looked to find new management to handle her Hollywood work. I was filling in wherever necessary, from finding law firms to developing material. The first show may have been wonderful, but there were six more to go, and then we had to look to renewal.

While this may have been business as usual for Rosey and me, for our parents, the situation was quite different. "When Roseanne got her show," our mom, Helen Barr, commented, "we had a couple of dollars in the bank – not a lot – by my husband decided, the night of her show, we were going to have the biggest party we've ever had. We had it at the Presidential Suite at the [Salt Lake City] Hilton. We invited all of our friends. Ben invited a lot of his friends. We had it all catered . . . this wonderful food. And then at eight o'clock, when her show came on, they had a giant TV in there for us, and we all sat down and watched the show. And then everybody kibitzed around awhile and left. And then Jerry and I had this beautiful, beautiful room we were going to spend the night. (We actually came home at three in the morning 'cause we missed the dog.) I think that party actually cost us more than anything we've ever done except a wedding [Stephanie's], but he was so proud. . . .

"I didn't want to do it. I thought, this is silly. This is every dime we own, and we just had this lavish, incredible party. And Ben had sent the press. . . . It was on all the [local] television stations."

Dad had the entire affair videotaped, and Mom recalled, "He was so proud. He got up and thanked everyone. He just said, how incredible to have your daughter on national television, and to make everybody in the world laugh. He was so joyous, and he was so proud! That was quite a party. . . ."

My father's joy was genuine. He wanted to share his daughter's success with everyone he knew. Yet by then he and Rosey had a communication problem that estranged them without either of them fully understanding why.

Dad did not understand all this. To him, the way he could best say "I love you" to his daughter was to show her off. He was like the laborer who hangs out in a family bar and periodically brings in his talented little son or daughter to tap-dance for the audience.

Dad wanted to move her from place to place to show all his friends. It was his way of saying, "I love you. I'm proud of you. I'm thrilled to be your Dad."

Roseanne did not understand any of this. All she saw was that her father wanted her, a major star in stand-up comedy, a rising star on ABC, to go back to the smoke-filled rooms where no one really listened to your act. When he threw the party in Salt Lake City, she gave the impression to my parents that she felt Dad was trying to ride on her coattails. Rosey felt that her success was not because of our parents but in spite of them. Her attitude was that she reached the top because she was smart and hardworking and had done it all on her own. And anyone who disagreed could go fuck themselves.

Both of them were wrong. Rosey's comedy was Dad's comedy. His influence on her delivery and stage presence was obvious to anyone who had watched them as we grew up. Perhaps she deserved more credit than Dad gave her, but Dad and others deserved more credit than Rosey became able to share as she became a star. Like too many who came before her and will come in the future, fame gave her blinders concerning her past and the people who were critical in helping her on the way to the top.

I never understood how anyone could deliberately want to undermine another person's dignity. I thought Roseanne owed our parents something positive for our past, if only taking them out to dinner. And before she truly reached the top, Rosey seemed to think this way as well. Mom had a story of Rosey taking her to a store and wanting to buy her a piece of jewelry. Mom declined, wanting only to enjoy her daughter as an adult, a success, a friend. There was nothing material she ever sought for herself, and when Mom thinks about large sums of money, she thinks how it might benefit her grandchildren, not herself.

Yet even this early hint of decency in Rosey became lost when our father called her. She not only declined to speak to him, she wanted to hurt him. And as I reflected on comments she had made over the years, and stories close friends and coworkers told about her, I realized that there was a mean-spirited side to her that was always inappropriately vicious.

Prior to this time I thought Rosey and I both shared what I called a win-win philosophy. There is so much money and power at the top, you can live well while helping immediate family, friends, and the women we wanted to empower through the various corporations and foundations we had planned. Success, to me, means that there is enough for everyone. I began to realize that for Rosey, success meant being able to build a castle with high walls, a deep moat, a secure vault, and a torture chamber for vengeance against real and perceived enemies.

I had seen the dark side of Rosey in the past. For example, I noticed her obsession with anyone who was critical of her. There could be ten people standing around to see her after the act. Nine would be adoring fans, men and women who could not stop praising her. They might bring her gifts. They could recite the jokes that made them laugh. They could tell her how her words touched their lives. They gave her the feedback we had worked for a decade to achieve.

The tenth person might be a friend or a fan, taken to the show to see what the fan adored. But if that tenth person was not enthusiastic, perhaps did not care for Rosey's style of humor, the moment Rosey realized that fact, she erased the nine fans from her mind. Rosey saw only the person who did not like what she did. She talked about the person endlessly, angrily. Trying to mention the other nine meant nothing, because they no longer existed for her. Only her enemy mattered.

Later, when she got a bad review from a critic, a review that in no way influenced the love of her followers, she would be outraged. She would send vicious faxes using the foulest language. She would use whatever point of weakness she thought the person had, such as being a closet homosexual, in order to attack them viciously.

Rosey was also fascinated with serial killers and the way they treated their victims. She told me that if she were such a killer, her pleasure would come from the fear she could cause them. She would live for the hunt, tracking the victims, capturing the victims, tying them up so that, when helpless, she could discuss how she would hurt them, how she would kill them. She wanted them to know what would happen, to smell the fear, to see the horror in their eyes before they would die. She said that was what would make her come.

At first I tried to understand her actions and feelings based on the fact that she was a Scorpio. People with such an astrological sign tend to have a sting to their attitudes. But objectively I realized there was something more to Roseanne, a dark side that had nothing to do with when she was born, how she was raised, or the experiences her life had brought her. It was deeper than all that, and it could be frightening.

One aspect of the dark side came when Dad's high school class had its fortieth reunion. Dad wanted Rosey to accompany him. He wanted to show her off, presumably to have her do a few jokes. He saw his desire as saying, "I'm proud of my daughter. This is my greatest accomplishment. Some of you are doctors and lawyers. I am not rich, not well educated. But I can make and raise a wonderful daughter who you love almost as much as I do."

Rosey heard something else. She heard a man wanting her to demean herself, to tell jokes to an audience of her father's friends when she could be on the road earning tens of thousands of dollars a night.

While I think it would have been best for her to put this in the context of how our dad looked at life, I knew by this time, her narcissism had made that point of view impossible. Roseanne was hurt and angry. "What the fuck's in it for me?" Mom and Dad remembered her asking. And there was nothing in it for her, nothing to be gained, and great potential emotional pain. Sis may have lost her temper and used language that was inappropriate with a parent, but my first reaction was to silently side with her for her refusal. The request, as I see it, was unfair, though the fact is that I believe in the Jewish family concept that you should give your parents *nachus*. This means that Jewish children are born to give their parents joy. It is the reason you often hear a Jewish parent talk about "my son the doctor," and you simultaneously see the delight in the eyes of the son who is being praised. He has given *nachus*. Thus I probably would have gone to the reunion. Even if I truly felt anger, I would have refused more gently, perhaps claiming a prior commitment, and then I would have sent a telegram to Dad at the reunion.

This is not to say that the idea of *nachus* is all good. There is the unconscious, unspoken agreement between many Jewish parents and their newborn children that the babies are about to become *nachus* machines. The results of this idea are like watching a screwball comedy of the 1940s. I can remember being in the fourth grade and having to play the song "Born Free" on my violin for my parents and a gathering of aunts and uncles. I put the violin in the playing position under my chin, raised the bow, and tears came to Dad's eyes. "Look how my Geraldine holds her violin," he seemed to be thinking. "Has anyone ever held a violin so beautifully?"

The bow moved across the strings. I was slightly off-key, trying to pretend the mistake was not noticeable as I worked to get the song right. Dad began sobbing, taking out his handkerchief and blowing his nose so loudly that an aunt told him to be quiet. "It is the music of the angels," Dad seemed to be thinking. "My daughter Geraldine has a gift from God."

Each time I made a mistake, each time the violin emitted a sound as grating as chalk on a blackboard, there were no grimaces, no cringing. I was a child performing, and that meant I could do no wrong. I was perfect just by standing up and trying to give *nachus* through my as-yet-unskilled effort at making music. And no sound was ever more beautiful to the Jewish family members listening in our living room. It was a scene played out in Jewish homes all over the world, for centuries past, and probably for centuries to come.

I remember the day I was visiting my sister Stephanie and my niece went to the toilet on her own rather than soiling her diaper. The moment she was seated on the seat, I raced to the room, accompanied by Stephanie and her husband. Her tiny face scrunched in concentration. Our faces beamed with pride. There was a sound, the passing of gas, and then the unmistakable noise of a bowel movement striking the water. My niece! Their daughter! The first time she potty-trained herself!

We would have brought strolling musicians to fill the by-then-slightly-foul-smelling room if they would have reinforced our pride in this milestone and we would have found them on such short notice. Instead, we applauded, delightedly saying, "You made a cocky in the potty! You're becoming a big girl." Nobel Prize-winners and beauty queens are the only people who receive as great adulation as she got that day.

While I am obviously exaggerating, I am only doing so slightly. Every achievement is praised. The children in such families are constantly rewarded, the reason so many became high achievers.

The flip side of *nachus* is guilt. Self-esteem is strengthened by the reward of meeting and exceeding parental expectations. Yet when a child makes a mistake, the feelings of guilt and despair can be as exaggerated as the rewards for success. This is why many of my faith can be both high achievers and somewhat neurotic. Yet at its best, *nachus* results in rewarding children for what they try to do, not just what they achieve. The children grow into adults who do not fear to try anything in life, for in the effort they find the reward; success or failure becomes secondary.

Nachus for the infant Roseanne was more exaggerated than for many other Jewish children born in America. For the first six years of her life, she was the only grandchild of Holocaust survivors. She was the first niece for my parents' siblings. She was living in Bobbe Mary's apartment building, a place filled with elderly Jews who had survived the ravages of the Holocaust. She was the first new life many of them had intimately encountered since the war. And as she became sensitive to the sadness that permeated their lives, she took delight in performing for them, in doing whatever was necessary to make them happy.

In return, Rosey was indulged, adored, and made to feel very, very special. But then I arrived, and my birth was shattering to her. I was not loved more than she had been. But I did take time and attention from her, there now being two girls giving *nachus*. As a result, a portion of her life would always be spent trying to regain what she had experienced during those first few years of life.

Louie Anderson put it best. He watched her on and off stage, then said to her, "Roseanne, I know who you are. You're successful, you're forty years old. People think you're saying groundbreaking, intellectual things, but I know you're really . . ." Then he put his hands over head like a baby wanting to be carried. With his head back, he'd use a little child's voice and say, "Pick me up! Pick me up! I'm Rosey. Pick me up!"

Louie was insightful enough to realize what I had always understood when I watched her perform. When Rosey goes on stage, facing her fans, hearing the waves of laughter and applause, she's still saying, "Pick me up." And as the applause continues, she is given the love she craves. They are figuratively picking her up, holding her, making "nice Rosey."

Looking at my niece in the bathroom, I realized that when Rosey is on the stage of life, she, too, is "making a cocky" and everyone applauds. That is why she gets a tattoo on her ass, drops her pants, and moons the press and all her fans. That is why she sings the national anthem off-key and grabs at her crotch. That is why she has hired thugs to beat up freelance photographers, roaring with laughter. And when she ultimately attacks family members, coworkers, and others, leaving a trail of destruction behind her, she is just making a giant cocky. And the unthinking members of her audience and the media explode with applause. What a wonderful girl our Rosey is!

Her refusal to attend Dad's reunion was one of the first

times she robbed him of *nachus*. And Dad was unable to understand one of the underlying reasons Rosey turned him down.

I thought Rosey's overreaction was partially caused by feeling unsupported for too many years. The way she perceived it, Dad didn't show his pride in her until she was a success. (In truth he tape-recorded all her television appearances and kept clippings of all her press coverage. There were pictures of her on every wall of their home, and Dad attended as many of her shows as he could from the very beginning. We all referred to Mom and Dad's living room as the "Rosey shrine." He knew at the start that she was going to be great, cheering her on every way he could.) It was all rather adolescent thinking. And, tragically, that pain built in both their minds until she wanted to truly hurt him, and he wanted solely to be reconciled on his own terms, without understanding her world.

In hindsight I now have other feelings. I idolized my older sister. Every important experience I had in life, she had experienced years earlier. Like every kid, I felt more comfortable asking my sister questions about life, sex, and related matters than I did my mom. I know now that Mom was not always as naive or unknowing as I thought. She had been a teenager. She had fallen in love. She had enjoyed sex for years. But few girls are going to see a mother as being anywhere near so wise as an older sister. Thus I always turned to Rosey, even when Mom probably would have been of greater help.

When Rosey went from being withdrawn to ambitious, I trusted her. I thought we were working together toward a common goal that would assure both personal financial success and the chance to give to others. That was what we talked about constantly. And I firmly believed that what was said was a mutual reality. Even today, with all I know, I think that the narcissism had not yet enveloped Roseanne, that she meant what she said, because having the money, the power, and the fame was still as much of a fantasy for her as a goal.

Real life has convinced me that if Rosey did say, "What

the fuck's in it for me?" and I'm certain she said something similar, she meant exactly that. She was and is self-serving, a reason she is successful in business and has so many personal problems. Dad was wrong in what he asked. But Rosey was incapable of compassion, understanding, or thinking about anything but what she could gain. She wants power and control, and she will throw away anyone who tries to stop her, anyone who reminds her of her past, anyone whose knowledge of her life seems to differ from her statements. Her response to Dad's request was cruel, but it was also a warning of far more vicious things to come.

Even harsher was the relationship between Roseanne and Maxine. Rosey hated Maxine because Maxine was not a fan. My life partner thought Rosey was full of shit. Maxine is intuitive, grounded, and extremely sensitive. She is a successful therapist who works with disturbed children. She knew the truth about Roseanne and could not be swayed to become either a fan, a victim, or silent about her opinions. Maxine thought Rosey should take responsibility for her actions, not play the victim, someone to be pitied, and Rosey hated her for her insights.

During this period, I had matured to the point where I wanted to know my parents on an adult level. Instead of viewing them as a child would, I was trying to build a new relationship, helping them get to know me and trying to know who they had become. I discovered that they were not rigid in their thinking, as was the case with the parents of many of my friends. Instead, they were people capable of change, sometimes embracing it on their own, sometimes choosing it after realizing that there was a better way to live or to think.

I had been an angry rebel against them in my twenties as I passed through adolescence. Now I was in my thirties, coming of age as a woman, and fitting that old joke where suddenly parents become smart. I began visiting them with more frequency, starting a dialogue about our past, enjoying their presence.

After the success of the show, there were two other enterprises in the planning stages. The first was a line of fat women's clothes. The second was a Saturday morning cartoon show.

The clothing idea was one we had shared for years. Rosey had style. She knew how to wear clothing in such a way that she could be glamorous even at her heaviest. But the clothing had to be right as well. The design and cut had to be meant for the breasts, hips, waists, and other key areas of a fat woman's body. It could not just be a large-size version of clothing whose lines, colors, and design had originally been created for a living Barbie doll. This usually meant seeking custom dressmakers. We wanted to create a line of clothing that would make large women feel beautiful.

The impetus was one of the many endorsement offers that regularly were presented to Rosey. Some designer, clothing line, or department store, I forget which, wanted Rosey to endorse a line of plus-size clothing no different than what she and I had always hated. We thought we could do better. We decided to produce clothing with flare, style, fine fabric, and yet at a price that could be sold off the rack. Rosey Wear would be developed with the aid of a designer, but it would be a hands-on project for her, not a meaningless endorsement.

I spent a lot of time working on this project. I did a feasibility study concerning the real costs of design, manufacture, storage, and distribution. I also did a feasibility study of freestanding Rosey Wear stores. If we pursued this, I would be CEO of a company that would have to begin with one location, then gradually be spread through the country. It would be one of the first of the businesses that had their beginning with the success of her television show.

We had fired Herbie Nannas before the Carsey-Werner deal was negotiated, so I added the manager's duty to my workload, just as I had done when we first came to Los Angeles. I continued with these duties through the filming of the pilot and the first few episodes. However, because I lacked the inside Hollywood contacts of a full-time manager, we felt we needed an additional person who could be used for such contacts, the same reason we had originally hired Herbie. The person we settled on was Arlyne Rothberg. Arlyne had experience working with women and the problems they encountered in the male-dominated industry. She had experience in film, an area we wanted to get into. She understood when we told her about wanting the production company and the various businesses that new power would allow. We liked her and trusted her advice. And she liked my and Rosey's relationship, since she had been raised without a sister.

Arlyne felt that since our primary goal was building a production company, we needed to keep focused on creative film and television projects. She asked me to delay the clothing line exploration until a later time. There was a constant tension on the set of Rosey's show, a situation Arlyne wanted us to deal with first. After fighting over credits and writers, we needed to find ways to make changes, and it was important to focus on the perfection of the show as well as the gaining of control. It was all about power and money, and Arlyne wanted our immediate focus to be on those areas that would achieve those ends. All of our energy had to be focused on the first renegotiation of the Roseanne contract.

During this same period, Arlyne worked on selling a Saturday morning cartoon show. The cartoon show was a merchandising concept. While we wanted quality product, the truth about Saturday morning is that it is a time to sell product.

In recent years, greeting card companies, cereal manufacturers, toy designers, and others have discovered that children influence spending. Create a demand by children, and their parents will generally yield to their desires.

There have been shows that were created to move product – *Strawberry Shortcake*, a creation of a greeting card company, for example, and *GI Joe*, which was created in order to sell a greater number of the dolls.

We wanted this market. A Saturday morning cartoon

show makes money from sponsors like any other. But unlike *Roseanne*, the Saturday morning cartoon show could lead to a licensing bonanza. There would be two main characters, "Little Rose" and "Sister," who would be eleven and nine years old, respectively. Rosie would be the rebel who was "a little hell on wheels with a four-barreled imagination and a thirst for fun and adventure," according to the concept ultimately prepared by an animation company called Nelvana. Sister would be the rather shy, reserved "intellectual" of the two. Both sisters would use their imaginations, and the show had the working title of *Little Rosie's Let's Pretend*, which eventually became *Little Rosey*.

There was a subtle subtext to all this. Just as the Domestic Goddess had a target audience and a specific agenda, so did the cartoon show. We were aware that studies showed that when girls reached puberty, the culture encourages them to stop being adventurous and curious. Their scholastic achievements start to decline, especially in science and math. They develop a serious loss of self-esteem. Yet none of this has to do with the reality of a girl's potential at that age. The biology of approaching womanhood is not destructive. Only the culture carries the subtle, overwhelming messages that change a girl's potential for the future. Thus the cartoon would stress girls' self-discovery and self-esteem through the stories of the adventures. Each episode would include a subtle message about life.

The nice part of the cartoon show was that it would take little of Rosey's time. I could easily produce it and work with the animators, who did most of the preparation on their own. Scripts and story ideas would have to be approved, but this was much simpler a process for *Little Rosie's Let's Pretend* than it was for *Roseanne*. There would be no rehearsals and no set. We had not considered who would do the other voice-overs; our concern was only with developing the concept and several episodes, work done by Nelvana.

Roseanne also was given the opportunity to star in a

movie entitled *She-Devil*, which began filming in the spring of 1989, and also starred Meryl Streep. The movie proved to be a bomb, though the premise delighted us. It was the story of a woman who is cheated on and generally treated poorly by her husband. She changes, becomes successful and desirable, and then returns to seek revenge. However, there were two problems with the ultimate picture. The first was that the director and the script writer diminished its potential by turning the movie into one long fat joke. Roseanne was used as much for her physical size as for her comic and acting skills. And the second problem was that the making of a movie is boring. You have to be on the set, in costume and makeup, for what might be ten hours of waiting in order to shoot a scene that will last ten minutes in the film. It is much slower than television, which can be as fast-paced as a stage play. Rosey had no patience for the process, and while she wanted the credit and wanted to show her versatility, she hated the slow pace of production.

In addition to all this, we decided to write a Roseanne Barr autobiography, a book that ultimately was released as *Roseanne: My Life as a Woman*. We went to New York and talked with a number of publishers, ultimately settling on Harper & Row.

The book, which eventually became a bestseller, was an accurate chronicle of her life, both the one we shared in Salt Lake City and Los Angeles, and the one she lived with Bill and the kids. There were tears and laughter, stories of Bobbe Mary, and descriptions of Daddy's storytelling. We documented the struggle, the time at Woman To Woman, and the gradual success that so closely followed our plan.

Rosey and I wrote together, shared together, relived the past together. Sometimes we cried. Sometimes we laughed uproariously. And when we were done, Roseanne touched me more than at any time in the past by adding the dedication:

"For my Sister, Geraldine, for being intense, passionate, committed, brilliant, fierce – for creating a large part of me, my career, the world. Where do you end, where do I begin? You believed in me always, as I believe in you.

Many of the words in this book come from you, and I look forward to *your* book, your film. The world is waiting for you, Sister."

Everything seemed perfect. We would soon be in a position to jointly share the executive producer role on her show, to implement all our ideas, to achieve what we had planned for almost a decade. We even named the business we would start – Beshert Production Company.

Beshert is a Yiddish word that was extremely important to us. It is a word that means that an event or a relationship is preordained. For example, if you meet someone, fall in love, and instinctively know that the other person is perfect for you, as though in the entire universe there could never be a more perfect soul mate, that is *beshert*. It is a situation which, in hindsight, you say, "of course, that had to be."

Rosey and I were sisters preordained to be Sisters. We made a good team. We had not only shared lives growing up, we had shared the struggle, worked to achieve the dream, and together would reap the rewards. Rosey was a star, the comic, the woman in the news. I would be the businessperson, the administration, the producer, occasional writer, idea generator, strategic planner, and coordinator of a variety of projects in business and the arts. With the Beshert Production Company we would make a greater impact on the world.

With the success of the *Roseanne* show, Roseanne had power, and she liked it. She liked the control. She liked being able to say anything, do anything, and still be treated with special respect by the media, who might have told someone else they were full of shit and denied them a forum until they had something valid to say.

What happened next was the start of a nightmare and a tragedy. And despite her growing success, despite her finally finding what she considered happiness in her personal life, Rosey's attitude toward power became a poison destroying the heart and soul of much of what once mattered to her. Tragically, the biggest victim would be herself.

8 Enter Tom Arnold

Many of the people who see Roseanne as a tragic, manipulated figure, sort of a plus-size Marilyn Monroe, like to blame Tom Arnold for her problems. He was a mid-level comic whose image was that of a big, mouthy, untrustworthy, lout who drank too much and took too many drugs. During the early days when Rosey first knew him, when he was sober or what passed for sober, she felt he was a fairly skilled writer. She found that he could produce jokes for her, and he was one of the free-lancers whose jokes she incorporated into her act. She even had him work as her opening act at times. I had to admit that he was far better than the previous person Carsey-Werner had hired, someone who just told fat-Jewish-woman jokes. I also knew that Rosey admired Tom's work, though his following was nowhere near to hers.

At first I saw Tom as just another or Rosey's somewhat self-destructive comic friends, one who seemed much more jealous of her success than any of the others. Later I realized that as the friendship deepened, he seemed to be seething at his inability to equal her achievements. He also appeared to be acting out angrily in thoroughly inappropriate ways. For example, I still remember when Tom, Rosey, and I attended an Orion Pictures private screen of her first movie, *She-Devil*. This was part of the prerelease process, a time to evaluate everyone's work, the editing, and other factors. Although the movie was not brilliant, it was Rosey's first and we were both anxious to see her on the big screen.

Afterward, despite having restrooms readily available, Tom went outside to the front of the building, unzipped his pants, and peed on the wall. He did nothing to conceal what he was doing from passersby.

My understanding was that Tom had been arrested in the past for peeing on buildings. However, no matter how any of this may have related to personal problems, I considered it shocking, offensive, and an angry action against Rosey's triumph.

Later Tom and Rosey would frequently have joke-telling contests between themselves to see who was funnier. Inevitably Rosey would tell Tom that he was the funniest. In fact, much of their professional relationship has involved Rosey reinforcing Tom's ego. When we were sitting around with a group of professional comic writers working on material for a new stand-up act for Roseanne, I remember Tom telling them which jokes in the new act were specifically his. He would say things like, "I wrote that," or "I told her to say that." He needed to take credit for the work with the other writers, a rarity in a business where everyone understands that a comic's routine is often a group product designed for a single voice.

Rosey first met Tom while playing a club in Minneapolis. It was around 1983. Tom had a reputation as somewhat of a smartass. He was like the classic high school class bad boy, constantly testing the limits of the teacher's patience without ever being so rotten as to risk expulsion. By contrast, Bill Pentland was an extremely passive man, somebody who accepted life. He accepted his wife when she was in her hippie housewife phase. He was not overly concerned during her period of semiagoraphobia when she rarely left their home. And he accepted her traveling from city to city as the act was being developed. Bill eventually became a writer of comedy, developed a stand-up act of his own, and even wrote and recorded some parody songs. By contrast, both Rosey and Tom Arnold were like two skyrockets exploding in the night, burning briefly though with unforgettable intensity.

Rosey didn't usually trust male comics. She didn't like their sexual humor. To have a male chauvinist opening for a woman whose target was primarily blue-collar, emotionally abused and/or neglected women was not something she looked forward to happening. She confronted Tom about all this, and as she later related, he first denied that he had any sexist jokes, then said, "I call women cum dumpsters and hosebags and stuff like that. Is that okay?" Rosey thought he was kidding. I felt that Tom meant every word he said. With women-hating wisecracks like this, I should have known that the dream we had so long shared was about to be shattered. Though I could not know how horrible things would become for me, I did instinctively realize that Rosey needed to legally protect herself in case my fears were valid.

Tom and Rosey didn't experience love at first sight, but Rosey had certainly met her match. He was as much an in-your-face comic as she had been when she had been told she wasn't feminine and had retorted, "Suck my dick!"

I did not see Tom's act until several years later, after he had moved to Los Angeles. However, from what Rosey told me, it was not that much different from what he had used that first night. He had goldfish he kept in a container that looked like an Igloo cooler. I remember him skewering them with toothpicks and putting them in his mouth while singing. Rosey said that he killed the fish and set them on fire that first night. His humor might best be described as offbeat.

I especially remember the night I heard him perform when he discussed the size of his penis. Other comics would talk about how big it was. Tom talked about his penis being unusually small, something Rosey later confirmed to me. She said it was like a little boy's. But whatever the case, I remember him discussing a pick-up line he'd use. As I recall, it was, "Hi, babe. Want to go out with me? I have this incredibly small dick."

Tom's sense of humor was different, but it seemed more like that of a small-town hick, a farm boy who had just discovered a big-city joke shop. Rosey liked him because he was able to write jokes for her act and he understood the character and attitude she had developed. Not that she paid him. Even though Roseanne, like most stand-up comics, budgeted money for new material, she felt that if Tom really cared about her, he wouldn't expect money.

Tom was a professional and teased her about her attitude. It was obvious from his statement that, had she sent him checks, he would have willingly cashed them. He needed the money, the work was good for her act, and yet she deliberately stiffed him.

Many of Rosey's comedian friends had similarly off-the-wall and self-destructive attitudes. There was Sam Kinison, another comic driven to personal excesses, who used to tell his audience to drink and drive, then was ironically killed by a drunk driver. And she also enjoyed Andrew Dice Clay's humor despite the fact that he built his act around degrading women, ethnic groups, and just about everybody.

Rosey loved the dark side of comedy, the acts that clubs used to empty the houses at two A.M. when the owners wanted to close and the audience wanted to continue drinking. Rosey howled over Sam, a perennial closer at the time because he was so disgusting that even a brain besotted with alcohol could comprehend what he was saying and not want to hear more. For example, Rosey delighted in retelling Sam's routine when he said, "I want everyone to take a pencil and their napkin and write down the names of their sacred dead on it." Then, screaming, he would add, "So I can wipe my ass on them."

Ironically, we came to learn that Sam had a few hard-core fans who would stay to hear the full act, and many of them proved to be off-duty Los Angeles police officers. I don't know what nerves he struck in them. I'm not sure I want to know.

For years there was neither an affair not the hint of a sexual attraction between Tom and Rosey. Not that they were saints. Tom eventually cheated on his girlfriend with Rosey. And she had been unfaithful to Bill. She and Bill were reconciled with each other, and Bill liked Tom. They were drinking buddies together. The fact that Tom had a fiancée during the years after Rosey met him helped keep Bill from worrying about the adultery becoming a part of his wife's friendship. Besides, Tom was doing drugs in a way that Rosey could not tolerate. She wasn't about to abstain when she was sitting with other comics, but she could live without drugs and alcohol. Tom seemed thoroughly addicted, especially to cocaine. In fact, during Tom's appearance on Rosey's first HBO special, she later wrote that his nostrils were caked with flecks of the white powder.

Our Dad, Jerry Barr, was troubled by Tom Arnold when he first met him in the early 1980s. The occasion was Rosey's show at Scott Hanson's Comedy Club in Minneapolis, and Roseanne, knowing that our father was raised in the St. Paul area, thought he might like to join her and see the show. "We got a room across the street from the comedy club in the Embassy Suites. . . . We had two double beds, and I stayed with her for two days and two nights.

"Anyway, I took her to St. Paul. I rented a car, and I took her to all my places where I grew up. I showed her the house I was born in, the neighborhood I was raised in, all my haunts as a child. I took her to where we used to go swimming in the lake, and we just shared."

Dad continued, "That night we go to the club across the street. She introduces me to Tom Arnold. I never knew Tom Arnold, but he was her opening act. We chatted, and he did his act. And I thought he was a good local comedian, good enough to do a local college. . . . It was strictly University of Minnesota students in this comedy club, and he was good for that.

"After it was over, he and Roseanne came out, and we sat around and had a couple of drinks. He asked me what I was going to do the next day, and I said, well, I'm a fanatic fan, a sports fan. I'm going to go to the Metrodome in Minneapolis to see the Minnesota Twins play baseball. I'd never been in a domed stadium. I thought it would be kind of an interesting concept to see baseball played inside. And he says to me, 'Mr. Barr, I'd sure like the opportunity to go with you. Would you mind going with me as my guest?'

"And I said, 'Tom, I'd appreciate it.' I mean, it's better to go to a ball game with somebody than to go alone. And I said, 'I appreciate that. Thank you very much.'

"And he says, 'Well, the game starts at two. I'll pick you

up at the room at quarter to two.' It was about a five-minute walk from where we were.

"One-thirty comes, no Tom Arnold that I could see. Quarter to two, no Tom Arnold and I'm sitting in the room, waiting with Roseanne, and he don't show up. And I said to Roseanne, 'It isn't the end of my life,' though I didn't get to go to the game. I thought something may have happened. And I just chalked it up to one of those things. Whatever.

"That night we go back to the club, and I'm sitting there, having coffee. This is early, before the show, and Rosey says, 'I got a problem.'

"I said, 'What's the problem?'

"She says, 'Tom doesn't want to come out and do his act in front of you.'

"I said, 'What's the problem?'

"'Well, he feels bad that he didn't show today for the ball game, and he didn't call you, wasn't courteous enough to let you know. He just didn't show.'

"So I says, 'What happened?'

"Roseanne says, 'He went out after the show [last night] and got drunk, and they found him in his car in a corn field in southern Minnesota.'

"I said, 'Well, that's the way it goes,' I said. 'It kinda speaks highly of the man's character.' That's what I told her.

"And I said, 'Go back and tell him it's all right, I forgive him, there's nothing to worry about.'"

The next time Dad ran across Tom Arnold was when Roseanne, still married to Bill Pentland, brought Tom home and told Dad she was going to marry him. "She was laying up with the guy, living in sin," Dad said. "If you want to call it adultery, call it adultery because that's what it was. And in front of her own children, she brings this man into her house." Dad was shocked by what he felt was a moral outrage.

Tom's early life was difficult. Both Roseanne and Tom told me that his biological mother, an alcoholic, abandoned him as a young child. He was a hyperactive kid placed on the drug Ritalin, which did little to affect him. He had uncontrollable muscle movements. When I first met him, I thought the movements were from cocaine use. Roseanne told me I was wrong, that he could not help it, that he had had the problem his entire life. He has more control now than in the past, but that has come from extensive work on his part. He also had emotional problems from being molested as a child by a young man who served as his babysitter.

On the Sally Jessy Raphael show of October 10, 1991, he stated that the young man who molested him lived across the street from his parents' home in Ottumwa, Iowa. "He'd take me to his house and have me play with him, and he'd play with me and do these things." He at first remembered that the youth was probably only a couple of years older, just old enough to be intimidating. Then he got hold of the Ottumwa High School yearbook and discovered that the youth was eighteen at the time that Tom was only seven.

At first none of us involved with the show and the families were concerned with Tom or his incest problems. We were just too busy.

At the same time, by April of 1989, when Rosey went to New York to act in *She-Devil*, she and Bill had officially separated. Thus she had to be concerned with the divorce settlement as well.

The Pentland home was never an oasis of peace for anyone. Bill was enlightened on women's issues. He was comfortable with doing the dishes, doing the laundry, being responsible for the kids. When a snotty little neighbor child in Denver commented that her father didn't do the work Bill did, Bill calmly explained that some dads have the wrong idea about housework.

Rosey had acknowledged the changes. She talked about how Bill didn't come the way he was, purchased off the shelf during a Blue Light Special at K mart. He had to be molded over the years. Yet Bill's relationship with Rosey was destined for failure for many reasons, among them the fact that he was as passive a man as Rosey was volatile.

Rosey was an explosive personality. She could be a screamer, a physical fighter who would destroy property when angry or having what she sometimes considered fun. The people who worked with her on *Roseanne* had two different reactions. Some people found her intensely demanding and hard to work with. But that was the professional side of the woman. Her demands were for the betterment of the show, the good of the character. She fought with the writers over the scripts and the characterizations. She fought with the producer and director over the best ways to get the most effective performances. And she fought alone, because John Goodman was the type of actor who comes on set and delivers whatever lines he is handed. He did it brilliantly, but he did not share her vision.

By contrast, the technical people – lighting men, cinematographers, prop people, and the like – adored Rosey. Being always present, they knew exactly what she was saying and doing. They saw her as a true professional, working for the betterment of the show, a fact that would be translated into ratings and long-term job security resulting from a quality product.

The fights sometimes made headlines in the press because powerful insiders knew that their days could be numbered. The people with the producer credit and similar titles control the show. They also knew that no one could be as effective at running things as Rosey, and they realized that when the show was a success, their positions would be the first to go during renegotiations.

The tension on the set was mostly due to the fact that Rosey and I had been undercut compared with what we had told Triad to get us. Rosey had to make the show work despite the people presently in charge or she would not have the power to properly renegotiate the contract. And the people in power saw Rosey and me only as Utah hicks who got lucky, who lacked their infinite wisdom which they were convinced had made all of the success possible. It became a war of product and talent. One side told Roseanne that she was on the set because Carsey-Werner had made her great. She and I argued that the show existed because of the years of work that made Roseanne skilled enough to make a vision that was translated into a product touching the hearts of millions.

As we learned the Hollywood power game, we were determined that nothing was going to stop Rosey and me from getting what we should have had at the start. I was fighting behind the scenes, hiring and firing the lawyers and managers, coordinating publicity, and rewriting scripts. Rosey was fighting on the set for the primary product that would make all our other plans succeed.

After we fired the two head writers brought in by Carsey-Werner and took charge of the hiring of a writer, a man named Jay Daniels, we finally had peace on the set. Jay, who had successfully been involved with the series *Moonlighting*, respected us. He knew where Rosey had come from. He knew she was funny, had paid her dues, and had the sense of comedy necessary to better handle her own show than anyone else. Once Jay was on the set, old writers were fired, and the new writers knew that their boss was Roseanne and that she was the person who had to be pleased with their scripts. This power position would be solidified when the contract renegotiations gave Roseanne the title of producer, the one she should have had from the start. As our manager, Arlyne, had so wisely said in the past, "You have to prove that you can deliver a successful product to the network. Once you do that, and the show becomes a hit, the networks have to give you anything and anyone you want to keep you happy, to keep the money machine rolling." She was right. If you want to have the network break Charles Manson out of jail so he can be your head writer, if the ratings are solid enough, they'll try to do it.

The one area that was spiraling downhill was Rosey's personal life. By the time Rosey was involved with Tom, she had become the type who wanted her sex bouncing off the walls, taking a man and being taken in every possible way, the least of which would be quietly on the bed. She was intensely physical when emotional, whether those emotions were rage or lust. And the tabloids would later run stories about the hotel rooms that were trashed after she and Tom stayed in them.

At first I heard the stories secondhand, reading about them in the tabloids. But as we talked, as I was present when Rosey spoke to favored reporters, I saw a growing dark side.

First there was her comment to one reporter that she enjoyed being "slap fucked." She liked being thrown against the wall by the man she loved. Then came an obsession with serial killers. The media seemed to eat up the antics of the new "Mrs. Arnold." I worried that the Domestic Goddess had been lost along the way. I was seeing less of the strong, feminist Rosey, and I worried.

We were in New York, finishing her movie and working on a book together. She had mentioned to her editor that she was fascinated by serial killers, so he sent her every book his company published related to serial killers, murder, and the like. She would devour them avidly.

The children were caught in the midst of all the changes in Rosey's life. Bill was content if the children were safe and quiet. He often let them watch television without editing their viewing, without deciding limits of time and appropriateness.

Discipline for the kids rarely involved clearly established boundaries. What was wrong to do one day might be ignored the next. Jessica was frequently enraged. Jennifer tended to be a screamer. Jake was the most outwardly stable, a sensitive child, curious about the world. He was reflective and quiet, like his father.

Rosey's success further separated her from the kids. She was often on the set for fourteen hours a day. She was frequently using marijuana as a means of coping. There was money for a staff, yet nothing was working. By her own admission in her book *My Lives*, by the end of 1989 her children had become "incorrigible at this point – the victims of bad parenting and L.A."

Tom arrived in 1988, trying to pursue his career as a comic while expanding his work with Rosey. I think Tom expected to be a regular writer for the show, with a regular weekly salary. He had never been in such a position before, and Jeff Harris, the second of our head writers, certainly was not about to hire him, but Rosey interceded and used him to warm up the audiences.

In his favor, it must be said that Tom had not gone to Los Angeles to work warm-up. I think even he senses that he was not going to hit the big time as a stand-up comic, no matter where he played. He was convinced of his skills as a writer, and since Rosey had been using his work over the years, he felt that she should be placing him on the writing staff.

Tom came on the set with few people skills and the attitude of a bulldozer. He acted as though he was entitled to be in charge. The show had been on for a year by then and was on top of the ratings. The actors had formed the close relationships that come with a long-term hit or when working for a repertory company. More important, they all knew Bill Pentland, liked Bill, and had mixed feelings about the marriage breakup because they would miss his regular presence on the set.

Suddenly Tom was there, talking about what "we" want and what "we" need. I should have known I was becoming invisible the first time I heard the word "we." He was talking as though the show was his and he knew what was best. And he demanded that his word be given respect. He was only occasionally on the payroll, for a small part written specifically to bring him in, and he was not very good in the role. With a show of Roseanne's caliber, even bit parts are normally given to actors who have paid their dues, who have proven skills. Yet Tom was there simply because of Rosey. He had no background in television production, no sense of working with the other actors, and certainly no previous connection with a successful show of any type.

I understood Tom to a degree. He desperately wanted to be good, to be liked, to be successful. He was willing to pay his dues. Certainly he had been doing that for years in the field of his stand-up. But he also wanted to take advantage of his opportunities, even if that came from being a long-term friend, occasional writer, and now lover of Rosey's. The trouble was that he did not understand the nature of respect in a business setting, and the cast and crew of a successful show have many of the dynamics of an office.

Years earlier, when I was in college, one of my management courses taught me the difference between earned and deferred respect. The most successful managers achieve earned respect. This means that they do their job so effectively, no one has reason to criticize. The staff will support their requests because they know that the person knows what he or she is talking about. The request comes from careful reasoning, from experience, from fairness, from knowledge of the total picture with which the business must be concerned.

During our work together I had always tried to get earned respect. Not only did I realize it was the best kind, it was also the type that allowed you to work through crises with the support of others. You could lose your job and get another one because you left a trail of proven abilities.

Deferred respect was the type Tom seemed to be demanding. Deferred respect comes from who you are, not what you have done. Certainly those who get deferred respect may be skilled enough to have earned respect, but they don't stay silent long enough to show that fact. Instead, the attitude is, "Kiss my ass. I'm the boss's son/daughter/spouse/parent/lover, etc. I have the boss's ear and you'd better do things my way or I'll make sure you're in trouble." They gain a position to be perceived as having power, then abuse whatever power they are given or can take.

Oddly, at times he reminded me a little of a schoolyard bully with a moral code honed on old western movies where the lone gunman rides into a corrupt town, one hand on his revolver, the other on the schoolmarm.

One day Tom told me that he had what he considered a traditional view of marriage. He said that he was going to become Rosey's husband, that his job would be to protect her and take care of her. He said he was going to beat up anyone who was mean to Rosey. Then he said that since I didn't have a husband, and since he would be my brother-in-law, he would be happy to beat up anyone I wanted as well.

I was stunned. I didn't know what to make of this generous offer. I just shrugged my shoulders and said to myself, "Heterosexuals! Go figure."

Later I realized it was the same type of attitude I had seen Dad convey toward Mom. Even today Dad still talks of being the cave-dwelling hunter who would gird his loins (though knowing Dad, he'd add suspenders for extra support), pick up his spear, and do battle for the beloved Helen Barr.

Rosey later said that she was also getting flack from Bill at home. Bill had begun writing jokes for his own stand-up work, and while he and Tom had become close friends, there apparently was some professional jealousy. Bill felt that if anyone was added to the writing staff, he should be the one. His work had also been used in Rosey's act. He had been involved with the first HBO special (Tom was paid a reported $15,000 to write the second HBO special Rosey did in 1988). He had written two shows for the first season of *Roseanne*, both of which had been used. And he was Rosey's husband.

There was no reason for Bill to have to ask for a contract from his wife concerning what would happen when the show was a hit, we got the producer credit, and the writing team could be changed. He had paid his dues and proven his worth with the two scripts of his that were aired. Thus, because of both the relationship and what fit the definition of earned respect, Bill rightfully thought that he should be first in line for a writing staff opening. This was reinforced by repeated conversations among Bill, Arlyne, Rosey, and myself. Verbal promises were made, and we all thought they were good enough to be binding.

During 1988 Rosey increasingly turned to Tom for emotional support. As a longtime friend, she could discuss with Tom the problems she was having with Matt Williams, her anger with the scripts, her frustrations at home. Both of them were drinking too much; in addition Tom was using cocaine and Rosey was smoking pot. Both of them had little life outside of bars and comedy clubs when they went out on the town. And while Rosey was married and Tom was engaged to a woman named Denise, they spent much of their time together, and not as a foursome. Still, there was nothing sexual taking place between them.

Rosey dates the admission of her love for Tom and the decision to divorce Bill as being Sunday, February 12, 1989. She and Tom attended a Grateful Dead concert at the Los Angeles Forum, and it was during that night that he not only expressed his love for her but also reportedly said, "You're always taking care of everybody, but I know what you really need is to be taken care of. And everybody's always taking care of me, but what I really need is to take care of somebody else."

The love affair that was about to develop was carefully followed by the *National Enquirer* as well as, to a lesser degree, some of the supermarket tabloids. This was because Rosey had a separate affair with the *Enquirer*.

It is difficult to explain the perceived importance of the *National Enquirer* as part of American popular culture unless you read it. I am speaking specifically of the *Enquirer*, not such publications as the *Sun* or the *Weekly World News*, where stories are frequently made up. The *Weekly World News* might have an article on the "fact" that aliens work with Bill Clinton or the "fact" that Elvis Presley is not only alive but has been photographed getting married. The *Enquirer* is closer in its information to *USA Today*, though without that publication's coverage of national and international hard news and sport. The celebrity stories are always obtained either through the work of the reporters or through reliable sources. The latter often consists of the stars themselves, their associates, loved ones, or publicity people. Even the more outrageous stories are true in the eyes of the people telling them to the reporters. In addition, a tape-recorded check-back system is usually used to be certain there are no surprises. The subject or subject's spokesperson is called and taped giving story approval. As a result, though the *Enquirer* is frequently sued for libel, it almost always wins.

Many Hollywood insiders are in love with the *Enquirer*'s money, taking payoffs for stories provided. The fees range from perhaps a hundred dollars for a tip to a thousand dollars or more for information leading to a front-page feature. One entertainment lawyer whose social circle includes the Kennedy family has earned as much as two thousand dollars a week in extra income by slipping stories to the *Enquirer*. The widow of a movie star, a woman who has been on intimate terms with rock stars, movie stars, and high government officials, has made tens of thousands of dollars through her connections. And others make just enough to provide them with little luxuries, such as regular dinners at more expensive restaurants than they could otherwise afford.

Becoming famous enough for the tabloids to pursue you is a little like living in a totalitarian state. Suddenly you can't trust your neighbors, your friends, or, at times, members of your own family. Tabloid staff writers generally start their careers with the highest pay in the newspaper field for new hires. They have relatively unlimited expense accounts so long as they don't abuse them. Such rewards make them want to keep their jobs, and a tabloid job is kept by getting the story first, getting it better than the competition, and getting the most fascinating, lurid, tragic, or hilarious details.

Tabloid reporters will come on to your street, walking door-to-door, canvassing the neighborhood. They will reward the neighbors with quotes, with respect, with cash, or anything else they want. Is someone an amateur photographer? That person will be paid for every picture taken that is different enough to sell newspapers. Is someone on the staff of a doctor's office? Arrangements will be made to get a copy of the celebrity's file.

Soon neighbors, tradespeople, and others who were once innocuous parts of your life are spying on your every move.

Certainly many of those people tell the reporters to go to hell, to give you privacy. But many do not, and you never know who is telling you the truth about their feelings concerning the offers made. It is easy to become paranoid, distrustful, deliberately going out of your way to shop, to eat, to play. You can withdraw or constantly change your behavior, much like a Mafia don trying to avoid surveillance by the feds. People talk of how fans change celebrities' lives. Fans usually have a sense of propriety, integrity, and boundaries. Tabloid reporters do not. Tabloid reporters will literally do anything to get that next story.

I had an unlisted telephone number. Each time a tabloid reporter got hold of it, I would have to change it. I changed it over and over again, but because they had contacts in the telephone company, I might have just as well been listed.

Over time I came to learn how sophisticated the most successful tabloids have become. I don't know what equipment they own and what they rent from surveillance experts. I don't know what is used by their staff people and what is used by hired personnel. However, I discovered that in addition to what you would expect – high-speed, low-light cameras, telephoto lenses, and tape recorders – there is an arsenal of high-tech equipment.

You've undoubtedly seen pictures of celebrity weddings where tabloid helicopters circled overhead. What you probably did not know is that some of them are equipped with special directional microphones. These supersophisticated "shotgun" mikes can pick up the sound of a pin dropping at fifty yards or more. Such mikes are used to sweep the house and grounds, searching for conversations that might be intimately revealing. There are also laser pickup units of the type the Central Intelligence Agency and other spy agencies now use. Telephone wiretapping is common. In addition, radio scanners covering both CB and FM lines are used to listen in on both portable and cellular telephones. Much of this is illegal, but you have to catch them in the act to prove it was done. Usually you learn about it after the fact, at which time they claim to have inside sources who gave them the information. And there is no way you can prove they didn't.

As the sister of the star, I had another type of reaction. Part of me wanted to preserve my anonymity, to be able to live my life as Geraldine, whatever that meant. Rosey was the performer. Rosey was the celebrity. I had always worked behind the scenes. However, if I am going to be in the tabloids, I want to be in for something I have accomplished. Let me be there as head of a foundation supporting the arts or because I murdered a dozen tabloid photographers and showed no remorse. To be known only as Roseanne's sister, to have your life be seen only through a relationship, is to live with the world's denial of your own existence.

Tabloid reporters' ethics are also different from those of traditional reporters. Normally, when you give a reporter a quote for a story, that is where it is used. Some tabloid reporters keep their quotes, using them again and again in radically different contexts for many years. The quote is real. When, where, and why you said those words becomes horribly distorted.

In 1986 Roseanne discovered the *National Enquirer* as a tool for self-promotion. She loved reading the tabloid and regularly went to the nearby twenty-four-hour Ralph's Supermarket at two A.M. in order to buy the latest copy the moment she knew it would be stocked at the checkout counter.

Rosey was popular with the *Enquirer*, which seemed to have a love-hate relationship with her. She was often ridiculed for her outrageousness, including her obesity and the somewhat annoying voice she used for the character in her act. Yet they also had favorable stories about her growing success. Like all celebrity-oriented publications, the *Enquirer* would regularly experiment with their coverage of a rising, existing, or falling star to see if his or her name and picture sold copies. Some stars needed negative coverage to excite their readers. Others had to be damned. And still others varied from day to day.

Knowing these facts, the tabloids could be used to preview a product. You could introduce a show, a rising star, or some similar concern in the tabloids in order to get free advertising.

Usually it was the Barbie or Ken doll type of person who was treated most favorably by the tabloids, such as John F. Kennedy, Jr., known more for his looks and parentage than his success as a lawyer. Rosey was so controversial that they tried both ways — favorable and unfavorable — to see which stories sold more. And as I discovered much to my shock, the stories were likely to originate with her.

I remember one time in 1988 she and I were sitting together while she answered a telephone call. As she talked, I suddenly realized she was speaking with a reporter from the *Enquirer*. After she hung up, I criticized her for dealing with the tabloids. She said something I have never forgotten. "Shut up! I know exactly what I am doing." Then she went on to say, "The tabloids reach millions of my fans per week." Despite that fact, in July of 1989 she wrote an op-ed piece for the *New York Times* attacking the tabloids. She called the cars the reporters and photographers used "the poop and scoop mobiles."

Over time I learned that Rosey liked to feed them both good and bad stories about herself. She wanted the fame, the attention. But she also wanted the control. That was why she was extremely upset when she discovered that the men in her life were picking up extra money by selling the *Enquirer* stories about her.

Rosey thought that Bill started making contact with the *Enquirer*, then passed the telephone number of his contact to his friend Tom Arnold. Whatever the case, eventually the *Enquirer* reporters and photographers began showing up outside Tom's apartment whenever Rosey was sneaking over to talk or have sex. Her infidelity and growing romance were well documented because Tom would tip them off. He did not care what Bill or the kids thought about the publicity. Rosey was a star, and her fans sought the titillation of seeing her with Tom. Since Tom's drug addiction and lack of major financial success kept him in need of money, he was happy to cash the *Enquirer*'s checks.

Later I met the *Enquirer* employee who was assigned to handle Tom's calls. She told me how Tom worked with them, calling to let them know when Rosey would be coming, where they would be going, and essentially coordinating the coverage. When the relationship became so serious that Tom knew they might marry, he became scared, I was told. He arranged for a woman to act as a go-between, calling them on his behalf and receiving the checks in his place. In that way the relationship with the *Enquirer* could continue without Tom's risking the loss of Rosey.

I tried to avoid the entire issue, but eventually I was brought into it as well. One story was sold about Maxine and me, one of the early examples of how Rosey and those close to her were beginning to think about using her family to promote her. (To be fair, we have not identified the source for the story. It was either Rosey or Bill or, less probably, Tom.)

I do not hide the fact that I'm a lesbian in a committed, long-term relationship Maxine and I both consider to be a life-time arrangement. This means a number of things, some spiritual, some intensely personal, and some having to do with the law. The issues that concern me are primarily women's issues relative to work and pay. Where I have unique social problems are with such matters as health insurance. Social Security benefits, tax deductions, living wills, and similar areas where espousal rights are not extended to same-sex couples. In all other areas, the lesbian and gay community is not all that different from the heterosexual community. There are liberals and conservatives, Republicans, Democrats, and Independents, deeply religious individuals and those who question the existence of God, urban dwellers, suburbanites, secretaries and CEOs, doctors, lawyers, and janitors. Unfortunately, our society hears the terms "gay" and "lesbian" and fantasizes public orgies, hidden agendas, and titillating kinkiness, ideas some tabloids, including the *Enquirer*, will exploit when given the right story.

The difference, for me, was where I came from. First there was Salt Lake City, then Denver, and while the Woman To Woman Bookstore may have flourished in

Denver, the community was not all that tolerant. Openly homosexual men and women were attacked there. Gay bashing was just common enough that newspapers regularly reported cases of men and women being beaten for nothing more than being suspected of having a same-sex orientation. "Outing" could literally be deadly.

The decision to come out is an individual choice that involves many factors. Most gays and lesbians go through a period of self-hate caused by what they have experienced within the culture. It is okay for someone to be aroused by a member of the opposite sex, but adolescents experiencing their earliest sexuality, a time when many people have sexual feelings towards both sexes, are taught that any feelings other than for the opposite sex are dirty and wrong. Heterosexuals eventually focus on the opposite sex. Homosexuals develop a strong same-sex orientation. Some can express their feelings openly; others are likely to hate what, for them, is the more natural choice.

Some communities are very tolerant of the diversity of individuals. I have felt that being a lesbian is a part of me but it is not how I wish to be defined. Coming out in Salt Lake City could cause me to lose my job, to lose people who previously professed to be my friends, to suffer humiliation. In San Francisco, I found a city that tolerates diversity, including that of sexual orientation. You are allowed to be comfortable with yourself, and when you are comfortable with yourself, others are more comfortable with you. Who you live with is not so important as whether you are interesting and compassionate or dull witted and racist. In San Francisco the straight people I know ask me how Maxine and I are doing, not how we "do it."

Even in San Francisco, Maxine and I are denied the legal and religious ceremony provided for heterosexuals. Our concerns include the spiritual, the reason why we belong to a Jewish synagogue and are active in the spiritual, ritual, and social life of our synagogue. If there is a difference, it is that the synagogue to which we belong in our home city is one that has been serving traditional families, gays, and lesbians for at least twenty-five years. The synagogue creates a family environment for traditional families and those gay and lesbian couples who are raising children either alone or in a shared situation with a former spouse. A recent study shows that 18 percent of the membership is comprised of children. We have a school for them, a library, and a sense of community for everyone.

The rabbi can perform marriages within the laws of the state and the traditions of the Jewish faith, but this currently means between men and women. Though many lesbian and gay couples would like a legally and religiously sanctified formal marriage, the rabbi is only able to offer affirmation ceremonies of deep meaning to the homosexual members making lifelong commitments, but these do not provide the legal benefits of marriage.

Obviously the synagogue is important to my spiritual journey, to my sense of history, culture, and community. My membership in it is not something I flaunt. Yet it figured prominently in one of the stories sold to the *National Enquirer*. Apparently it was a slow news period for Rosey and she was looking for yet another reason to shock. Having a "queer" sister would make good copy. But telling my story accurately was not interesting. I was too much like the average person's sister, aunt or daughter. Instead, the story that was placed was a lie, a story about Maxine and me being "married" in a formal ceremony. It claimed that Roseanne had given us a large cash gift, and it sounded so believable that friends from my past called in outrage. They were happy for me and were irate that I had not invited them to the wedding that never happened.

Not only did the story depict us as "queer," I felt the implication was that we perverted the sacred institution of marriage in a synagogue catering to Jewish deviants. I was later told by one of the reporters that they felt the story was fair, that they tried to show such a marriage in a positive light. I think that was a naive assumption. But what was important was that none of this ever happened, yet Enquiring minds were told anyway.

The story was bad. The effort to make an even "better" one was vicious. Neighbors came to us, telling us that the

284

reporters had knocked on their doors, trying to learn what they thought of having women like us living near them. Our neighbors were called and asked if people like us should be involved in the lives of young children. No one would raise that issue concerning the work of a heterosexual therapist whose brilliance and success helping children had nothing to do with her personal life. As a result, Maxine was forced to "come out" to her employers. Fortunately they felt much of the sense of outrage that we did. But the situation was one that, in a different community, could have destroyed our lives. And all for one week's circulation of a tabloid newspaper my sister and her husbands thought could boost their income or careers.

I was angered and hurt. Rosey, Bill, or Tom, whoever sold the fiction, probably just chalked it up to one more headline coup. Yet I should also have seen this as a warning that the family was about to become fair game in Rosey's quest for attention.

Tom seemed to settle for letting his courtship be documented. When he went to New York to be with Rosey during the filming of *She-Devil*, he called his primary tabloid contact before he left. However, at least he was enough of a gentleman so that the first time (as far as I know) that he and Rosey consummated their affair, the only semiwitness was our sister Stephanie, who acted as chauffeur.

It was around March of 1989 and Tom was still doing stand-up comedy. He had a tour about to start, and Rosey was planning to leave for New York during the time he would be away. As she related the incident, she decided to fuck him that night and took Stephanie along to bring him down from his apartment without arousing suspicion. Since Tom had no idea this was going to happen, there were no reporters camping out, but Rosey was still married, and not willing to take any chances.

The threesome drove to a motel in Encino where Tom and Rosey discovered that neither had the cash for the bill. Instead, Stephanie was asked to put the room charge on her credit card, then wait in the car. They were back quickly, having partially trashed the room in pursuit of what apparently was rather violent sex. Shortly thereafter, Rosey decided she had to break formally with Bill.

I've always felt that the biggest appeal of Tom Arnold was that he was Rosey's bully. He was part lover, part adversary, part big brother who liked to beat up the bad guys who were tormenting her, even when she may have helped create the atmosphere in which she found herself. (In fairness, while I continue to not be friends with Tom, much of his early misbehavior was the result of admitted alcoholism and coke abuse. He has had the courage to face his various addictions, to get into treatment programs, and to conquer them one day at a time. Yet it was in his wild, out-of-control days that Rosey first fell in love with him, a fact that probably says more about her than him.)

For example, there was the night that Roseanne and Tom went to Spago, a luxury restaurant in West Hollywood that is a favorite dining spot of stars who want to be seen. Hollywood has two types of restaurants for the rich and famous. One type carefully protects their privacy and expects them to come to eat, to relax, or to work. Musso & Frank's on Hollywood Boulevard, for example, is a popular lunch and dinner spot where rubbernecking is discouraged, and seeking autographs, photographs, or anything else from the celebrities can result in extreme hostility from the management. They provide a quiet haven for professionals despite being in the heart of a tourist area. Surprisingly, they are also modestly priced, something even the rich appreciate when not trying to show off.

By contrast, other locations are known to be celebrity hangouts, and a gathering of photographers and autograph seekers is encouraged just outside the premises. Sometimes the staff alerts the press to a star's dining there. Sometimes the star's staff makes the contact. And sometimes the freelancers just drop by during lunchtime and dinnertime, when they are most likely to catch someone coming in or going out. Spago's is one of those locations where Hollywood insiders know there will be an audience, and I think both Tom and Rosey were aware of that fact.

Whatever the case, Tom and Rosey went to Spago's the night of July 13 to celebrate the fact that Roseanne had finally filed for divorce. The press was there when they arrived, as well as the autograph seekers. In addition, there were three young tough guys who offered to clear out the press for fifty dollars. Rosey and Tom took advantage of the offer, and a brief fight began.

While the photographers who were not hit caught the action on camera, Rosey paid the youths, then looked on delighted as people were beaten right and left. Eventually there was a settlement, reported by Rosey to be twenty thousand dollars that she had to pay, but I know she felt it was worth the money. She got to enjoy the outside equivalent of a barroom brawl in her honor, and she also got tabloid headlines. She even mentioned the incident in her book *My Lives*.

Rosey was becoming increasingly outrageous in her public actions during this time. She was becoming fascinated with the effects of her power and fame, including the extreme way the fans reacted. She felt that when you were famous, you could get away with anything. In fact the twenty thousand dollars she paid the photographers came from the insurance company, not from her.

For example, she and Tom joked to me about the idea of getting in a motor home and traveling around the country. They would randomly stop at a fan's house, go inside, eat all their food, write on their walls, piss on their carpet, then trash the place. Then, Rosey believed, as they left, the family would gather at the door, all smiles, and say to her, "Thanks for coming by, Roseanne. We love ya." Then they would tell their grandkids what a wonderful experience they had had.

The other concern during this time was the issue of Rosey's attitude toward truth. Celebrity had given her a credibility I felt she deserved until I noticed her actions contradicted her words. During one lunch we had together, I said to her, "I love how you throw statistics out, Rosey. You'll make an observation and say it as if it's a fact."

I recall her replying, "Oh, no, dear. As soon as I say it, it becomes true."

I then said, "Well, please tell me you don't believe that."

"Of course I do, Sis. Everything I say becomes true as soon as I say it."

And then I went on in that conversation to say, "Well, what in the hell are you going to do when you get caught in one of your creations when it's not true?"

I remember her saying, "Well, then, in that event, I'll just say, 'Well, give me a break. I'm a comedian, you know. I get paid to tell jokes. It's my job. I'm supposed to tell jokes. It's just a joke. Give me a break. I'm a comic, for Christ's sake.'"

And she said, "So you know, it's foolproof. I can always do that. That's why being famous is the greatest scam of all."

And then I said, "What happens if even that doesn't work?"

And she said, "Well, then, my dear, we will be forced into the ultimate nightmare – we'll have to go on a diet. And then everyone will say, 'Oh, she looks great. She's really getting healthy.'"

Our mom would ultimately put it better. After one particularly vicious attack by Rosey, Mom said, "God doesn't change history. Roseanne changes history."

Tom's cocaine problem might have caused her to delay her second marriage, but she was committed to marrying Tom, even if she had to wait until he was clean. My world was not expected to change during all this. I would continue working on the show and the various side projects, in what we hoped would soon be a coproducer status with her. However, I did advise Rosey from the start that before she married Tom, she needed to have a prenuptial agreement.

This does not mean that I was looking at the relationship coldly. Rosey told me of her love for Tom back in May of 1989 when we were at the Mayflower Hotel in New York. My first reaction was that of a sister who loved her, who had always wanted her to be happy in life. I told her of my joy concerning the happiness she expressed. I said to Roseanne that she deserved to be loved well.

Rosey understood what I was saying. She told me that he did love her in that way. "But I'm not stupid," she added. "I'll never marry Tom without a prenuptial agreement."

Tom made it clear to Rosey and me that he was marrying her for love, not money. He promised her that he would also sign such an agreement.

California is a community property state. Rosey was marrying at the high point of her career. Tom would be marrying someone about to start a series of businesses that could make her one of the wealthiest women in show business. Without a prenuptial agreement, he could be legally entitled to half of everything she did, without ever having done any work for it. And if the marriage failed, certainly a possibility since she had never had a relationship with him while he was fully sober, she could lose massive sums of money to someone who might be in her life only briefly.

I was at risk as well, I expected all that Rosey and I discussed to be completed as planned. With the next contract renegotiation, I would share the producer status with her. I would be in charge of the cartoon. I would be developing the side businesses. We would be our own little conglomerate, and I would never worry about poverty again.

In hindsight I know that I should have separated the world of sisters from the world of business. I should have left a careful paper trail of contracts and memos with Roseanne. I should not have worked for years on her word and my integrity. But there seemed no reason for concern. We had gone almost a decade together, following my business plan, and my work had put Rosey where she was. She knew full well that she was the comic genius and I had the business sense that enabled her to reach a level other comics who had been her mentors never were able to achieve. I saw no reason to question, to mistrust. Yet I did see the sense in the prenuptial agreement.

It was inconceivable to me that nearly a decade of work would ever be challenged. Rosey was my big sister and I knew she would always do what we had discussed for so long. I had neither the time nor the inclination to consider how changes in her life might affect my own. I was happy, productive, and thinking only of where we were headed. It was naive on my part, but someone who was jaded could not have helped Rosey achieve the type of success she had earned. To me, doing anything other than what I was doing might ultimately hinder Rosey, not help her.

It was in June 1989, when Rosey and I were in Washington, D.C., as part of the book tour for her first autobiography, *Roseanne: My Life as a Woman*, that the engagement to Tom almost came to an end. She was appearing at the American Booksellers Association convention, and we had spent the morning and early afternoon talking with people, attending meetings, and working on a speech she had to give. We were both tired, but she was especially exhausted, having just finished six weeks of work on *She-Devil*.

It was approximately three o'clock in the afternoon. Arlyne was also in the hotel, and I was in her room, talking. Rosey had been in a luxury suite down at the end of the hall, but all of a sudden I heard the door to her room slam shut. Then she came running down the hall, shrieking, wailing, and crying her heart out. We opened our door and Rosey rushed inside, weeping uncontrollably as she sobbed, "I just lost the best thing that ever happened to me. I just lost the best thing that ever happened to me."

Rosey threw herself on Arlyne's bed, overwhelmed by grief. I lay down next to her, holding her, comforting her, trying to understand what was happening.

She said something about having to fire Tom, then broke into sobs again. I finally got her to her feet and helped her back to her room, where I tried to get the full story.

At first I tried to get Rosey on a chair, but she began pacing the room. I learned that Tom had been fired from the show, though I could not get more details from her. All I could do was listen to her, try to comfort her, and eventually get her on to her bed.

This was not a time for questioning. This was a time to

be a sister in the special way that each of us had experienced with the other over the years. The one unique aspect of our relationship was that we each knew we could trust the other with a side of ourselves we would never allow the public to see. If one of us was in emotional pain, we could let the other see the depth of grief, let the other reach out to that place we considered most private, and gain comfort from the love sisters can share. We might be curious about the cause of the pain, and I certainly wondered about the details of what happened with Tom, but we knew that was not what the other needed. It was not a time for talk or questioning. It was a time to let the other bare her soul without judgment, without pressure, and without fear. There were many times when Rosey had done the same for me.

Then the telephone rang. Rosey answered it, telling me it was Tom. I gave her the cup of tea I'd made, then left the bedroom and closed the door while she talked with Tom for what proved to be three hours.

I spent the time in a different part of the suite, writing, and sometimes meeting with Arlyne. Finally Rosey emerged, the tears gone, a smile on her face. She said, "It's going to be okay. We had a long talk. I think things are going to be really good and even a lot better."

I then said, "You have to give a speech," but I was no longer worried. She was as peaceful after this three-hour conversation as she had been despondent before it.

To Arlyne's amazement, Roseanne calmly wrote the speech she had to give in an hour and fifty minutes. The speech overwhelmed the audience because she spoke as a woman and a feminist. She talked about how everything started in a bookstore. She did not come on as a comic telling jokes, but as a person of depth and concern who respected them and gave them a side of her few in the public had ever seen. It was the sister I loved almost beyond all others in my life. And the death of that side of her was one of the greatest losses I would ever endure. I believe that show business killed that woman, and the person who remained was someone the Roseanne speaking that June day of 1989 would have considered an object to be pitied, not envied. She would have been horrified to think it could be herself.

It was in late August or early September that Tom hired Mickey Robins to be Roseanne's attorney, replacing the law firm she had been using. He struck me as the classic stereotype of an old-time, very aggressive, Hollywood attorney. I remember one time, apparently trying to impress me with his toughness, he said that he liked nothing better than getting a witness for the opposing side on the witness stand, then using his questioning to rip their throats out. I did not care for him, but I liked the idea that we might have a "badass" on our team during renegotiations with Carsey-Werner.

Rosey seemed to feel comfortable with Tom's choice, and eventually I hired Mickey's son-in-law to be business manager. One of Mickey's daughters, also a lawyer, became part of Rosey's legal team. And another of Mickey's daughters works for the insurance firm Rosey uses. Mickey himself is an officer on all of Roseanne's corporations. Today the Robins family has almost a cottage industry with Roseanne.

This was a tumultuous time for Rosey. The divorce from Bill Pentland was still be finalized. She was taping the new season of her television show. Arlyne was working to sell *Little Rosie's Let's Pretend*, as well as working out a development deal with a motion picture company for new material. In addition, Roseanne was planning her wedding to Tom, sending out invitations based on when she felt the divorce would be finalized, and dealing with her kids. She was constantly exhausted, constantly overstressed, and I felt she was unable to think as clearly as usual.

In November Rosey had a birthday party in Hollywood. Tom was there, and Rosey was like a little kid, feeling loved because she was surrounded by friends, gifts, and her favorite food. Then, several times during the evening, she noticed Tom was missing. He would leave the nightclub where we were celebrating, get into a limousine the couple had waiting outside, and drive somewhere for a few minutes. Each time he left, Rosey looked as distraught as a small child who had just received a coveted toy, only to have it break when removing it from the package. Then, when he returned, her face could light up and she would be joyously happy.

The absences troubled two of our mutual friends more than they did Roseanne. One was a woman who was not present but who Rosey talked to on the telephone with great frequency. She told Rosey that she felt the frequent absences meant that Tom was still using cocaine. She felt he left to repeatedly get high. She also suggested that Rosey make Tom pee in a bottle, then get his urine analyzed to prove that he was not still a heavy user of cocaine.

The other person was Maxine Margaritis, by then a part of Rosey's staff. We had known her in Salt Lake City, where she had spent fifteen years as a fund raiser for the Red Cross. She was a skilled organizer and manager. We hired her to take my place on the set of Roseanne, coordinating the myriad of details that previously drastically limited my time.

I had switched into a more creative area, as Rosey and I had planned. In addition to training Maxine, I was writing one of the shows, establishing a fan club, helping to rewrite her stage show act, planning a comedy album, and preparing for the development of the Saturday morning cartoon show. This was one of the creative areas in which I had longed to be, an area which Roseanne and I felt was my reward for the years of business work I had done. Rosey told me when I made the switch that I had taught her well, that with the team I had helped create, the business knowledge I had passed on to her, we had reached the next level for both of us. I could begin focusing on the art, the creative end that I dearly loved.

Maxine worked well with Rosey, the cast, and the crew. However, she did feel tension with Tom, who she felt was treating her more like a gofer and maid than a skilled, management-type person.

Maxine coordinated the birthday party, bringing in a band from Minneapolis, the members of which were

293

friends of Tom's. What he did not realize was how much they cared for him. After Rosey insisted Tom get a urine sample checked for drugs, Bobby, the drummer, went to see Maxine. He was troubled by what Tom was doing to himself, and troubled that he might have added to the problem by helping Tom. Maxine said that Bobby told her that Tom paid him five hundred dollars to pee in the jar that was to be analyzed. Tom knew Bobby was clean. He also knew that his own urine would not pass the test.

Rosey went ballistic when she first discovered what he had done. She told Maxine Margaritis and me that she wanted Tom's name off of everything related to the business. Then Tom came on the set, very distraught. The tension between the two was disruptive and distracting. I was told to get him off the lot.

Then Rosey said she was afraid to marry him, that he was much too damaged for a committed relationship. She couldn't be his wife, but she was going to try to be his friend. And soon Rosey was working on getting Tom into a drug detox and rehab center. As I recall, he agreed, eventually leaving from the studio lot, taking a cab to the hospital where he checked himself in.

I never wanted Rosey to marry Tom until she was certain he was sober. I thought that anyone who married an active addict was a fool. Even the twelve-step programs feel that a year of sobriety is necessary before someone can begin to exhale, and even then, continued sobriety requires dealing with life one day at a time. She did not know Tom Arnold. She knew a man who had a history of outrageous, self-destructive behavior. Maybe the relationship would work, but I felt Rosey should stay a single parent for a while, letting Tom get his life together before she made a commitment.

Rosey was at a breaking point. She needed to get away, and when the show stopped taping for the holidays, she and Maxine Margaritis flew to Hawaii. I thought the relationship with Tom was over, but instead, she and Tom talked many hours by long distance telephone.

Rosey returned to Los Angeles on New Year's Eve, 1989, and we had a small party at Maxine Margaritis's house. We were relaxing, eating turkey, and toasting 1990.

Rosey left the party early, taking Jake and going to see Tom. A few days later Rosey told me that her lawyers were in the final stages of finishing the divorce with Bill. The financial aspects and other details would be completed by the middle of January, and she was going to marry Tom the next day. Tom, who was active in Alcoholics Anonymous, using his AA sponsor to arrange the wedding and security. A justice of the peace would perform the ceremony, but Tom had too few days of sobriety to trust himself with all the pressure. He had the good sense to utilize the skills of someone who had been there, who understood and could help him if he felt he might get into trouble. The wedding was alcohol-free.

I went to Mickey concerned about what was about to happen. Rosey was in love. Tom was in love. But there was obviously a serious drug use issue no one knew for certain had been resolved. The marriage could be perfect, or it could break up in a matter of days or weeks. No one knew, though with California a community property state, the issue of the prenuptial agreement was more important than ever. I told Mickey that his job was to protect Rosey's interests, and I asked him where the prenuptial agreement was.

Mickey told me that the prenuptial agreement was a personal matter between Roseanne and Tom. It was none of my business.

None of my business? I should have seen that to Mickey and Tom I was the evil stepsister they needed removing from the scene. For the first time in a decade, I had reason to be concerned about the future of what I had helped create. Within a matter of weeks, everything was supposed to come together. There would be a renegotiation of the contract, and Rosey and I would be able to share the producer credit. Everything I had worked for was in place. I just had to wait out the brief period before it was finalized. Or so I thought.

One of the producers on *Roseanne* called me into his office to discuss Tom. "What are we going to do about Tom?" he asked me. He was worried about Tom's presence, worried that he might be disruptive.

My first reaction was that as long as Tom remained clean and sober, we had little to worry about. "I think things can get a lot better."

I believed Rosey and I were about to begin sharing the executive producer credit. No one knew the show better than Roseanne. Everyone realized that if there was any way to make the show stronger and funnier, she had the talent and the drive to do so. Tom did not belong in the midst of all this, yet Tom was a factor for all of us.

This producer and I discussed the development deal that would soon be finalized. We talked about channeling Tom's energies away from the show and into the development area, where he could work on his own project. It would be a valid use of his time and talent, and we felt that both Rosey and he would benefit as a result.

The money did not matter. I had always felt that there was enough money and power to be shared by everyone appropriately involved. Rosey would marry. Tom would have his work. I would have the creative work I had spent ten years of effort to achieve. Carsey-Werner's influence would be diminished. We would have Beshert. And everything could be better through the arrangements this producer and I were discussing.

During this same period, Arlyne had completed the deal for *Little Rosie's Let's Pretend*. The importance of this cannot be stressed enough. I understood product merchandising and knew that a successful cartoon would bring millions of dollars in licensing arrangements. Rosey and I agreed that I would handle the licensing and merchandising campaign for the cartoon, a fact that excited me. Nelvana, the animators, had already successfully marketed the animated versions of *Beetlejuice* and *Babar, the Elephant*, and they would be working with me as partners on the business end. We all knew that the real money would come from the dolls, lunch boxes, T-shirts, and countless other spin-offs that had brought so much money for The Simpsons, Strawberry Shortcake, Care Bears, and numerous other similar creations.

Some of my share of the profits from the merchandising would fund my dream. My family would leave the poverty in which they had lived for so long. We would all get off Lincoln Street, where we had known the family stress of seemingly endless hard times. Our parents, our brother and sister, would share in the financial success I would be achieving for Rosey's and my company.

Another portion would establish Beshert, the company that would help empower working-class women through-out the arts. It was as though we were about to awaken from a happy dream, only to discover that real life was even happier and more exciting.

On February 1, 1990, a meeting was held on an empty sound stage on the production lot where *Roseanne* was filmed. The executives from ABC Television's children's programming and those concerned with Saturday morning scheduling were there, along with Arlyne, Mickey Robins, Rosey, Tom, writers, producers, and merchandising people from Nelvana, a child psychologist, and myself. The child psychologist worked for ABC and was present to assess the impact of the show we had in mind.

The executives were concerned about any cartoon Rosey might create. Her reputation was not that of someone who the average American family might want to have writing material young children might watch. Her stand-up act used blue material. *Roseanne* was very much adult in nature. And they feared that the cartoon might be an animated hybrid of the act and the prime-time program.

I understood the fears and began working the room. I stressed that we were dealing with separate, unconnected products. I explained how concerned we were about the lack of role models for preteen girls. The cartoon show would be aimed to give positive role models and morally appropriate stories for younger kids.

There was something odd taking place during the meeting, though it didn't seem to be particularly noticeable to the executives we were trying to impress. Rosey was distant, as though her mind was on something that mattered to her more than what we were about to develop. By contrast, Tom was making comments that I felt were meant to diminish me. He seemed mean-spirited, as though trying to put me down without going so far as to hurt the deal. It made no sense, yet it was not something we could discuss right then.

It was perhaps a week later. I had known something was wrong for several days. Nothing specific had been said, though it was obvious from the tension that something was changing. In addition, I knew that all the business contracts and corporations were being established. I kept waiting to hear from Mickey about the structure, to see the documents I would need to sign. But no one telephoned as I expected. Then Rosey called me to her home, and both Tom and Mickey Robins were present. They left the room long enough for Rosey to fire me, saying, "I don't want you to clean up my shit anymore."

That's what it ultimately came down to. Rosey was a brilliant talent. No one has ever challenged her on-stage abilities. But I was not and had never been a gofer or "pooper scooper" in her life.

I was shocked. What do you say at such a time to the sister you love, your business partner, the person with whom you shared your dream? What do you say to someone for whom you have devoted years of work without meaningful reward because of a vision about which you both talked a thousand times? Women have often been shafted by men whose careers they have guided and supported, working selflessly behind the scenes as a purported partner. We had railed against such actions in our growing feminist awareness. And now Rosey was acting in a way she had once stood against. The only words I could utter to Roseanne were, "I'm sad. I'm very, very sad." But there were far more feelings racing through me.

I left dazed. I remember Mickey Robins, the attorney, standing outside near my car. He didn't have the decency to look me in the eyes, to say "I'm sorry" or "Have a good day" or even that very California comment, "Have a nice life." He didn't even have the courage to be vicious, to say, "Glad to see you out of here, you bitch." He just turned his back to me, folded his arms, and stood there as I drove away.

By the time I reached Maxine, I was apparently a blithering mess. She met me at Jerry's Deli near the Sunset-Gower Studio where I had my office. I had a corned beef sandwich and talked, though Maxine later said that I really wasn't very coherent. I just rambled about everything, still in shock, unable to comprehend what had happened, how it could happen, and the loss of my sister.

My mind was a blur for the next few days. I walked along the beach a lot. I played the violin. I wrote in spurts, including a short story about two sisters who have a plan to take over the White House. One is the charismatic front person, a little like Jack Kennedy. The other is the strategist, the person who puts together the campaign, who uses her political savvy to get her sister elected. Then the sister who becomes President has an affair with a drug-addicted male version of the Marilyn Monroe character, who simply walks into a dynasty that took years to build.

Obviously the work would never be published. It was a way of working out my anger and pain on paper.

I had to return to the lot. I had to pick up my possessions. Ironically, the show was being taped when I arrived, and the script they were using was the one I had both written and gained on-screen credit for with my life partner, Maxine.

There was a surrealistic aspect to what was happening to me as I walked through the lot. I felt like an artist who conceives of a painting and assembles the canvas, the oils, the brushes, and other items needed to make a vision become reality. Next the painting takes shape, step by step, starting

with one small corner of the canvas and gradually envelop-
ing everything. Those who see it declare it a masterpiece,
yet suddenly the artist is told it is not hers. Someone else's
signature is on the corner. And when she tries to study it, to
see what happened, she is pulled in and out of the painting,
sometimes experiencing the world of the creation, sometimes the world of the studio, and never being certain
which is truth.

The soundstage held my masterpiece. Not the writing of
that week's script, though I was proud of what Maxine and
I had done. Rather, it was the conception of what began as
an act, became a weekly series, and had come to dominate
American television ratings. The show was conceived brilliantly, and I knew I could take credit for that. I knew what
began a decade earlier in Denver and the reason Rosey was
in the position she had achieved. Yet my name had been removed from the canvas. I was a lost soul in the midst of a
world that should have been mine to share.

I was demoralized, defeated, betrayed on every level. I
saw a golf cart parked by the side of the building. Suddenly
I was present and past in my thinking. I remembered the
day *People* magazine did a story on Roseanne's climb to
fame, and they wanted to include the two of us because I
was a part of that story. I had agreed only to one photo session involving us having fun on the set.

We were doing what we always did when we traveled
the lot, riding that golf cart together, laughing together,
sharing the joy of being sisters, sharing the triumph we had
achieved. I remember the reporter's reaction, the delight of
the photographer who was capturing our relationship. It
had been a time when our lives were showing the world
what Sisterhood could mean, what Sisterhood had
achieved.

I stared at the empty cart and saw the excitement of the
past. I stared at the active set and saw the Denver kitchen
where we first started writing.

I saw someone who looked as though she might be a reporter and remembered a Barbara Walters television
special Rosey had done the previous year. I still have the

tape, but I did not need it that day. I suddenly saw her telling Barbara how much I had done for her, how much she cared about me. And I saw the tears. The camera had gone to close-up when they first began falling. Barbara's question and Rosey's joy that she and I had reached the top together touched one of those deep places in her soul she normally tried to avoid letting others see.

I felt as though I had been struck on the head in such a way that past memory and present reality blended together to such a point that I could not be certain which was which. It was as though each step I might take could put me one step closer to my office or one step back on to Lincoln Street, and I had no idea which would occur. My youth was gone. My future had been stolen from me. And to make matters worse it had been handed, gift-wrapped, to Tom Arnold. If this was how a woman comes of age, I wanted to return to the womb.

As I left the lot, my mind began to clear. Suddenly I understood everything.

As I made my way through that miserable day, I tried to compose myself by talking to Rosey in my head, writing her imaginary notes that went something like this: "So, Rosey, after we worked so hard for so long, you have deliberately written me out of the picture. You have everything and I am left with nothing. Less than nothing, only bitterness. You have decided that Sisterhood is dead and you have chosen to kill it.

"I am afraid to go without you, Rosey, but I know that I will. I will reinvent myself. I will be reborn. You will choose to repackage yourself as a talk-show cliché. What a total waste."

Roseanne had made a very conscious decision to eliminate me. She had become "Mrs. Arnold," and in her mind that meant embracing Tom's world by replacing all those she had loved, worked with, or who had known her well in the past. It was a defining moment, a time to rewrite history the way they rewrite scripts on shows like Roseanne's.

On television, first there is the creator's truth, the pristine pages of black ink on white paper that form the original script used on a weekly show. That script comes on Monday, and as readings and rehearsals begin, changes are requested. Blue pages are inserted for the first rewrite. Green pages are used for the second. By Friday, when the show is taped, the script is a seemingly seamless story, yet it is quite different from the original.

Only the writers, cast, and crew of a television show know the true story. Only Rosey's sycophants were aware of the facts in her past, and they were too fawning, too concerned with sharing her money, power, and celebrity status, to ever remind her that the truth was what she knew from the beginning.

I felt that Rosey was surrounded by pure evil. These were men and women whose points of view were different from mine, who lacked vision, patience, the willingness to share in order to achieve a positive end for everyone. At that level of stardom, it is the rare exception who tells you no. They tell you only what you want to hear. With my dismissal, the last person in Rosey's life who understood the need for limits and was willing to say so was gone. I had been willing to expend the tremendous amount of energy and reasoning needed to keep her grounded and focused. The people left behind to advise her were ones who found her Drama Queen tactics explainable and adorable. They would encourage her instead of trying to get her to establish appropriate parameters of behavior.

I felt enraged that we had worked so hard to earn a voice in society, and suddenly she had slashed my vocal cords. Like a martial artist who sees the black belt as the beginning of knowledge, not the ultimate achievement, so Rosey's success was to mark my beginning. Everything I thought we believed in doing could finally be achieved because of ten years of effort. And suddenly it was gone. It was *narishkeit*, a Yiddish word that means nothingness or emptiness, with no redemptive quality. Ten years of opportunity had been wasted.

Then I met briefly with Arlyne, who added a sharper focus to the reality Roseanne had just created. "Geraldine," she told me, "you did all the work, and now Tom will get all the money and all the credit."

9 Can You Top This?

The story that Roseanne and I had written, the story of two Jewish sisters from Mormon country working to take on Hollywood and the world, was over. She wanted something new, something different. It was time to reinvent herself in a way she felt would be more pleasing to her fans, more interesting on the talk shows. Roseanne the hardworking professional was about to be replaced by Roseanne the soap opera queen, Roseanne the victim, and Roseanne the heroine of a story-book romance.

The basic story that went before the media was the one that would cause her fans to vicariously share in a fantasy that is only supposed to come true for the svelte, the sophisticated, and the beautiful. Roseanne had been saved from the drudgery of the trailer park and the too small home, the wasted marriage and the evil sister, by the hero on the white horse. He had come into her life, swooped down, and carried her off. No one had ever known such love. No one had ever known such happiness. She was the heroine of a thousand movies, the covers of ten thousand paperback novels.

To achieve Roseanne's new reality, she had to do more than appear on all the talk shows, holding hands with Tom, looking adoringly into his eyes as he gazed adoringly into hers. She had to do more than open her home to magazine and newspaper photographers. She had to exaggerate the quality of her new life by vilifying the old.

I was one of the first to be "awfulized." The good sister became the ugly, evil stepsister of fairy tales, Hollywood, and the new Roseanne. She had to be banished.

Rosey's dismissal was like the war cries heard centuries ago when feudal siblings turned against one another. The wars were not about ending evil or righting wrongs. They were about money, power, land, and family dominance. And now they were about production companies and producer credits.

Rosey was the landowner, I was to be the serf. Tom would become the landed gentry through marriage. The rest of our family and I would be excluded from within the castle walls, where the history of the kingdom would be continually rewritten.

But we were Jews in twentieth-century America. Our sibling wars would be fought in Hollywood, U.S.A. We would gird our loins with lawyers and do battle on the soundstages of talk shows. We would surround ourselves with journalists, each hostile to the other side. We would make the covers of magazines, create headlines in newspapers, and gain segments on such respected news shows as *60 Minutes*. And it would all happen while hundreds of thousands of people faced death and starvation in Rwanda, Serbs and Croats were destroying each other's cities, hospitals, and industries, and hostile troops massed on the border between North and South Korea. The world was in turmoil. Millions of suffering men, women, and children were desperate to bring their plight to the eyes and ears of Americans. But their time was limited. The media chose to first focus on Roseanne. The Barr-Arnold War was more titillating to the viewer than Croatia, Rwanda, Israel, South Africa, Haiti, and all the other hot spots of the world combined.

As the media focused on the "hard work" and "well-earned success" of Rosey and Tom, I realized that my contributions were being written out. My story with Rosey was to become like the stories of women in ancient times which had been partially lost from or written out of history. We know of the lady of ten thousand names so important in ancient society, but only a handful of those names have survived, and her full history has been lost. We know of Lilith, the first wife of Adam, but her history is usually mentioned only among Jewish scholars, and then only briefly if at all. We know the names of Isis, Sarah, Mary, Celene, Kali, Demeter . . . women whose lives and stories changed their world at different times and in different places. But we no longer can recite their stories, nor do we know the breadth of their accomplishments. Women warriors. Women spiritual leaders. The stories, the lives, and the voices of women scientists, artists, authors, and others have all influenced their times through the centuries. Yet today we have only fragmental knowledge of their existence, and that knowledge is not part of traditional history courses. Rosey was about to rewrite history in the manner of the patriarchs.

As pressured as Roseanne was during the period before and after she fired me, she had been finding time for hypnotherapy with a woman who was a counselor in Van Nuys. She began around 1987, using the therapy for stress management and to help her focus on her work despite the pressures around her. She may also have been using it to help herself diet and quit smoking, though I don't recall.

The place where Rosey went had a large celebrity clientele and was quite respected in the state. However, I think a mistake may have been made in 1989, two years after she began with the hypnotherapist. As I understand long-term treatment, hypnotherapists often leave their clients with some code or key word that, when spoken, quickly puts them back under hypnosis. They are considered quite sensitive to suggestions throughout the treatment; for example, they may watch an advertisement for a product they normally do not like and seriously consider buying it during the period they are in a suggestible state. I don't know if that is what happened with Rosey, but I do know that late in 1989 I received a troubling telephone call from her.

Rosey began attending what I believe were group therapy sessions with Tom and some of the other patients after returning from Hawaii. He had been through detox and was in the most intense therapy portion of the program. She was hearing stories of child abuse, at least from Tom and possibly from others. And while I have no reason to be certain of this, I suspect that in her ongoing suggestible state, she may have begun to fantasize that what she was hearing had also happened to her.

Rosey called me to say that she was having longrepressed memories of being raised in an abusive environment. There was nothing specific about her recollections, so I tried to be sympathetic. After all, Dad could be sexist, condescending, inflexible at times, and neither Mom nor Dad was consistent in their expectations and discipline of us kids. However, by then Mom, Dad, Stephanie, Ben, and I had been talking. We were all adults, all deeply involved in our own lives and work. We knew that we had unresolved issues from the past which we needed to discuss as a family.

With the exception of Rosey, who I feel was too narcissistic to think about anyone else, we were trying to genuinely understand each other from adult perspectives. Stephanie, Ben, and I needed to know about not only our parents but also the way they were raised, the influences that caused them to raise us as they did. We talked, but more importantly, we listened. We came to understand Mom and Dad's reasoning so that, even if in hindsight it may have been faulty, we recognized the logic of it. And they came to understand how, from our viewpoints as children, we sometimes misunderstood what was happening or placed an emphasis on their actions they never intended.

There were periods when I returned home to Salt Lake City in order to go into therapy with my mother and to truly talk with my father. All childhood leaves some scars, because no two people in a family are likely to share the same perspective during the formative years. But I found my parents truly wanted to listen to me, to understand why I felt they were less than perfect parents. And they were able to tell me why they had done what they did.

I learned that as an adult, I had to end the idealized version of my parents and come to grips with who they were and are. They were neither perfect, the font of all knowledge, nor terrible, ogres in human form. Instead they were loving, caring people who lacked effective parenting themselves. They had children too young, with too little information and too little family support. In an ideal world they would have learned about life and parenting before Mom got pregnant. But they didn't, and so we all had struggled through rough times, the only consistency being their love. More important, as they have gotten older, they have tried to change, to adapt to the world as it is, not as they once thought it to be. The three of us kids who have chosen to share this journey through their later years with them have reaped rewards that Rosey, with her inner focus and unique spin on history, will never understand.

Despite all this, as Rosey was talking about problems she was remembering, Mom telephoned her several weeks after the wedding. She was worried about Roseanne, worried about what she was apparently going through. She wanted to come out to Los Angeles to talk with her, to learn what was troubling her, to see how she could help. Mom was also willing to be a part of group counseling, meeting with any therapist Roseanne designated. Mom wanted a healthy adult relationship with Roseanne as well as with the rest of us.

Rosey refused to talk with Mom, though at first an angry Tom Arnold got on the line, demanding to know how Mom could have the nerve to even call. Didn't she know what she had done to Roseanne? But Mom tried to explain to him that she didn't know. That was why she wanted to come out. (Eventually there would be statements that Mom put her fingers in Roseanne's vagina as early as six *months* of age, a time for which no accurate memories have ever been proven. Later such allegations were seemingly retracted, Roseanne focusing on abuse by our father, reducing her charges against our mother.)

Mom understood Tom Arnold's anger. Rosey had obviously told him God knew what, and being a man who loved her deeply, he would naturally want to protect her from further pain. It was a trait Mom respected, even though she was frustrated by not being able to speak directly with Rosey, with or without Tom on the line. In fact, Mom would have been concerned had Tom not loved her daughter enough to trust her to tell the truth, then to protect her from those Rosey claimed hurt her. Tom could not know that Rosey's version of history was skewered away from what all the rest of us lived.

Mom continued to try to make contact, offering to meet with Rosey in a neutral place – a therapist's office, a doctor, whomever Rosey was seeing and trusted to mediate without pulling punches. She wanted to know the worst, whatever that meant, because she knew that unless she could hear Rosey's troubles, there was no way to resolve whatever was wrong. However, all Mom got in return were responses from Roseanne's lawyers, responses Mom felt were both hostile and threatening.

Even after I was fired, Rosey and Tom planned to go ahead with *Little Rosie's Let's Pretend*. Everyone in our family would be likely to become a character in one or another episode, though the focus would still be on the sisters. The family members would receive a percentage of the merchandising and licensing, since there would be a mom, dad, and siblings loosely based on our family. They were asked to sign a release so there would be no problems when characters based on them were created. This seemed a minor concern before the unexpected firing, because they liked the fact that I would be hands-on involved with the production, and they trusted me to ensure it was in good taste.

Once I was fired, the rest of the family became wary as the concept was modified. Release forms for a new version, which would feature Tom and Little Rosie in a completely redrawn format, were sent, along with a dollar bill each. The dollar bill was a formality Mickey Robins thought was legally necessary to make the signed agreements binding. He felt that at least some money needed to change hands. More important, the release gave the creators the right to portray everyone in any way they desired, and that did not have to be favorable, accurate, or otherwise connected with real life.

Naturally, the family asked me what they should do. I told them I could not get involved. I explained about my being fired and what that meant. However, I also knew that each of them would financially benefit if the program was a success. The dollar amount was much less than originally planned, though perhaps Mom and Dad could have stopped working so hard. Stephanie might have the rest of her education paid for. Ben would also be able to more easily finish his education. They could all use the money, and it would be a conflict of interest for me to advise them what to do. Of course, even this assessment was very optimistic. Originally they would have received a percentage of the net from the show and the profits from the merchandising campaign. The new contract gave them nothing from the show, and the only merchandise from which they would have profited would be characters bearing their names and/or likenesses. All the merchandise would have had to be enormously successful for them to truly benefit.

Stephanie went so far as to call Roseanne. She was told that the money to be made would put her through college. But Stephanie told me that she replied that if Rosey was concerned about helping her, she shouldn't wait for the show and the check that would pass through the lawyer's hands. She needed thirty thousand dollars to complete her degree program, money that was small change to Roseanne. If Rosey was seriously concerned with Stephanie's education, why didn't she just loan her the money directly, separating a caring act from her business? Rosey took Stephanie's cynicism as blackmail. Stephanie was hurt by the coldness of the situation and the fact that signing really only meant that, for the foreseeable future, she would get a dollar from Rosey's lawyer. And in truth, if Stephanie really wanted her big sister's help in her life, she would have gone to Rosey long before the show became an issue.

Although nervous, Dad was willing to sign to keep peace with Roseanne. Mom, however, refused, saying it was a matter of principle. The situation to which she originally agreed was over and she was not going to participate in the new concept without me having the position originally planned.

310

Roseanne was irate. Tom said that his parents didn't have a problem signing the releases. Yet neither he nor Rosey understood how, after I was screwed, everyone in our family would be nervous. Rosey went ballistic, cursing my mother for letting our family hurt her future. She felt that Mom had deliberately misled her concerning her intentions to sign. And everyone was upset that the characters had to be changed to include Tom's family, not Rosey's as originally planned.

Later Mom would look back on this time with amazement and horror. In hindsight, she realized that this was the first time she had ever said no to Roseanne. She felt that, like a spoiled brat in adult shape, Rosey was determined to get even. She wanted to throw a temper tantrum, and when you're worth close to a hundred million dollars with instant access to *People* magazine, a temper tantrum can be as destructive as an earthquake.

Eventually the show, under the title of *Little Rosey*, went on the air for the 1990–91 season. There were thirteen episodes produced and run between September 1990 and spring 1991, all produced by Nelvana. What might have brought millions in revenue with the original concept was taken off the air in its final form.

Later, on May 15, 1992, Nelvana and Little Rosey Productions teamed up to create the family-oriented animated satire called "The Rosey and Buddy Show." Nelvana's Patricia Burns oversaw the production, though Rosey and Tom shared executive producer credits as well as handling the voice-overs for their characters. The press release that came from Bill Saul at ABC described the special:

"Two fun-loving, havoc-wreaking animated characters voiced by Roseanne and Tom Arnold ('Roseanne') drive their RV into Cartoonland, where power-hungry weasels have locked some beloved, classic cartoon characters away in a padded cell. . . .

"Amidst periodic raids on their fridge, where foods come to life in self-defense, Rosey and Buddy try to present their ideas for a television cartoon to The Powers That Be. But they run foul of the network power weasels, who pack them off to the Betty and Veronica Clinic in an attempt to discover why they prefer outrageousness over cuteness."

Bill Saul remembers the special as being meant for one time only. However, the *Hollywood Reporter* noted that while the *Little Rosey* show was meant specifically for kids and featured Roseanne as a ten-year-old trying to cope with an adult world, "The Rosey and Buddy Show" had older characters in the hope that it would appeal to a family audience. I never saw the show, never read a review of it. And for whatever reasons, Bill Saul said there was no follow-up production.

Even if the original *Little Rosie's Let's Pretend* had gone on the air, I felt Rosey would have jeopardized it by the stunt she pulled within months of firing me. It was an incident that generated tremendous controversy, enough to cause the sponsors of the merchandising campaign to pull out.

The problem began when Tom Werner, who owned the San Diego Padres baseball team, was having a promotion called Working Women Night. Tom Arnold suggested that Roseanne be used to sing the national anthem on July 25, 1990.

Rosey was not a professional singer, but she certainly was competent. She could carry a tune, including one so difficult as the national anthem. Many opera singers have trouble with it, though there was no question in my mind that Roseanne could do an adequate job.

What happened next is hard to know. I did not talk with Roseanne until the end of August when we met in a hotel to talk about our business and personal relationship. At that time Roseanne was still high from the incident, considering it the finest comedy she had ever done. Later, in her second book, she explained that part of what happened was an accident, part suggested by several of the ball-players. I question this largely because of what I had seen her do in the past, such as our October 1989 attendance at a ball game in San Francisco where she and Tom pulled down their pants and mooned the crowd.

The joke that was planned was that Rosey was going to

sing the national anthem, grab her crotch, and spit. I don't
know what it is about some men that causes them to
scratch their scrotum in public, and I don't want to know.
Dad was like that at times, and I have seen other men do
that. But it is almost a stereotype among ballplayers to
grab or scratch their crotch. And because of their use of
chewing tobacco, spitting seems to be second nature to
them.

The Roseanne character created for the act used to
parody men all the time. She would talk about men peeing
in the snow. She would talk about husbands who never let
their wives drive a car, acting like, "If I don't sit behind the
wheel of that vehicle, the entire universe will blow up!" She
would then talk like the men as they drove and watched the
sights, saying things like, "Look at the hooters on that
one." Parodying the macho baseball players and their
eccentricities seemed a logical extension of her act. The
only question is whether she deliberately or accidentally
sang the national anthem off-key.

As Rosey related the story, she had to sing without any
musical accompaniment. She was standing before 64,000
people, many of them conservative, and some of them
drunk. She was nervous, uncertain how to sing the extremely difficult song without an organ or piano to help,
and her voice cracked after the first few notes. People
assumed that she, a comedian, was deliberately sabotaging
her own performance for laughs. Almost from the start,
Rosey was being booed.

Perhaps the incident could have died down had Rosey
finished the anthem and left the stadium. A singer is
allowed to have an off night. But she had to complete the
act, had to grab her crotch, then spit. The entire performance was a mockery of both ritual and sport, funny to
many, inappropriate to most, and foolish given the hostility of the crowd when she sang off-key.

Rosey never cared about limits. She liked to see how outrageous she could be and still keep her fans loyal.

Rosey and Tom probably should have considered the
sacredness of baseball to many Americans, but there was

also reason why she would think the players were fair targets to parody. Back in 1989, when Rosey, Tom, Maxine, and I went to the World Series, we were seated next to the ballplayers' wives.

The women were dressed up to the nines, wearing expensive dresses and furs, and showed a total lack of interest in the ball game. They seemed bored with their husbands' work, having more fun talking among themselves and joking with Tom and Rosey. Soon they were becoming more and more outrageous with their jokes, and no one in the area was bothering with the game. The show in the stands was more fun. Finally, when they knew some of the cameras were on them, Tom and Rosey dropped their pants and mooned the photographers and the crowd. They made the news shows, but most people laughed. I'm certain Rosey later felt that people would understand the parody if she deliberately mocked the ballplayers.

The combination of the off-key singing, the grabbing of the crotch, and the spitting was high comedy to her because she had tweaked the noses of middle America. Even worse, the next day Kuwait was invaded, the possibility of war was announced, and Rosey was seen as unpatriotic. (Later, however, Rosey did entertain the wives of some of the soldiers serving in Desert Storm.) Even President George Bush, an avid baseball fan, denounced her actions. Yet this just fueled Rosey's excitement. She later told me how thrilled she was that she could get even the President of the United States pissed off at her.

And then I thought about Roseanne's act, not only what she did at the two ball games (mooning, scratching her crotch, and spitting), but the raunchier visual material she used in nightclubs. I realized whose crude humor was both identical to Rosey's and her earliest inspiration. Roseanne had become just like our Dad. She was doing Jerry Barr schtick.

Bobbe Mary used to call our father a gorilla. He was lewd, crude, and had a sick sense of humor, just like Roseanne when she engaged in the more visual aspects of her stand-up routine.

You have to understand that Dad intensely loves Mom. Yet the way he was raised led him to not understand that there can be inappropriate behavior in the privacy of one's own home. His attitude was that if no one got hurt, who cared? And if he did it in the comfort of his family surroundings where a man is "king," why not?

For example, Dad often sat around in his underwear, completely covered, yet looking like a slob. Every once in a while he would scratch his crotch, just like Rosey did at the ball game. I don't know why. It was gross and made no sense. It was just Dad and men like him, including the ballplayers Rosey was mocking.

The more I thought about it, the more I realized that Rosey's vulgar physical humor was like Dad's. He loved to gross us out with body-function and body-odor jokes. In fact, I knew a number of Jewish families in Salt Lake City in which the height of home humor involved talk of flatulence and belching. For quite a while I thought that Jewish families had an obsession with bodily functions – how often they went to the bathroom, the sound, smell, and enormity of a fart, and similar matters.

Yet when Rosey began working the clubs, no matter what the background of her audience, the greatest laughs, the kind where people are left gasping for air and racing to the toilet to avoid peeing in their pants, involved body functions. She could do brilliant political satire, the type that might get quoted in newspapers, and it would only get a fraction of the laugh of a good fart joke.

For example, one of her favorite jokes involved nose picking. She loved Louie Anderson's talk about the way nose picking is a mystical experience for some people, a cross between Zen and using a narcotic. She used the joke in her act, mentioning people who sit in their cars at traffic lights and run their fingers up their noses. Then she would combine the comments with slowly working her finger as deeply up her nose as she could. Once she reached the limits she could achieve, she would let her eyes roll back in her head. Then she would stand there, finger up her nose, eyes rolled back, a look of ecstasy on her face, letting the laughter build before going on to the next joke.

Rosey also loved to talk about the male obsession with creative peeing. She had a routine about males standing around a campfire in the midst of a winter snowstorm. They could take out their penises and proceed to etch their names in the snow while peeing. This would be combined with a graphic rendition of unzipping her pants, then pantomiming taking out her penis, and carefully peeing the letters B-I-L-L in the snow.

The gross part of her act was clearly inspired by Dad. It was pure Dad and men like him. In fact, in her first book, Rosey discussed an incident where she was being interviewed by *People* magazine. She and my parents were in Las Vegas together. She had been on *The Tonight Show* a couple of times, and now she was opening for the Pointer Sisters. As Rosey recalled the incident:

"The reporter was listening to me say that my father taught me all about timing, and jokes." Then Mom explained that when Dad was in high school, he had to write what he always called a "thesis." It was a paper that told what you wanted to do after graduation. And Dad's said that he wanted to become a stand-up comic when he left high school.

"I looked into my Dad's eyes," Rosey wrote, "and he looked into mine, and it took only one-tenth of a second for us to say, silently, and me first, 'You made me a comedian,' and his eyes said, 'Yes, and I made you a good one.'"

How true it was. Rosey loved the visual gross-out material. That was why she would later tell me that scratching her crotch and spitting after the national anthem was such high art.

In fact, Rosey thought Tom Arnold's peeing on buildings in public view was hilarious physical comedy. As much as she would later avoid the issue, Tom looked and acted very much like Dad when he was Tom's age. The only difference is that Tom had an alcohol and drug problem fueling his exhibitionism. Dad could be crude without thinking. But in their hearts the two men were very much the same — loving, fiercely protective of family, sometimes violent, and gross as hell.

316

Tom Arnold admitted in the June 1993 *Playboy* that "I threw her [Roseanne] around a few times. She'd be screaming at me and I'd throw her on the floor." And Roseanne, speaking in the same interview, admitted that she threw a plastic-encased baseball at Tom's head. She complained of my father's physical outbursts of anger, then married a man with whom she admitted engaging in worse fights than I ever remember from home.

Rosey was able to love both Dad and Tom until she went emotionally off the deep end. That was when she decided to seek a new cause, a new way to shock America. That was when she decided to announce that she was the victim of incest.

I had no idea when I met Roseanne in that Santa Monica hotel room in August of 1990 that she would soon turn against our parents in a manner so vicious, her words were like knives meant to maim for life. We were meeting, to discuss our business arrangement, but she was still on a high from the incident with the national anthem.

I arrived at the hotel early, going to the room to prepare myself for whatever was to happen. I sat cross-legged on the floor, my hands resting palms down on my legs, my eyes focused on a corner of the room. I began by inhaling slowly, then exhaling slowly. My body began to relax and I let my eyes close as I did a series of visualization exercises I have used in the past to increase my energy while calming my body.

Eventually there was a knock at the door. I rose to answer, and there was Rosey, looking really great. We stared at each other, then melted in each other's arms. We hugged, weeping. We "squoze" each other like friends who had been parted too long, who thought the last parting had been final, who could not believe their good fortune in rediscovering life where they previously thought there was only death. Neither one of us knew that it would be the last time we would ever again be together.

Finally we sat down. Rosey spoke first. "I can't believe you didn't call me after the anthem thing," she said, her

317

voice filled with surprise and a little pain. It was as though she had forgotten that the anthem incident occurred after I was fired. It was as though she had never understood how much what we achieved, and what we were about to achieve together, meant to me. "It was incredible to have even the President of the United States pissed off at me. I consider this to be the greatest art I ever created."

I looked at Roseanne, the first I had seen her in the six months since she fired me. I had chosen to not call her during that period, to give both of us time. I was both angry and distraught, but she also did not try to call me. Then I phoned and arranged the meeting to discuss our unfinished business together.

Much of the time before our meeting was spent grieving and in shock. I was demoralized. However, as I began to harden to the reality of what we were facing together, I went to a lawyer, explaining our partnership. I felt that Rosey and I had an oral contract, as binding as anything in writing. I felt that the people who had worked with us over the years would confirm the truth of our working arrangement as accurately as a paper trail. But I wanted confirmation of that fact, and so I checked with the attorney who told me I was right, but that I had only a two-year window of opportunity for my suit. If I waited any longer from the time I was fired, the case would be thrown out of court.

The attorney also said that the case would be a difficult one, as are most oral contract cases in California. What he did not realize was that the difficulty would be increased by Rosey's deep pockets and her Baltic attitude of war. It was a fight to the death. If I took Rosey to court, I knew she would see it as a declaration of war, never seeing that she had fired the first round in the way she dismissed me from my work.

The reason for the hotel room was so I could meet with her alone, away from Mickey Robins, away from Tom Arnold, away from the sycophants. I had not worked with Mickey, Tom, or anyone else except as a result of my working with Rosey. They had only been in our lives and our business for three or four months before I was fired. We needed to talk. We needed to settle things between us. We needed to assure *shalom bayit* – peace in the family.

There also may have been a touch of fear on my part. I knew the dark side of my sister. I knew the Roseanne who talked about serial killers and delighted in the idea of tracking someone, tying them up, and torturing them with words even before she began to kill them. Not that I thought Rosey would ever act out such fantasies. But I did know there was a cruel streak to her, and I felt that meeting in private would be a situation unlikely to trigger that dark side.

More than all those factors, I believed in the type of conflict resolution that had taken place among the other members of our family. I decided to follow the management philosophy of a win-win situation which is used in a conflict where both parties are valued and both need to be retained in the corporation. If we could work out an agreement where both of us left the room happy, perhaps the entire family could be healed.

I spoke next. "I want to talk with you about a fair settlement," I told her. "I planned my life and based my future on promises that you made to me."

I tried to sound stronger than I felt, not confrontational but sure of myself, sure of my words. In truth, I want to run like a son of a bitch whenever I face conflict. Before I went to the lawyer, I tried to justify Rosey's actions. I tried to blame what she had done on stress, on the pressures of the show, the residual exhaustion from the movie and book tour, from the stress of a new marriage.

But I knew that such thinking had been a way of avoiding the truth and delaying the inevitable. That was why I was forcing myself to deal with Rosey in ways that seemed firmer than I felt.

I did not expect to "win." I may have considered myself a brilliant businesswoman who helped get Roseanne to the pinnacle of success, but I am also a realist. I may have made mistakes. I knew I had done nothing that warranted my being let go, but I could accept the idea that she no longer wanted to work with me in business. I could accept that, though I wanted some answers as they related to our past long-term partnership and my future. I had to understand why she had made her decision as she had. If we had been in a large corporation, I would have considered the meeting to be an exit interview where the employee has a chance to go through the records and truly understand the reasons for the dismissal. And as such, I also expected to be able to negotiate a payment and benefit plan based on my years of service.

"If you don't want to work with me, okay. However, I worked with you for ten years and based my future on promises you made to me." I wanted to give her the opportunity to do the right thing, to just be fair. The financial settlement would provide my new beginning, the beginning I had worked so hard for.

Had I not involved myself with my sister, I would have started a series of small businesses, probably running them with my friend Rick. I had an entrepreneurial sense that made such work more fun than any other. If Rosey chose to follow the win-win concept, a fair payoff for the work involved would be enough for me to start such businesses on a limited scale. And the pay-off I came up with was 1 percent of her current net worth at that time. I would not lay a claim to future earnings, even though some of those future earnings would be the result of work I had done.

The 1 percent figure would enable us to each attain our own success. Then we could renegotiate how to be sisters, establishing a new relationship of equals. One of the things that had caused me such intense pain earlier was the fact that she dismissed me with the attitude, "I have everything, you have nothing."

I told her that I believed that the future I had worked so hard to create for myself by design, she had given away to Tom Arnold. "Sorry," said Rosey. "You don't get any money. You're not one of my husbands."

Inside I lost it. California is a community property state. Marrying Rosey assured a piece of her success. I was just the sister who had created and guided her career. I wondered if a woman's work could ever be considered real and

320

valid. What is the price of living behind the scenes when you are female? I suddenly understood the horror of the woman who joins a one-man business, handling all phases of the office operations while he focuses on gaining clients. She eventually does the hiring, with his checking only the finalist. She coordinates manufacturing, acts as a liaison between new management and the work force. And then, when the company is a major success, she is replaced by a "trophy" secretary. She is dismissed because she is a re- minder of lowly beginnings and the many times she had to save his ass through her greater competence. And all she re- ceives is a nice letter of recommendation for any next employer, and a warning from his lawyer not to try to obtain any extra benefits from the corporation she helped create.

Outwardly I was calm, but I kept remembering the past, the words she had spoken, the words she had written. This was the same woman who dedicated her book *My Life as a Woman* to me.

Then, shortly after I was fired, she sent me a letter that both movingly touched my heart and caused me great frus- trated rage. Instead of looking to herself, to her own actions, she spoke of the supposed resentments I had in- wardly harbored toward her. By her reasoning, these unspoken resentments somehow gave off an invisible force field. Or maybe some slightly warped aura as unpleasant as deodorant fade-out. Whatever it was I radiated, she felt it was destroying both the good and the bad in our relation- ship.

Yet the letter also talked of her love for me. She re- minded me of the years of planning, of working together to build the act, to develop the future. She spoke of our scheming to "out wit, out think, out maneuver everyone" in Hollywood. She spoke of our laughter. And she spoke of how I always was there for her, always helping her. The way that I "gave all that you could and more."

She spoke of the future, of a time when there might be renewed love between us. Yet the ending to that letter was one of personal denial. It might have been written by a long married spouse who abandoned his wife for a lover with whom he had been cheating for months. Instead of saying, "I'm guilty of hurting you," the adulterer was telling the faithful partner. "I know how much you have longed to be free of me."

I thought of all that before speaking. Then, choosing my words carefully, I said, "What about the spiritual dimensions of everything we talked about? What about you took the name of the goddess for your own? You claimed her name and you're killing your sister. What about our promise to build a corporate philosophy that would not be based on hierarchy but on power shared, and change the way that power is used?"

Roseanne replied, "Sisterhood is dead. Motherhood is where it's at. I don't believe in any of that stuff any more."

Many people talk about murder as society's ultimate taboo because it is an irreversible act. In truth, child molestation is the worst crime of which anyone can be accused. It involves an innocent victim who is too small to physically defend himself or herself, too young to know how to avoid it or get help, and so easily intimidated, the child can fear he or she will be blamed for the act. It also carries with it the image of an adult so perverted that sexual pleasure can only come from someone who has yet to reach physical maturity.

The charge of being a child molester is so horrendous in the United States that to be accused is to be convicted in the minds of most people. To be charged is to be guilty.

There is also no defense against the allegation of child abuse when brought by an adult against his or her parent. A person caught in the act can be convicted through a variety of scientific tests involving pubic hairs, semen, DNA testing, and the like. A witness who can speak of the recent past can be interrogated closely, the story checked against physical evidence, the testimony of witnesses to the movements of all parties involved, and so forth. But when the charge comes many years after the fact, the accused is presumed guilty because it is believed that no one would make a false accusation.

322

There is no better way for a celebrity to make headlines in the 1990s than to be a survivor of incest. During the 1970s the rich and famous seemed anxious to brag about drug addiction and alcoholism. When the Betty Ford Clinic was opened, experiencing their program became a necessary part of an actor's resumé. However, no one gets hurt if someone wants to lie about drug abuse, as Rosey admitted to doing when she was in the state hospital in Provo. When someone chooses to exaggerate family problems, to turn a troubled but safe childhood into one of endless terror, the falsehoods hurt many people. Perhaps those ultimately hurt most of all are the many legitimate victims of child abuse whose plight is demeaned by those who want to say "me too" for the sake of getting attention.

The problem in trying to discuss what happened with Roseanne is that I feel she has come to believe what she says. I can never forget that conversation we had where she said that the words she speaks become true the minute she says them. This does not mean an objective person looking at the facts would come to the same conclusions she does. It just means that this is Rosey's new "truth," the pronouncement that is "real," solely because she has made it enough times that she can no longer envision her life without it.

Rosey's "memory" began to come back when Tom was in the hospital going through rehabilitation and getting all the attention. She "remembered" our mother's abuse (from six months of age, she told Sally Jessy Raphael, up until the age when she could talk) and then "something ritualistic, sickening and sadistic," according to *My Lives*. Rosey's stories included tales of being forced to assume nude poses with Mom in various sexual positions, "pornographic" movies of Roseanne and Stephanie and me taken by Dad, being threatened with death, Dad masturbating in front of the family, and other horrors.

The family heard about what was taking place in the usual manner Rosey had begun to choose to handle so many of her personal concerns – on the national media.

Dad doesn't sleep well and hasn't for approximately

fifteen years. He has heart disease, diabetes, and macular degeneration of one eye that limits his sight. As a result, he tends to sleep in spurts in the manner of many who are growing older and whose bodies are not well. He will sleep for a couple of hours, then get up for an hour until tired again, returning for another couple of hours. He gets adequate sleep each day, but he does it in a series of what amounts to long naps instead of continuously.

Dad's favorite pastime is listening to the late-night talk shows. Because he has a good radio, and because the all-night stations often have unusually strong signals, he gets programs out of Denver, San Francisco, Los Angeles, and elsewhere. As Dad explained:

"One morning I wake up around five o'clock in the morning. I'm laying in bed and I listen and I'm hearing this radio program, and I hear this story, and it just blows me away. And I nudge the wife, and I say, 'Dear, you better get up. They're talking about us.'

"She says, 'Oh, what're they talkin' about?'

"I says, 'Roseanne's talkin' about us on the radio.' On CNN Radio. It is simulcast. When you hear it on CNN Radio, it is also being shown on CNN Television.

"She says, 'Well, what's she sayin'? Is it good?'

"I says, 'You won't believe it. Wake up.' And she was in a half-asleep situation. I kept buckin' her. Finally she woke up and I says, 'Roseanne's in Denver with Marilyn Van Derbur Atler saying that we sexually abused her as a child.'

"And Helen says, 'Roseanne who?'

"I says, 'Our Roseanne. Our daughter.'

"So I says, 'Come on. We'll go watch it on TV.' So I pulled her out of the bed half asleep, took her in here in the front room, turned on the television, and every thirty minutes — I don't know if you're familiar with CNN — it comes on every half hour. They do the news over, you know. And ever half hour, here we are. They got us on television. Me and my wife, and Roseanne at the Kemp Institute on the stage addressing five hundred therapists — eleven hundred people and five hundred of them were therapists — 'I am a victim of sexual abuse.' And me and my

324

wife sit here and we couldn't believe it. That's when we first heard the story."

I was vacationing in Santa Fe with Maxine when I learned of the accusations. I had not seen the cable show, not talked with my parents. Instead, I was in a grocery store to buy some Tampax when I glanced at the magazines on the checkout counter and saw Roseanne's picture on the cover of *People*. Her being on the cover did not surprise me, but the clothing she was wearing did. She had on a pinafore, something she has not worn since she was in fourth grade. I don't know if she bought it especially for the cover shot, but the obvious attempt to provide a symbol of schoolgirl innocence struck me funny. I wondered what she was trying to do this time, and then I noticed the headlines: "Roseanne's Brave Confession: 'I AM AN INCEST SURVIVOR': For the first time the TV star tells her harrowing story of childhood sexual abuse."

My first reaction was a combination of shock and anger. My sister was such a fucking asshole! She was the only person I knew who could take a little bit of truth, then filter it through her own narrowed vision, refuse to see the whole picture, refuse to take anything in context, and then come out with a story that has nothing to do with the life she led. Although she and Tom would later talk about his influence in the process of discovery (Rosey would awaken from a nightmare and say something, which Tom would write down before she fell back asleep. In the morning there would be no memory of what was said, though Tom's notes would be there), Tom was not a concern. Nor were the prescription drugs she was taking – Prozac and a couple of other antidepressants, she said later. Rosey, the Drama Queen, had found her new cause, Victim Chic, a perfect way to avoid taking responsibility in her own life. In fact, over time she would claim that her obesity was partial proof of what she endured (i.e. *all* fat women were the victims of child abuse). She also claimed that our youngest sister's being thin as a child when the rest of us were fat was also proof of abuse. She never did admit that both of us got fat because we like to eat and we don't like to exercise! Likewise she conveniently forgets the variety of

Stephanie's food allergies that kept her from eating like the rest of us. (Never mind the incongruity of saying that both obesity and being thin are "proof" of the same problem.)

Equally frustrating was the fact that, at that moment, the magazine gave her a forum without any opposing viewpoint. Other publications tried to interview my parents and Stephanie, Ben, and me before running their stories, regardless of who they believed. But this one let her write her own story without seeking any other information. After all, what did they have to lose? Roseanne was a star. Her picture on the cover was likely to sell additional magazines. The topic was controversial enough to probably sell even more. Besides, the magazine was not responsible for what Rosey said about Mom and Dad. Only she could be sued, and that was my parents' first thought. They believed that Melvin Belli was the finest lawyer in the country and immediately flew out to see him in his San Francisco office.

My parents were devastated when I met them at Belli's office. I had moved to San Francisco after being fired because it was an area that Maxine and I both loved. My parents looked like wounded, terrified animals. I realized we had to do something. Melvin Belli made it clear to my parents that if he thought they were guilty of any form of child molestation, he would not represent them. He hated anyone who could do such a thing. And while, in theory, an attorney must defend the guilty as well as the innocent, Belli was old, his reputation such that he did not have to take a case. He wanted to take a polygraph test from the best examiner in California. Then, if they passed the test, he would work on their behalf in whatever manner seemed best. The next day, after what was probably little rest, my parents went to see the polygraph examiner. The questioning was intense, personally humiliating for them, and quite thorough. There was also no question about the results. Neither of my parents had ever molested any children, their own or others.

30 September 1991

CONFIDENTIAL REPORT: Our Case No. P-22554-J

Melvin Belli, Attorney at Law
Belli, Belli, Brown, Monzione, Fabbro & Zakaria
722 Montgomery Street
San Francisco, California 94111

On 27 September 1991, Jerome H. Barr and Helen R. Barr came to the San Jose offices to undergo polygraph examinations in regard to allegations of sexually molesting their daughter, Roseanne Barr. Roseanne Barr, a comedienne and actress, has recently made public statements before audiences and on television to the effect that her parents both sexually molested her and that at age 16 they forced her into a mental institution. Both Helen and Jerome Barr are denying these allegations.

Prior to taking the polygraph examination, both Helen and Jerome Barr signed consent forms, indicating they were undergoing testing voluntarily. These consent forms are retained in the files of this office, along with other polygraph related documents on this case.

During the pretest interview of Jerome H. Barr, he denied that he ever sexually molested Roseanne in any manner and he advised that Roseanne had turned herself in to the mental institution in Utah against his wishes and that it was her decision to go to the institution. It was his opinion that Roseanne's current husband is somehow instrumental in her suddenly making allegations of sexual abuse.

Polygraph testing of Jerome Barr was conducted utilizing the following negatively answered relevant questions:

"Did you ever engage in any intentional sexual activity with your daughter?"

"Did you ever engage in any intentional sexual activity with your daughter in Utah?"

"Were you ever aware of your wife doing anything sexual with your daughter in Utah?"

"Did you force your daughter into a mental institution?"

At the conclusion of testing, it was the opinion of the examiner that Jerome Barr was being TRUTHFUL [emphasis in original report] in his denials of the relevant questions asked during this examination.

Helen R. Barr was administered a polygraph examination utilizing the following relevant questions, which she answered "no":

"Did you ever engage in any intentional sexual activity with your daughter?"

"Did you ever engage in any intentional sexual activity with your daughter in Utah?"

"Were you aware of your husband engaging in any sexual activity with your daughter?"

"Did you force your daughter into a mental institution?"

At the conclusion of testing, it was the opinion of the examiner that Helen Barr was being TRUTHFUL [emphasis in the original report] in her denials to the relevant questions asked during this examination.

> *Yours very truly,*
> *Albert L. Lary*
> *Harman & Shaheen Associates, Inc.*

Roseanne has refused to reexamine her "memory" in light of the polygraph or statements made by the rest of us kids in which we deny without question that we were ever our parents' sexual victims. She also has not taking a polygraph of her own, nor is she likely to do so since she is the "victim" and should not be questioned. Instead, she points out that people without any conscience can pass the polygraph. Thus the fact that my parents are clear according to the test means, by her twisted reasoning, that they are guilty.

At dinner following the polygraph test, I wanted to treat my parents like shock victims who had survived a disaster. I wanted to wrap them in warm clothing and blankets, feed them with chicken soup, rock them in my arms. Instead, we went to the Tumbleweed Café on Van Ness, where they ordered sandwiches, though I could not eat.

I looked at my parents, my anger building, I was outraged with Rosey. She had needlessly shattered two lives. They were like beaten puppies huddled in a corner, shaking, knowing they had done nothing wrong, yet victims all the same because someone wanted to vent their anger inappropriately.

Dad started talking about what had happened. "It was horrible," he said. "It was humiliating. They made us sit in a little chair, and then they strapped us into the chair, and tied something around our chests, and they put straps on our arms." In my mind they were sitting on the electric chair or in the gas chamber. I could only imagine them suffering the horrors of the damned, and while the physical reality was not so harmful as my fantasies, the psychological damage was evidenced in their drained faces.

"And then the guy starts asking me questions," said Dad. "And I tried to answer them, but then the questions started getting weirder and weirder."

Mom interrupted, saying, "I was humiliated because I was asked if I practiced autoeroticism. And I said to him, 'Could you turn off that machine for a moment?' And he said, 'Yes,' and he turned off the machine and I said, 'I don't understand the question. What does that mean?' And he explained to me that it meant, 'Did I have sex with machines like vibrators.' And I said, 'Heavens, no!'"

And then my Dad said, "And then the son of a bitch says to me, 'Mr Barr, have you ever gone into pornographic movie theaters to watch pornography? Have you ever masturbated in public?'

"I'm thinking to myself, I can't believe the question. So I said to him, 'What do I look like? Pee-wee Herman?'"

And then I lost it. After all the emotions, Dad's comment made me laugh so hard, I had to leave the restaurant to get control.

Originally, Belli was going to be hired to sue Roseanne for slander, defamation of character, and any other appropriate charges. He came to truly believe my parents after he talked with them, then saw the results of the polygraph tests. However, he refused to let them sue their daughter. He encouraged them to instead consider the option of suing the publications if they continued to print lies. He felt that a lawsuit would irrevocably end any chance of my parents' being involved with the child they loved. Yet to his shock, when he tried to act as intermediary, Rosey was so hostile, it was impossible to even start a conversation about the allegations and family conflict.

Still, Belli felt a lawsuit could only hurt the family, since no one wanted to have Rosey be permanently estranged. My parents decided to take his advice, a decision about which they continue to have mixed feelings.

Kevin Sessums, in his February 1994 *Vanity Fair* article on Roseanne, quotes Belli as saying: "I told them [Mom and Dad] that I don't believe – no matter how bad it is – that interfamilial lawsuits should be brought. So I got ahold of Roseanne and tried to square it all away. But I didn't make any headway. I just kept the parents from suing the daughter so that it didn't make it any worse than it was. I remember I was doing something with some celebrities involved, and *oh* Roseanne came up to me and cussed me out 10 ways from Sunday! Just cussed the hell out of me! That's what I got for keeping the mother from suing her."

When the family gathered to talk about Rosey's charges, we were so emotionally overwhelmed that we resorted to humor. I decided that with Rosey's love for media attention regardless of what she had to do or who she had to hurt to get it, we could turn her charges into a game show. It would be called *Dysfunction Junction* and would have as the guest panelists all the entertainment stars who either have been abused as children or have claimed to have been abused. Roseanne would be on, of course. But also La Toya Jackson and several others.

Actually, I wanted two versions, one of which would be a board game. Mormons in Salt Lake City enjoy family home evenings every Monday night. There are all manner of written materials to help families become closer, and my mother had us follow these. For example, one of the activities is for everyone to write down how they feel about something – what is taking place in the family, what is taking place in the neighborhood that concerns them, etc. Then the notes are folded, put together in a container, mixed, and drawn. Everyone has to read one, then guess who wrote it. Sometimes these are a little surprising. Sometimes they are funny or sad. Whatever the case, after a little light-hearted banter, the person who wrote it gets to express his or her feelings. The rest of the family is expected to truly listen, then discuss all this. It is a way of communicating and bringing everyone closer together, something in which the Barrs engaged as part of my mother's ecumenical activities.

This format was perfect for Dysfunction Junction: The Board Game. But first there had to be the television show.

Each show would have guests from Middle America. The person would have a chance to tell every lousy, rotten thing their parents ever did to them. Some of the guests would probably have horror stories to tell. Others might have complaints about being denied a favorite candy, being grounded for six weeks for coming home ten minutes later than curfew one time, or not being allowed to buy the same sneakers that "everybody in school" was wearing. There would be a mixture of the tragic and the petty, much like the ways of the world.

In order to make Dysfunction Junction more entertaining, the guest victims would have to act out the abuse. Naturally, the Barr family would be first because we had become America's best-known victims and victimizers. But that would be just a means for grabbing high ratings at the start. The "little people" from everyday families would be a major part of all this. And the celebrity judges would have slate boards and chalk on which they would rate the victims' stories by a numbering system similar to that used by the Olympic Games. Then the person whose point total made him or her the biggest victim would win fabulous prizes including a two-week stay at the treatment center of their choice.

The more we tried to refine the rules, the more ridiculous it became. We thought we might have categories like Incest, Covert Incest, Inappropriate Behavior, Hidden Messages You Didn't Know You Were Sending, and the like.

We all laughed at the image of the Barr family starring on *Dysfunction Junction*. We laughed until there were tears rolling down my face. And then I realized that the tears were not of happiness. I wept for the pain Rosey's misinterpretation of life/mental illness/quest for headlines – or whatever the hell else was driving her – had caused our family. She was shattering the lives of people I love deeply, whose only real mistakes had been living in the same family.

A little later my Mom called me just to talk. She said that when she was seventeen and just married, my Dad said to her, "Let's make a baby." In hindsight, as much as she truly loved us kids, she said, "I should have told him, 'Hell, no. We'll just buy a Doberman puppy.'"

Perhaps the angriest among us has been Stephanie. She is not in show business. She is not in awe of Roseanne. Since she is also eleven years younger than Roseanne, her life and experiences have been radically different. She is happily married with two children, neither of whom is likely to ever need therapy. Yet when Rosey first decided to go public with her allegations, she focused on Stephanie as further "proof."

Stephanie has come forward on a few occasions to deny Rosey's claims, but she is trying to avoid doing so. She does not want her privacy invaded. She does not want to become a public figure who has the media camping on her doorstep, calling her on the telephone, and studying her own children for signs of abuse. Yet she also does not want our parents to suffer more than they have. Nor does she want Roseanne's fantasies to be seen as the truth.

Stephanie has repeatedly expressed her outrage, as, to a lesser degree, has Ben. Roseanne has made clear that if they tell the truth about our past, they are in "denial" of what Rosey claims happened. The only truth is her truth, and if any of us think our childhood was anything other than a nightmare, it is for Rosey to discuss that "delusion" with the world. Rosey has been the creator and arbiter of family history. Rosey must reveal what the rest of us refuse to discuss, even if the reason we refuse to discuss it is because it did not happen.

I have come to look upon Roseanne as the destructive individual in the family, not the seeker of truth or healing. Technically, I consider her the active perpetrator of abuse, not the people she accuses.

A perpetrator is someone who crosses boundaries, disrespects another person's privacy, is invasive and violative, breaks trust, lacks empathy, is self-centered and narcissistic, blames, does not take responsibility for his or her actions, and claims a hierarchy of oppressions and pain. A perpetrator is someone who makes choices for you that you would not otherwise make yourself. Perpetrators have power. Confronting the perpetrator requires confronting the imbalance of power. Roseanne uses her celebrity status, which is her specific kind of power, to cross boundaries.

We in the family recognize that Roseanne is an actress. We recognize that there is a public and a private Roseanne. We believe that the private Roseanne is blinded by rage, is vulnerable, is defined and manipulated by others.

I recognize that "healing" is a process. I know that different people are at different stages of "recovery." I believe that forgiveness is the ultimate victory of healing.

I know that a healthy family honors difference and respects boundaries. I know that anger and disagreement are not reasons for withholding love or justifications for violating trust.

Roseanne may say that her latest round of publicity about the supposed incest is part of the "healing process." I see it as another episode in the cycle of violation of boundaries and privacy. I believe that Roseanne is an addict, and that her drugs of choice are power and celebrity. I also fear that the people who surround her, and the media which canonizes her, are her enablers. She is also addicted to being a victim. Unfortunately, she has no regard for the people truly afflicted with the tragedies she has falsely adopted. They are real incest victims. Their problems are real and need treatment. They do not have the luxury of appearing on talk shows and pulling publicity stunts.

I fear for the safety of my parents and the emotional safety of Ben, Stephanie, and myself. I also fear for the emotional well-being of Roseanne's children.

Stephanie certainly has had good reason to fear the media reaction, because she has seen what happened to my parents. Mom would like to be left alone. Dad wants to go on the offensive. Both have joined an organization that fights what is becoming known as "false memory syndrome." Many of the members are innocent parents accused by their adult children of being molesters. The "memories" are often brought out by therapists who misuse suggestion, hypnosis, and therapeutic interpretation to "prove" molestation. In several instances the adult children come to realize they were misled by the therapist, even to the point of uncovering evidence that what they had believed was fact never happened. In a handful of headline-grabbing cases, these adult children have successfully sued their therapists, sometimes winning large financial judgments against them, and sometimes costing the therapist his or her practice.

I am intensely grateful for the existence of the False Memory Syndrome Foundation, which works to unite families who have been victimized by false memory syndrome. These people are nice, intelligent, loving individuals who, like my parents, have often discovered failings that had nothing to do with abuse. The problem with false memory comes, in part, because a child has feelings without knowledge of the cause. Some adults remember the feelings, then are convinced that they must

334

have been caused by abuse. They might not remember the abuse, but why else would they be fat? unhappy? unable to stay married? or whatever situation has made their lives more difficult and for which they have taken no personal responsibility.

Life is tough. Adults recall the emotions they experienced with their primitive minds as children. The feelings are real, some good, others bad. When they are analyzed in the adult mind without putting the childhood into perspective, the conclusions can become skewered. It is the misapplication of deductive reasoning, as in "Man likes dogs; dogs like bones; therefore man likes bones." In this case the reasoning is, "I am obese; some obese people have been molested; therefore, I have been molested."

The truth is that many families, including our own, are not perfect. Pain is caused where it shouldn't be. Rules are applied unevenly and inappropriately. We live in a round-robin world of perpetrators, victims, enablers, rescuers, peacemakers, clowns, and others as defined by therapists such as John Bradshaw. And all of us take on all of these roles in the family setting.

In some ways I want to bless Roseanne. In her skewered view of family, she has also brought attention to an important issue. She chose a cause that, for whatever reason, she has fully embraced. She testified before the United States Senate, and while her words are not true of our parents, they are true of others. Child abuse is real. It is ongoing. It is multigenerational. Celebrity spokespeople have helped pass legislation others have been unable to achieve.

Child abuse is real. Incest happens. False accusations are real. They happen, too. Many of the false accusations are made during divorce cases in which parental custody issues are at stake. The problem is that false memories, when exposed, hurt the credibility of real abuse victims. Likewise, many victims of FMS attack all therapists for the failings of a few. And many therapists refuse to engage in active peer review to weed out the few bad ones. The tend to go on the defensive, like a police department that can accept the fact that a police officer gone bad must be removed, but that doesn't want the public reminding them of that fact. They become defensive instead of entering into a partnership to clean up their profession.

Adult children and their parents need to learn to communicate in new ways. They need to confront their past and their memories, and share in the journey of mutual understanding. Ultimately all families need to learn to listen to one another, to hear in a new way. That is what Ben, Stephanie, and I did with our parents.

Young adults often have misguided rage toward their parents. Yet what they're really discovering is that life is not fair. Leaving the protection of home and family forces us to confront experiences from which we had previously been sheltered. There is much to understand, much of the early years to review and to comprehend.

That was what Rosey failed to do. Narcissism prevents communication, and without communication, false understanding is likely. And whether she was putting her unique spin on the reasons behind her feelings, was influenced by Tom's group therapy sessions, or developed her Victim Chic in some other way, Rosey refuses to take the steps that lead to true family healing.

Both my parents have spoken at various FMS group events, trying to share their horror and their pain. Yet they are still hounded by the media. Reporters have questioned their neighbors on everything from their sex life to how the neighbors like living near Jews. The latter, bringing anti-Semitism into the issue, is the most horrible. Rarely has any writer tried to report totally objectively, though the *TV Guide* writers did admit that they were given copies of the polygraphs.

Even worse have been television talk shows. These are meant to provide entertainment, not news. Some try to be honest and objective. Others become little more than a forum for one side of an issue or controversy. And because she is the more interesting of the family, Roseanne is usually the one given the forum. The family is not brought together in any way, nor is the family given a chance to refute her allegations.

336

Roseanne did not stop with her earlier accusations, though. She thrives on controversy. Stephanie and her husband feel that, prior to Tom Arnold, she tried to stir up some controversy every three months. Dad feels that she becomes outrageous whenever industry talk implies her show might be dipping in popularity. And I know that Rosie keeps monthly scrapbooks of clippings, along with a library of videotapes of her shows and personal appearances.

Perhaps her most horrible allegation is that my parents molested Roseanne's oldest daughter, Jessica, on the day of Rosey's wedding to Tom. I have agonized over how to discuss these charges. I have talked with my parents, Ben, and Stephanie. Jessica is now legally an adult, yet the charges that were brought were made when she was a minor. And they began with Roseanne.

Jessica has been a victim of a woman who, in my opinion, will only win Mother of the Year awards when they are given in hell. I am outraged that she would concoct such a story involving her own daughter and use it as a public ploy. The fact that the investigator on the case, after talking with all parties, felt that my father was innocent of a crime has not been reported.

I have finally decided to say to hell with it all. I can't discuss the allegations related to Jessica without doing to my niece what Roseanne did to Stephanie and Ben. The fact is that Rosey makes charges while admitting to being emotionally disturbed (she asserts that she is in therapy, on prescription drugs, and even that she has a multiple personality). She does not make the charges as a healthy person in recovery able to look objectively at her life and the lives of those around her.

Bill Pentland has become a man in crisis in recent years. He loves his children, and for many years might as well have been a single parent. Good or bad, he was their father, their mother, their nanny, disciplinarian, and maid while Rosey was on the road, having affairs, or otherwise focused on her personal life. The divorce was messy, and Roseanne had to pay Bill because he was the primary caretaker of the kids. It was in many ways like what happens to a successful businessman when he starts messing around with his secretary, then divorces the woman who devoted herself to his career, not her own. The difference was that Roseanne was a celebrity, and celebrities hold the same status as the gods of old in the minds of far more people than anyone wants to admit.

Mom and Dad love their grandchildren. They were the caretakers of the kids when Rosey first went to Los Angeles to become successful. They were able to instill such discipline in those children, using Mom's educator friend, that Rosey and Bill asked Mom and Dad to keep them a little longer. Despite all the charges, no one has ever questioned how much they helped their grandchildren begin to learn self-control.

Prior to the kids' coming totally under Roseanne's control, everyone was in therapy to try to heal. Bill and Jessica had been going every week for months, in addition to seeing therapists separately. The therapy had been intense and intimate, and nothing had gone unrevealed. Yet the issue of my dad's alleged improper behavior, Jessica's discomfort with Dad, or anything similar never came up. I think Bill's side of the family is convinced it never happened.

The latest topper has been to "discover" in 1994 that Roseanne has approximately twenty different personalities. The only problem with this allegation is that her multiple-personality claims seems more likely to come from books she has read, such as *Sybil*, which she read at twenty-two, than from therapy. My understanding from experts in the field is that she is not going to suddenly discover so many personalities if she is, indeed, what is technically known as a dissociating hysteric. And, as always, Rosey is the victim, so she needs offer no proof for public scrutiny. She does not release her medical records, though she talks freely about her problems caused by Mom and Dad. She does not release the names of her therapists, though she claims to be in regular therapy, as well as periodically checking into hospitals and treatment centers. She says enough so there is no reason for her to claim a right to privacy, then fails to back up her allegations by letting people talk with the same experts she claims are helping her.

And in the meantime she is destroying our family's reputation. Mom and Dad are relatively accessible to the media. They are quite willing to provide the polygraph results. And I am going public with what I think is a more accurate perspective. Yet the truth is that to be accused is to be convicted.

As for me, all I can do is weep for whatever caused Rosey to come forth as she has. This is the sister I still love, my onetime role model, mentor, idol, teacher, and friend throughout childhood and into our early adult years. I know I can never have Sisterhood again. The tragedy is that the only way to have my sister back is to pretend that there are dirty little family secrets about which everyone but Rosey is in denial. Yet I refuse to allow lives to be destroyed so my rich and famous sister can have headlines.

Ironically, I am certain that Roseanne believes that what she is speaking is the truth. I am equally convinced that it did not happen as Rosey has pronounced it. Even sadder, as of Valentine's Day, 1994, Rosey and Tom admitted on Oprah Winfrey's show that he now keeps a separate apartment because she is in such turmoil. Since they are rich enough to build on to their home to give him a private space, I have to think this is an indication that there are serious problems for the couple.

My feelings were reinforced on Sunday, 17 April, 1994, when Roseanne announced that she and Tom Arnold were getting a divorce. She allegedly had a fight on the set of her show with him, tore up his credit cards, fired him, and fled to Europe. The "divorce" plan seemed timed to coincide with a *60 Minutes* report that brought serious questions to bear about Roseanne and others who have what appear to be false memories of childhood abuse. Within a week, Rosey stated that it was all a mistake, that she had been misled by people on the set of her show. Yet her divorce proceeding claimed that Tom physically and emotionally abused her. If the divorce papers were false, then this means that Rosey again used dishonest allegations of violence to gain public sympathy.

There was a dramatic reconciliation, declarations of undying love, more hints that they might try to have a baby during the summer of 1994, and then the announcement that the marriage was really over. Rosey back-pedaled a bit on the reports of abuse, though others around her claimed that they would not have made such allegations if they had not been true. Whatever the case, "forever" in love with Tom proved a lot shorter than "forever" in love with Bill.

At this writing, I suppose I am waiting for the next revelation. Will Rosey, who had many in the media turn against her when she began attacking Tom in so contradictory a manner, now try to reconcile with Mom, Dad, or her sisters and brother? Will she say Tom led her astray? Or will she attack him all the more, saying that he abused her because she was vulnerable as a result of the abuse she endured as a child?

It is impossible to guess. She is the Drama Queen, and when one drama seems to have run its course or no longer plays in Peoria, the next saga has to be mounted. With Rosey, the show always goes on. The only question is on which stage the next corpses will be littered.

10 Today

After four years, two thousand pages of documents, three judges, one referee, eleven days of deposition, and $1.2 million in billable hours spent without recompense by my lawyers, my lawsuit against Roseanne was thrown out on a manufactured technicality. I was told that I had waited six months too long to file my lawsuit.

I have come to believe that justice is a commodity in America. You can get as much of it as you can afford. And with all the effort of my attorneys, Roseanne had deeper pockets.

I have not watched *Roseanne* since I was fired. People ask me what I think about the portrayal of the lesbian sister or the handling of homosexual issues on the program, and I have to say that, in general, I honestly do not know. From what I read in the paper, Roseanne has not allowed the sister character to develop as we originally planned. There will be no spin-off featuring a normal career woman who happens to have a same-sex orientation. The one "groundbreaking" issue I do know about because it made headlines in all my local papers is the lesbian kiss on the show. In a March 1994 episode Roseanne Conner unwittingly is taken to a lesbian bar where one of the women kisses her on the lips. Roseanne, disgusted, angrily wipes her face with her hand.

The gay community applauded. I found such meaningless caricatures an outrage, a perversion of what we had originally planned.

But that era of my life is over. I'm grateful that I had the opportunity to write this book, and I look forward to moving on to the creation of other things. My ultimate fantasy is that, now that this book is done, I never have to write the word "Roseanne" again.

Power corrupts. Absolute power corrupts absolutely. And as our mom has so wisely commented, "God doesn't change history. Roseanne changes history."

On March 1, 1994, I was in Salt Lake City to visit my parents and work on this book. My father has taped almost every television show on which Roseanne has appeared. At first it was because he was proud of her achievements and delighted in her work. That part of his taping continues, because he still respects her comic genius. However, now he also must tape the shows where her appearances are attacks against him. And I returned, in part, in order to review the tapes, to look for contradictions, to understand the venom in her assault against our family.

Needing an escape, and perhaps looking to get a laugh at the expense of people I always mocked, I went walking through Salt Lake City's Temple Square. Mormons had been the fantasized bane of my childhood. Even at the time of my return, I was shocked to learn that the hierarchy had stated that there were three enemies of the church. These were feminists, intellectuals, and homosexuals. Thus I was as hostile toward their ideas as I had ever been.

Despite this anger, I have also always thought of myself as spiritual. Yet I did not understand how God works in our lives until I received a telephone call from one of the boys – now a grown man – who had been a much-joked-about figure in our childhood productions. He was, is, and probably always will be a Mormon, but he called to say hello, to tell me of his support for our family.

Next I learned something else. When Roseanne announced that my parents were child molesters, the news caused everyone who knew the family to reevaluate our lives. They thought about each of us, and especially Mom and Dad. Then they unanimously came to the conclusion that whatever motivated Roseanne had nothing to do with the truth.

342

In accordance with their beliefs, many members of the ward where my parents live fasted as part of their effort to pray to God to help my family. Then my parents' names were placed in the Mormon temple for regular prayer. The Mormon people so love my parents that they are doing everything within their belief system to end the unjust ordeal. After thought, discussion, and prayer, they are convinced that Roseanne has changed history, and they want God to help Mom and Dad through these trying times.

This knowledge shocked me. The people I looked down upon as misguided at best, inferior at worst, have become a solid base of needed, welcome support. It is like the New Testament story of the Good Samaritan, in which the person considered to be the lowest in society upheld the greatest love humans can have for one another.

I suddenly felt very wise and very foolish. I still have a hard time understanding many of the tenets of the Mormon faith. What I perceive to be the bigotry of the church's power structure still troubles me. But the people ... the love that has poured forth ...

I came home despite the Mormons because Salt Lake City is where my parents live. When it was time to leave, I parted not in anger but enriched in spirit by the people I once thought I never wanted to experience again.

Roseanne, I have to thank you from the bottom of my heart for what you have unintentionally done for me. As kids growing up, you were my mentor, my teacher, and at times, one of my spiritual guides. Then you turned against our parents in a way I find dishonest and reprehensible. You also turned against me in a way I feel reduces a decade of work to the type of perverted business dissolution we vowed Sisters would never do to one another. Yet it is because of your verbal violence against the family that I have been able to experience the love of people I formerly refused to see for what they are. Your hate has been a breeding ground for my discovery of selfless giving in people I thought were all self-centered, isolated, and bigoted.

I don't want to think that God is working through you. Rather, I feel that when you chose to speak your own "truth," you gave God a vehicle for touching my heart. I would rather have experienced almost anything other than what Mom, Dad, Ben, Stephanie, and I have endured in the last few years. But we have experienced it, and because of what I found after returning to the land of people who once seemed to be the enemy, my life is enriched. My soul now soars on wings of love I never before knew existed. May you one day also come to know such peace despite currently being in the midst of a hell of your own creation.

Will the Real Roseanne Please Stand Up?

National Enquirer, November 15, 1988, from an interview with Alan Braham Smith: "'I had some problems when I was a kid. I drank beer, stole my parents' car and hit a car,' said Roseanne, 36, recalling the troubles that led her parents to put her in Utah State Hospital in Provo.

" 'My parents didn't think I was going to kill myself, but they thought I was out of control.

" 'I was in the mental hospital for 8½ months. I was tranquilized. I was in a stupor for those 8½ months. . . . But I didn't go to bed every night crying my heart out. I just learned to live through it. And I grew.'"

TV Guide, January 4, 1992, from an article by Mary Murphy and Frank Swertlow: "She left home and *checked herself* [emphasis added] into a state mental hospital in nearby Provo, Utah. 'I now say this was the most desirable place I ever went to in Utah. There was sanity at last, structure. It was safe.'"

Vanity Fair, February 1994, from an article by Kevin Sessums: "Subsequently, her parents . . . put her away for almost a year in a state hospital. To this day she refuses to go into details about her life there."

On October 10, 1991, Roseanne and Tom Arnold appeared on *Sally Jessy Raphael*, where Rosey discussed the horrors of the damned she had experienced as a child. The program itself was entitled "I Am an Incest Survivor," and it was obvious that Sally was deeply and honestly moved. In the closing minutes of the program, Sally said: "I have been interviewing and talking to people as a way of life, for thirty-three years. I have never – I, personally, have never met anyone who lied about being an incest victim or being an abuser of substances. No one would choose that way to go. So if you're saying to me, 'What do you think? What do you feel? Do you believe her?' The answer is, darn right I do."

On page 89 of Roseanne's book *My Life as a Woman*, she tells of the time she was in the state hospital in Provo and had the chance to go to schools to be on a panel to discuss mental health. Each youth would introduce himself or herself by first name, then explain why they were in therapy. "And then I'd go, 'My name is Roseanne and I'm in here for heroin addiction.' They'd ask me drug questions but luckily there were other kids in there for drugs so I just used all their language – 'yeah, I was shooting crystal and meth' – they had no idea why I was there. . . .

"I never did do drugs. I was so afraid."

USA Today, September 29, 1989, from an article by Ann Trebbe: "Though she vowed never to hire a publicist, she now has two who rarely return phone calls and protect her from the press.

"Before she took the stage at the American Booksellers Association summer conference, she chain-smoked, acted exasperated at having to pose for a picture with a fan, and refused to walk anywhere without her sister and her manager on either side."

Playboy magazine, June 1993, from an interview with Roseanne and Tom Arnold by contributing editor David Rensin: "She [Geraldine] means my firing her as my manager. I thought she was there for me because she was my sister. But I think now she was there for a payoff, and obviously that's true. My sister and I were very close, as close as two sisters can be. I supported her for ten years. It's over now. She has to get a job, do some work."

Roseanne, writing in her second autobiography, *My Lives* (Ballantine Books, New York, 1994; p. 189): "My sister, Geraldine, decided to quit working for the 'Roseanne' show, maintaining that she 'needed her freedom.'"

Index

351

ANTHONY HOPKINS

The Authorised Biography

Quentin Falk

'... written with style, humour and humanity, knowledge and affection for its subject and solid understanding of a great actor's craft' Bryan Forbes, *Sunday Express*

Winner of the Best Actor Oscar in 1992 for *The Silence of the Lambs* and knighted in 1993, Anthony Hopkins has established a magnetic personality and a dangerous vitality. But there is a downside: alcoholism and hell-raising almost wrecked his career, and only through sheer determination has Hopkins been able to reform his life. Definitive and fully updated to include his latest work in *The Road to Wellville, Legends of the Fall* and *August*, this biography has been written with the full cooperation of Hopkins and those who know him.

ISBN 0 86369 632 5

SEAN CONNERY

The Untouchable Hero

Michael Feeney Callan

'A necessity for Connery and Bond fans' *Los Angeles Times*

Sean Connery is a study in contradiction. Balding, argumentative and reputedly tight-fisted, he is also regarded as the sexiest man alive. He despises the fame he found in Bond – yet it is the cornerstone of his multi-million-dollar fortune. More than a career chronicle, this biography includes the frankest and most in-depth interviews to date from Connery's family, friends and co-stars.

ISBN 0 86369 755 0